Provence A-Z

Provence A-Z

Peter Mayle

Alfred A. Knopf   New York   2006

THIS IS A BORZOI BOOK
PUBLISHED BY ALFRED A. KNOPF

This book was originally conceived as part of the *Dictionnaire Amoureux* series
published by Les Éditions Plon of Paris, France.

Library of Congress Cataloging-in-Publication Data
Mayle, Peter.
Provence A–Z / Peter Mayle.
p. cm.
ISBN 1-4000-4442-1 (alk. paper)
1. Provence (France)—Description and travel.   2. Provence (France)—
Social life and customs.   I. Title.   II. Title: Provence A to Z.
DC611.P958M385 2006
944'.9—dc22   2006040885

Manufactured in the United States of America
First Edition

For Ailie Collins,
without whose help I would still be floundering around
somewhere in the middle of the alphabet

Introduction

I am now in the land of corn, wine, oil, and sunshine.
What more can man ask of heaven?

—THOMAS JEFFERSON
in Aix-en-Provence, March 27, 1787

I t's an impossible business, trying to squeeze Provence into a single volume. There's too much history, too much material. Thousands of years of human habitation; an encyclopedia's worth of churches and châteaus, towns and villages; a small army of distinguished or notorious residents, including Petrarch, Nostradamus, Raymond de Turenne, and the Marquis de Sade; artists, poets, and writers galore: Vincent van Gogh, Paul Cézanne, Frédéric Mistral, Marcel Pagnol, Alphonse Daudet, and Jean Giono; legends and myths, mountains and vineyards, truffles and melons, saints and monsters. Where to start? What to include? What to leave out?

It's a problem that many writers have faced, and their solution has often been to specialize. They have confined themselves to particular themes—ecclesiastical architecture, the influence of the Romans, the cultural significance of *bouillabaisse,* any one of a hundred facets of Provence—and they have produced comprehensive, often scholarly books. Admirable though these are, I haven't attempted to add to that collection. Probably just as well, since I'm no scholar.

Instead, I have compiled an autobiographical jigsaw of personal interests, personal discoveries, and personal foibles. That may sound like a cavalier way to approach a book, but I can at least say that I have observed certain rules and restrictions.

As much as possible, I have tried to avoid the more celebrated landmarks, buildings, and monuments. I have left to others the Pont du Gard, the Roman amphitheater at Arles, the Abbey of Sénanque, the Palais des Papes in Avignon, and dozens more historic marvels that have already been so frequently admired and so well described. For the same reason, I have neglected great tracts of glorious countryside, like the Camargue, and one of the most beautiful stretches of the Provençal coastline, the Calanques east of Marseille.

My choice of subjects has been guided by a set of simple questions. Does the subject interest me? Does it amuse me? Is there an aspect of it that is not very well known? It's the technique of the magpie, hopping from one promising distraction to another, and it has the great advantage of being virtually all-inclusive. Anyone or anything can qualify, as long as it has piqued my curiosity. That, at any rate, is my justification for assembling a collection that includes such unrelated topics as a recipe for *tapenade* and a morning spent with a public executioner.

In the course of my research, I have often been reminded of the Provençal love of anecdote, conversational embroidery, and the barely credible story. I make no excuses for recording much of what I've been told, however unlikely it may sound. We are, after all, living through a period in which the truth is routinely distorted, usually for political advantage. If I have sometimes overstepped the limits of verifiable accuracy, at least I have done so in a good cause, which is to make the reader smile.

In the same spirit, I have not questioned too closely some of the specialist information passed on to me by experts, and Provence is full of experts. Almost without exception, they are generous with their time, their advice, and their opinions. The problem comes when you ask two of these experts the same question. When is the correct time to pick olives? How can I keep scorpions out of the house? Is the Provençal climate changing for the warmer? Is *pastis* the cure for all ills? Invariably, you will receive totally conflicting answers, each delivered with enormous conviction. I admit that I always choose to believe the most improbable one.

Among these experts, one in particular deserves to be mentioned here, even though he also appears several times in the pages that follow. He is the emeritus professor Monsieur Farigoule. Now retired from the mainstream of academic life, he has established a charitable course for the education of backward foreigners, and I am his favorite pupil. In fact, I think I may be his only pupil. Lessons are held in the local café, and the curriculum is remarkably wide-ranging, since Monsieur Farigoule seems to be an expert on everything. Among other things, I have tried him on hornets' nests, Napoléon's love life, the use of donkey dung as fertilizer, the poetry of Mistral, the essential character differences between the French and the Anglo-Saxons, and the Avignon Papacy. He has never been short of an answer, is usually contentious, and is always extremely opinionated. It is to this unconventional muse that I owe a considerable debt, which I now acknowledge with great pleasure.

Some Unreliable Geography

It seems to me that almost everyone, from the first Roman mapmaker onward, has had very definite ideas of exactly where Provence is. But unfortunately for the seeker after geographical truth and precision, these ideas have varied, sometimes by hundreds of kilometers. I was told, for instance, that "*Provence commence à Valence,*" way up north in the Rhône-Alpes *département*. Recently, I made the mistake of passing this information on to my personal sage Monsieur Farigoule, who told me that I was talking nonsense. One might stretch a point, he said, and include Nyons in Provence, as a reward for its splendid olives, but not one centimeter further north. He was equally adamant about the eastern boundary (Nîmes) and the western limit (Sisteron).

The fact is that, over the centuries, boundaries have expanded and contracted; a bulge here, a dent there, sprawling or shrinking. Names have changed, too, or have disappeared from popular use. Not long ago, the lowly Basses-Alpes were given a leg up in the world and promoted to the Alpes-de-Haute-Provence. And who nowadays could tell you with any conviction where the Comtat Venaissin begins and ends? It is not an exaggeration to say that the whole area, for many years, was an affront to the French sense of neatness, order, and logic.

Clearly, this haphazard, almost medieval state of affairs couldn't be allowed to continue in the modern world. Something had to be done. And so eventually, throwing up their hands in frustration, the officials in charge of such matters decided to consolidate several *départements* of southeastern France into one new, all-embracing region. Naturally, this needed a name, and who better to provide one than that shadowy but influential figure, the minister in charge of acronyms? (We can thank him for such triumphs as CICAS, CREFAK, CEPABA, CRICA—and these come from just a brief glance at the Vaucluse telephone directory. There are literally thousands of others.)

The minister was called in. He rummaged through the alphabet and deliberated. And having deliberated, he brought forth. PACA was born: Provence–Alpes–Côte d'Azur, stretching from Arles in the west to the Italian frontier in the east—a single, tidy, administratively correct geographical unit. What a relief. At last we all knew where we were.

Or did we? Today, people spending their vacations in Saint-Tropez, in Nice, even in distant Menton, still send postcards home with enthusiastic descriptions of the wonderful time they're having in Provence. Foreign journalists have only to catch a glimpse of lavender in the hills above Cannes to write about the glories of the Provençal countryside. A fish supper in Antibes is promoted as a true Provençal *bouillabaisse*. And in the lexicon of real estate agents—those incurably creative souls—any stone-built villa with a tiled roof, albeit within spitting distance of Monte Carlo, is automatically classified as a Provençal *mas*.

In other words, "Provence" and "Provençal" are finding themselves in areas where, strictly speaking, they have no business being.

Introduction

So where is Provence, and what are its boundaries? Maps vary. Opinions differ. Confusion reigns. But in the end, I find myself agreeing with Monsieur Farigoule's geography, which you will see reflected in the map that follows. Provence—in this book, at least—consists of three *départements:* Bouches-du-Rhône, Alpes-de-Haute-Provence, and the Vaucluse. It is, of course, possible that many people will denounce this as a purely arbitrary decision. It is even possible that some of the entries you will find on the following pages might overstep these arbitrary boundaries by a hair's breadth. Forgive me. All I can offer by way of apology and excuse is, in the Provençal manner, a shrug.

Provence A-Z

Accent

There is a popular misconception that the language spoken in Provence is French. It resembles French, certainly; indeed, in written form it is almost identical. But remove it from the page and apply it to the ear, and Provençal French might easily be another language. If words were edible, Provençal speech would be a rich, thick, pungent verbal stew, simmered in an accent filled with twanging consonants; a *civet*, perhaps, or maybe a *daube*.

Before coming to live in Provence, I acquired a set of Berlitz tapes in order to improve my grasp of French, which I hadn't studied since my schooldays. Evening after evening, I would sit and listen to cassettes of the most mellifluous, perfectly enunciated phrases—spoken, I believe, by a lady from Tours. (I was told that the accent of Tours is considered a jewel among accents, the most polished and refined in France.)

Every morning in front of the mirror while shaving, I would do my best to imitate this accent, pursing my Anglo-Saxon lips until they could pronounce something close to the Gallic *u*, practicing the growl from the back of the throat that is so necessary for the rolling Gallic *r*. Little by little, I thought, I was making progress. And then I left England to come south.

It was an instant farewell to the lady from Tours, because the sound of the words I encountered in Provence was unlike anything I had heard before. And to make matters even more incomprehensible, these words were delivered with an incredible velocity, a vocabulary gone berserk. My ears were in shock for months, and for at least a year I was unable to conduct any kind of sustained conversation without a dictionary. This I used much as a blind man uses a white stick: to identify obstacles and try to find my way around them.

To this day, many years later, there are times when words, even sentences, pass me by in a glutinous blur of sound. Living as I do in the country, I have noticed that the rural accent is perhaps a little thicker—or, some might say, purer—than in bastions of urban civilization like Aix or Avignon. But then there is Marseille, a special case. Here the unsuspecting visitor will have to contend not only with the accent but with an entire sub-language. How, I wonder, would the lady from Tours react if she were offered a *pastaga,* directed to the nearest *pissadou,* cautioned against employing a *massacan,* accused of being *raspi,* invited to a *baletti,* or admired for her *croille?* Like me, I suspect, she would find it all extremely puzzling, even *comac.*

Translations:

> *pastaga* = *pastis*
> *pissadou* = toilet
> *massacan* = a bad worker
> *raspi* = miserly
> *baletti* = a small dance; what used to be known as a *bal populaire*
> *croille* = arrogance, effrontery, chutzpah
> *comac* = extraordinary

Ail

It has been said that Provence is a region that has been rubbed with garlic. Whether you think of garlic as *le divin bulbe* or the stinking rose or the poor man's panacea, there's no getting away from it—in soups, in sauces, in salads, with fish, with meat, with pasta, with vegetables, on or in bread. And if there isn't quite enough of it for your taste, you can always resort to this old Provençal habit: Take a clove of garlic (probably the one you always carry in your pocket for just such a gastronomic emergency), peel it, and hold it between the thumb and index finger of your right hand. With your left hand, hold a fork with its tines facing downward on a plate. Grate the garlic briskly across the tines until you have enough aromatic

juice and fragments on your plate to season the food to your liking.

When considering garlic's history and reputation, it is often difficult to sort out fact from legend. We are told that the laborers building the pyramids of ancient Egypt went on strike because their garlic ration was late in being distributed. This is confirmed by several sources and is probably true. On the other hand, you have the vampire-repellent theories—carry a head of garlic with you at all times, and rub garlic on window frames, door handles, and the floor around your bed for nocturnal protection—which probably aren't. Other slightly dubious claims include garlic's supposed ability to neutralize snake and insect venom; to cure leprosy, asthma, and whooping cough; and to protect against cholera and the evil eye (*"Bon ail contre mauvais oeil"*).

But nothing in the medical history of garlic, at least in Provence, is quite as impressive as the tale of the four thieves. It takes place in Marseille in 1726, when hundreds of inhabitants were dropping like flies from the plague. Our four thieves (today their nearest equivalent would be ambulance-chasing lawyers) visited the empty houses of the recently dead and ransacked them. Growing careless, the thieves were eventually caught and brought to trial. Fortunately for them, the judge had an inquiring mind. How was it, he asked them, that you were able to enter all those contaminated houses without being stricken yourselves by the plague?

Plea-bargaining ensued. In exchange for leniency, the thieves revealed their secret, a powerful elixir that made them immune from the plague. It must have seemed at the time as miraculous as the discovery of penicillin, and from that day on it was called *le vinaigre des quatres voleurs*, or four thieves' vinegar. The ingredients are vinegar, absinthe, rosemary, sage, mint—and, naturally, garlic. (Absinthe is difficult to find nowadays, but *pastis* would probably be an acceptable substitute.) Not surprisingly, the Marseillais quickly found themselves among the most enthusiastic consumers of garlic in France. They still are.

There is no doubt about some other, less dramatic health-giving properties. Garlic is an antiseptic, a disinfectant, and an inhibitor of bacteria. It is rich in vitamins B_I and C. Medical studies suggest that garlic eaters show a lower incidence of stomach cancer, may be less prone than average to strokes and cardiovascular disease, and possess blood of exceptional purity.

Alas, the same cannot be said for their breath. Garlic-induced halitosis has been something of a social obstacle ever since man popped that first clove in his mouth thousands of years ago. King Henri IV of France used to eat a clove every morning. It was said by one of his contemporaries that his breath could knock over a steer at twenty paces. And yet he was also a renowned ladies' man, which leads me to believe that his lady friends had discovered the only truly effective solution to the problem of garlic breath in others. Which is, of course, to eat garlic—and plenty of it—yourself.

Aioli

The Provençal poet Frédéric Mistral, a man with a lyrical turn of phrase and a practical turn of mind, praised *aioli* for possessing, among its many other virtues, the ability to keep away flies. I have also known it occasionally to repel humans, particularly those delicate souls accustomed to a cuisine that is largely innocent of garlic. *Aioli* is not for those with timid taste buds.

Technically, it is mayonnaise. But it is mayonnaise with guts, and to compare it to conventional mayonnaise is like comparing a slice of processed cheese to a ripe Camembert. This classic recipe explains why:

For eight people, you will need sixteen cloves of garlic, the yolks of three eggs, and nearly half a liter of the best olive oil. Peel the garlic, put the cloves in a mortar, and crush them to pulp. Add the egg yolks and a pinch of salt, and stir until the yolks and garlic are thoroughly blended. Then, drop by drop, start adding the oil, stirring (and never stopping) as you go. By the time you've used about half the oil, the *aioli* should have thickened into a dense mass. The rest of the oil can now be added (and stirred) in a continuous, steady flow. The *aioli* becomes thicker and thicker, almost solid. This is how it should be. Add a few drops of lemon juice and serve with potatoes, boiled salt cod, peppers, carrots, beetroot, hard-boiled eggs, and maybe some Provençal snails, *les petits gris.*

As you can imagine, a plateful of this poses a significant challenge to the digestion, and you may wish to follow the advice of one Provençal writer who recommends a *trou provençal* in the middle of the meal. This is a small glass of *marc* that has the effect of cutting through the pungent ointment of eggs and oil to form a hole, or *trou,* through which the rest of the meal can pass. The practical Mistral would surely approve. But I wonder what he would think of a recent development in the social life of *aioli* that I find fascinating, although I haven't so far had the chance to experience it personally. It is an event—one can hardly dismiss it as a mere meal—known as an *aioli dansant.*

If one takes this literally, it sounds like a dangerous combination, mixing the careless rapture of the dance with the consumption of a rich, heavy, oily dish that is quite difficult to eat accurately even when sitting still. But perhaps it is an athletic substitute for the *trou provençal:* an exercise to shake down what has been eaten to make room for second helpings. Who knows? It might even take over from the *paso doble* that is traditionally danced at village fetes.

Air

A man in a bar once told me that the air in Provence was the purest air in France, perhaps even in the world. He was a large and somewhat aggressive man, and I thought it wise not to argue with him. In fact, I was delighted to believe what he had told me, and for several years I would pass on the good news to friends and visitors. "Every breath you take of Provençal air," I used to say, "is like ten euros in the bank of health." It wasn't until I started to research the subject that I discovered the truth.

Here it is: The *départements* of Bouches-du-Rhône, the Vaucluse, Alpes-de-Haute-Provence, and the Var make up one of the four most polluted zones in Europe, a distinction they share with Genoa, Barcelona, and Athens. (Source: Greenpeace France.) Apart from the emissions coming from heavy traffic on the *routes nationales* and the *autoroutes,* the principal villains are to be found in the industrial complex—*l'industrie-sur-mer*—that straggles along the coast from Marseille to the Gulf of Fos and the oil refineries at Berre.

How bad is it? By August 2003, there had been thirty-six days during the year on which the level of air pollution exceeded the official limit of 240 micrograms per cubic meter. More was to come as the summer heat wave continued. And, so we were told, the pollution was not necessarily confined to the area immediately around those who produced it, but could spread as far away as sixty to ninety miles.

Since each of us breathes about thirty pounds of air each day, statistics like this make uncomfortable reading. And yet, walking every day in the Luberon as I do, it's difficult to believe that such a thing as pollution exists. The air looks clear and tastes good. Vegetation seems untouched. Butterflies thrive. Birds and game go about their business, apparently in rude health. Can it be that the mistral is protecting us by blowing away the foul breath of industry? I must consult the man in the bar. He will know.

Alpes et Alpilles

Once upon a time, geographical names had a certain logic about them. They indicated, with varying degrees of accuracy or sometimes optimism, the physical or historical characteristics one might expect to find in that particular place. For instance, the town of L'Isle-sur-la-Sorgue is surrounded by the river Sorgue; Pernes-les-Fontaines has thirty-six fountains; Vaison was settled more than two thousand years ago by the Romans, and eventually became known as Vaison-la-Romaine. These were names that made sense.

Other names, however, seemed to have made too much sense, and here we have a good Provençal example. For many years, the *département* to the west of the Vaucluse was known as the Basses Alpes. It was a name that reflected the fact that in the neighboring *département,* immediately to the north, there were significantly higher mountains whose height was officially confirmed by their title—the Hautes Alpes. This clearly rankled in the Basses Alpes, and local pride was bruised. It is possible that some of the more sensitive residents developed alp envy. Whatever the reason, the name of the *département* was changed in 1970 to Alpes-de-Haute-Provence, which had the great advantage of suggesting a certain alpine loftiness without being too specific.

How high does a bump in the landscape need to be before it can be classified as an alp? The dictionary is of no help here, defining the alp simply as "a high mountain" without telling us how high. This, of course, is open to interpretation, and therefore very useful to those whose task it is to provide names for natural outcroppings. One can imagine such a man, many hundreds of years ago, scratching his head as he gazed at the range of sun-bleached limestone crags that runs from west to east between Fontvieille and Saint-Rémy-de-Provence. His problem was that the crags were certainly taller and more impressive than mere hills. And yet not really high enough, at 900–1,200 feet, to be described as mountains, let alone alps. Our man sat and pondered.

Who knows what caused inspiration to strike? Possibly the dazzling limestone reminded him of the snow-covered peaks of the Swiss Alps. Ah yes, that was it; what he was gazing at, in fact, was a miniature alpine range. Fortunately, in his search for a name he chose to ignore the dinky French habit of adding *-ette* as a diminutive suffix—*alpettes* somehow sounded too much like a group of female mountaineers—and so he decided to call them Les Alpilles.

9

They are charming, picturesque, small enough to be almost cozy despite their jagged silhouettes. Harsh white rock, dark green *maquis,* deep blue sky, brilliant light—it all seems like another world from the sunflowers and fields van Gogh painted in the softer countryside just a few kilometers away.

If you have the legs for it, the best way to explore Les Alpilles is to leave the car behind and rent a bicycle. This will let you appreciate the smell of the scenery—thyme and rosemary and warm stone—as you make your way up and down the D5 on the twists and turns between Saint-Rémy and Fontvieille. A morning of this is an excellent preparation for lunch.

Amandes, Les

Commercially speaking, the almond is the world's top nut. California alone produces 250,000 tons a year. Provence comes almost at the bottom of the international list with anything from 500 to 3,500 tons, depending on which statistical source you choose to accept (as with so much else in Provence, official figures are subject to interpretation, argument, and frequent disbelief). However, on one matter I feel sure that all Provence is in total agreement, and here I quote from information supplied by the Regional Ecological Association of Béziers: "Over the years, it has become clear that the American almond doesn't have the same taste as the

French almond, being less good and a long way away." So there you have it: our almonds are not only better but more convenient than foreign nuts.

The almond was introduced to Europe more than two thousand years ago by

the Greeks (it was once known as the *noix grecque*), although serious culti-vation didn't begin in France until the sixteenth century. But even after four hundred years, domestic production is only equal to about 10 percent of domestic consumption, such is the voracious appetite of the French for this remarkably versatile nut.

To start with, there is the simple salted almond to accompany your *apéritif,* and the gently sautéed almond to add a little crunch to your trout, your chicken, your couscous, even your cauliflower cheese. After that the sweet tooth takes over, and we find the almond in cakes and biscuits, cov-ered in a shell of sugar, dipped in chocolate, pounded into marzipan and nougat, embedded in ice cream, or transformed into that most delightful Aixois specialty, the *calisson* (q.v.). Or you can sip it as a liqueur in its dis-tilled form, Amandine.

Almonds are good for you, too, helping to lower the level of bad cho-lesterol and keep the arteries clear. And if you're fortunate, you will one day be in Provence to see a field of almond trees in February, their white-and-pink blossoms bright against the somber, gray-green hills, an early announcement of spring.

Warning: there is a less amiable kind of almond—the bitter almond—that should be avoided, as it contains prussic acid. Eat ten of them and you will feel very ill. More than twenty, and you could die, and what more undignified end could there be than death by nuts? Luckily, bitter almonds taste horrible.

Amis, Les

Living in Provence has convinced me that there is a strong correlation between popularity and climate. One's social desirability tends to increase with the temperature, and it isn't long before you become more than just an acquaintance, or even a friend. You become a destination.

Around the second half of February, when the first sprinkling of white almond blossoms is decorating the countryside, and there is an occasional

14. June '06

Guess what — we shall be passing
through Provence in July. Any chance
of a couple of beds for a week or two?
There are four of us and a dog (don't
worry — he's house trained).

All you own,

yours

Boll

HOUSE OF LORDS

delicious tremor of warmth in the breeze, the calls start to come in from the frozen north. There are inquiries about your health, complaints about a long and miserable winter, and casual questions about the Provençal weather. These are the first signs of an overwhelming urge to migrate— although at this point, the when and the where of the migration are not disclosed. Be patient. They will be.

As the weeks go by, the calls continue but the questions change: When is it warm enough to swim? How crowded is it in June? How long does it take to drive from Calais to Aix? And then, edging ever closer to the real purpose of the call, what are *your* plans for the summer?

This apparently innocent question is enough to impale you on the horns of a dilemma. If you should say that you will be off butterfly hunting in Siberia, the caller will offer to come to Provence and take care of your empty house while you're away. If you should say you're spending the summer at home, even better: the caller will offer to come to Provence and let you take care of him.

It has taken me several years to admit to myself that I would be lost without these annual visits. If nobody came to stay, I would be free of all obligations except to lie by the pool; potter around the garden; have long, peaceful lunches on the terrace; and take siestas. What kind of summer is that?

Anchoiade

This is a fierce, fishy, and delicious purée made from crushed anchovies, garlic, and olive oil. (As far as I know, there is no precise, definitive recipe; it very much depends on your tolerance of garlic.) Spread on thin slices of toast, it is one of the few canapés with a flavor assertive enough to stand up to the taste of a predinner *pastis*. In the form of a sauce, *anchoiade* is equally good as a dip for raw vegetables.

NOTE: Anchovies, whether bought in a can or straight from the barrel, may be too salty for you. If so, soak them in a mixture of milk and water for ten minutes before using them.

Âne

In my ignorance, I had always thought that all donkeys were created equal: gray-coated, smaller, more stubborn versions of the horse. It wasn't until my neighbor acquired Celeste that my donkey education began.

So far, I have learned that there are at least ten different members of the donkey family resident in France, from the *grand noir du Berry* to the *baudet du Poitou,* each with its own particular features and, I imagine, per-

sonalities. The lovely Celeste is an *âne de Provence,* and displays the classic characteristics of the Provençal branch of the family: smaller than most of her cousins (but with slightly larger feet), a handsome coat in shades of gray, a distinctive rim of white around each eye, and a prominent dark-brown cross, *la croix de Saint André,* running across the shoulders and down the spine. She also has a most engaging smile when offered a carrot.

The Provençal donkey is possibly the most celebrated donkey in France, thanks largely to guest appearances in the writings of Giono, Pagnol, and Daudet. Even so, the breed wasn't officially recognized by the national stud farms until 1995. Now it has its own studbook, in which are laid down in great detail the physical characteristics required of a donkey before it can be classified as a genuine *âne de Provence.* The height must be within certain limits, the cross clearly marked, the ears of a certain length and color—everything down to the size of the foot is included. But there is one important omission: no mention is made of its bray. This, so I'm told by experts, is never the conventional *hi-han, hi-han* of other donkeys but the Provençal version: *hi-hang, hi-hang.*

Anglais, Les

When, in the nineteenth century, the English first came to Provence in any significant numbers, there was no word in the Provençal vocabulary for tourist; *anglais* was used instead, whatever the visitor's nationality. To some extent, it still is. Americans, Dutch, Germans—indeed, any foreigner with a pink face—they all run the risk of being taken for English.

I am an Englishman myself, and I can easily understand why my compatriots are drawn to Provence. Brought up as we are on a small, damp island under a semipermanent pall of cloud, the promise of blue skies and long, predictable summers of a Mediterranean life free of socks and umbrellas is infinitely alluring. Many of us have been unable to resist. And so, over the years, we have come to Provence in what a French friend of mine describes as "industrial quantities." I have found it interesting to see that these refugees from England fall, very roughly, into three groups.

The first, and I hope the largest, consists of those who are happy just to fit in. They work at their French, which on their arrival is often only a few rusty fragments left over from their schooldays. They do their best to adapt to the rhythm of Provence. They take advice from the natives, tread carefully with their neighbors, and observe local customs, from the ritual kisses and the two-hour lunches to the often elastic rules of punctuality. On the whole, this group tends to stay.

The second group should never have left England. Physically, they may be in Provence, but in every other respect they live in an Anglo-Saxon cocoon. Their social life is restricted to other English people. They receive their news from the BBC and English newspapers. During their frequent visits to the mother country, they ransack the supermarket shelves to bring back English cheese, English sausages, English bacon,

and—of course!—canned baked beans. They are not comfortable in the heat and are suspicious of the Provençal character, which they regard as slightly louche. It is only a matter of time before they migrate to the more familiar joys of the Dordogne, where there is a good deal of rain, a large English colony, an English-language newspaper, and a cricket team.

The third and smallest group is the exact opposite. They are determined to overcome their English origins and become, if possible, more French than the French. While not going quite as far as wearing a beret, they bristle with rural Gallic accessories: the local newspaper, *La Provence;* a wooden-handled Opinel pocketknife (which they will produce with a flourish at mealtimes, to cut up their food); French cigarettes—preferably black tobacco wrapped in *papier maïs;* a selection of Loto tickets; canvas ankle boots; and, if they can find one, an ancient Citroën 2CV in the faded blue color of the old Gauloises pack. Thus equipped, they will spend many happy hours in their chosen role of the surly peasant, glaring at strangers from their personal table outside the café.

I used to be a little sensitive about my nationality, and I could never quite escape the feeling that I was no more than a permanent and possibly unwelcome tourist. Then one day, a neighbor with whom I was having a drink set my mind at rest. "You are English," he said, "which is, of course, unfortunate. But you should know that most of us prefer the English to the Parisians."

After that, I felt much better.

Antiquités et Antiquaires

Where did it come from, this passion to acquire relics from other people's attics, this fascination with eighteenth-century chamber pots, cracked and fuzzy mirrors, murky pre-Revolution tapestries? Do we really need, in our already well-equipped homes, an umbrella stand made from the lower portion of an elephant's hind leg? A worm-eaten armoire? A daybed designed for midgets? Of course we don't. And yet thousands of us—nay, hundreds of thousands of us—spend hours, sometimes entire weekends, poking through the jumble in dusty showrooms and cluttered warehouses. So popular has this pastime become that it has spawned its own ungainly Anglo-Saxon verb: we go antiquing.

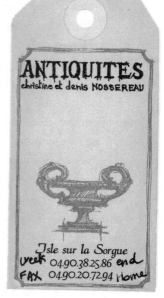

Provence, being a region in which history has left innumerable odds and ends, is fertile ground for the antiques hunter. You will find *brocanteurs* and their more expensive colleagues, *antiquaires*, lying in wait in villages or tucked away behind the walls of country houses and renovated farms. On the RN7 outside Aix, for example, there is a small colony of dealers. Their neighbors up the road are merchants who appear to specialize in dismantled châteaus: fireplaces, staircases, arches, pediments,

17

statues, iron gates, flagstones, gazebos—all thrown together like items in a giant's clearance sale. There are similar establishments selling ancient domestic spare parts outside Apt and Cavaillon.

But for true addicts of all things old and rare, the place to go in Provence is L'Isle-sur-la-Sorgue, a town of some 17,000 inhabitants between Cavaillon and Carpentras. Here, on Saturdays and Sundays, the population explodes. Dealers from Paris, from the rest of Europe, from New York and Los Angeles mingle with locals and vacationers on the lookout for that most elusive purchase, the bargain. And there are scores of resident dealers more than happy to help them.

A building now known as Le Village des Antiquaires was converted some years ago into a kind of shopping mall for antiques. Sixty or so stands on two levels offer temptations of all sorts—chandeliers, copper bathtubs, club chairs, obelisks, busts, ancestral portraits, butcher's tables, boudoir stools, dinner services, nineteenth-century parrot cages, trompe l'oeil chests, leather-bound books sold by the meter, grandfather clocks, trinkets, medals, *objets* of astonishing diversity and no immediately apparent function. In other words, everything for the enthusiastic homemaker.

But if, after seeing all that the stands have to offer, you still haven't come across the commode of your dreams, don't give up. On the Avenue des Quatre Otages you will find a row of establishments fully furnished with chairs, tables, sofas, paintings, and cabinets (with or without ormolu). In the infuriating way of antiques dealers, the prices of these elegant items will not be shown. You must ask, and my belief is that the amount quoted will vary according to the appearance and nationality of the customer. There will be one price for, let us say, an American woman encrusted with jewelry, and another for the Frenchman in shabby corduroys. As a general rule, one should avoid looking too prosperous. And leave your checkbook at home. Dealers prefer cash.

Apothicaires, Rose des

Seldom can a single rose have had so many names: *Rosa gallica* 'Offici-nalis', the Red Rose of Lancaster, Roso-ebriago, Rose de Provins (despite the name, nothing to do with Provence) or, more simply, the Apothe-cary's Rose. Take your pick. There is no question, however, that it is a rose of great antiquity, having been brought to France from the Middle East in 1242, so the legend goes, by Thibaut IV, the count of Champagne.

Apothecaries came to recognize not only that the rose was a beautiful flower but that it also had "medicinal virtues." As a preserve or as a syrup, it was found to calm a turbulent digestion; in the form of lotion, it cleansed and purified the skin; prepared with barley sugar, it soothed the throat. And in Provence it also assumed supernatural qualities, a mixture of myth and manicure.

"More or less everywhere in Provence, one cuts the nails of young children for the first time under a rosebush, so that they will be honest throughout life and will have a beautiful voice." This optimistic message appears on a plaque that is most handsomely set off by a display of Apothecary's Roses in the magical garden of the Mas de la Brune, outside the village of Eygalières.

The Alchemist's Garden, as it is called, is in fact an assortment of botanical gardens. The three largest are laid out in giant squares—one black, one white, one red. As you wander through them, you have the impression that you're walking through a series of paintings in which the artists have used flowers and plants instead of pigment and paint. An extraordinary creation, in the grounds of an equally extraordinary house.

Le Mas de la Brune, built in 1572, is a particularly fine example of Provençal Renaissance style, complete with all kinds of features—lead lattices, round tower, decorated cupola, pilasters, niches, entablature— that make today's architects swoon with nostalgic admiration. The house is also home to a curious selection of permanent residents: a mermaid, a

Tarasque (Provence's favorite man-eating monster), four Christian evangelists, and two carved heads representing anger and gluttony. All that, and the magnificent garden. Who could ask for a more fascinating place to spend an afternoon?

Apta Julia

What was Apta Julia (named after Julius Caesar in Roman times) is now just plain Apt. The town calls itself "the world capital of crystallized fruits," although it is probably better known for its seething Saturday-morning market. This is busy throughout the year, but in July and August it seethes so energetically that one is lucky to escape superficial flesh wounds caused by glancing blows from loaded shopping baskets. In the winter, the market is smaller and calmer, and there are usually one or two

truffle dealers outside the Café de France or the Café Grégoire, where visitors are often surprised by the sight of men with their heads thrust deep into blue plastic bags: truffle sniffers, inhaling before buying.

Two very different establishments in the center of Apt shouldn't be missed. In the Cathedral of Sainte-Anne, dating from the late twelfth century, you will see stained glass from the fourteenth century, a portrait of John the Baptist, and various reliquaries, one of which contains "the shroud of Saint Anne." In fact, this is an Arabian banner, a souvenir brought back from the First Crusade.

Two minutes away, in the Place Septier, is one of the best wine merchants in Provence, where I have spent many happy hours. Hélène and Thierry Riols, in the Cave Septier, specialize in wines from the south. They have a formidable selection of Côtes du Rhône, Côtes du Luberon, some treasures from the Languedoc, and an assortment of *eaux-de-vie* that will restore your faith in the alcoholic virtues of fruit.

Fruit of another style can be found at small, artisanal establishments such as the Confiserie Saint Denis and the Confiserie Marcel Richaud, where all kinds of *fruits* are *confits à l'ancienne*—that is, mainly by hand. The water is extracted from the fruit and replaced with a sugary solution that preserves and coats it. This is, of course, dangerously addictive for those with a sweet tooth, and irresistible for those who like their sugar in a rush.

Artichauts à la Barigoule

It is only in the oldest of cookbooks that you will find any mention of the hero of this dish, the original *barigoule* (or *barigoulo*). It was a mushroom of the morel family, an extraordinarily tasty mushroom, and it was used as the base for a variety of recipes that, naturally, were described as *"à la barigoule."* From its birthplace in the area around the Alpilles, the original recipe spread through the rest of Provence and eventually, as Provençal chefs traveled, even farther. I myself have seen versions of it on menus as far away from the Alpilles as New York and San Francisco. Sadly, although the dish has become increasingly popular, the unfortunate *barigoule* has been extinct for centuries; only its name has survived.

Despite this, modern recipes provide a much more interesting way of eating artichokes than simply dunking the leaves in vinaigrette sauce. For a proper *barigoule,* the artichokes must be young, tender, and small (a suggested serving is four per person), which is easy enough. The problems start when it comes to making the bed on which the artichokes rest, and here even that valuable volume *L'Inventaire du patrimoine culinaire de la*

France is a little hesitant in offering a definitive recommendation. Finely chopped onions, carrots, shallots, olive oil, and white wine are a start. And then what? Mushrooms, diced bacon, garlic, ham, bread crumbs, lemons, parsley, chives, butter—they all appear in one recipe or another. But should they be used as a bed or as a stuffing?

Occasionally, questions of this importance and complexity can only be resolved by calling in the gastronomic police, otherwise known as the guardians of Les Appellations d'Origine Contrôlée. I think this may be a suitable case for them. They should put their heads together—probably under the direction of a good Provençal chef—and decide upon an official *barigoule* recipe. That done, they can organize an artichoke evening at the Élysée Palace to introduce AOC *barigoule* to the world.

Automne

Gunfire in the hills as the hunting season starts. Green turns to russet and gold in the vineyards. Wine turns from pink to red on the table. The frogs finally fall silent, and the fish disappear to the bottom of the *bassin*. The return of the *daube* in the oven and the fire in the kitchen. One final, chilling swim. A whirr of speckled partridge rising from the wheat stubble. *Vignerons* breathe a sigh of relief now that the grapes are in. The village shakes off its summer languor, and there are more locals than strangers in the weekly market. A few hardy butterflies, seemingly impervious to the change of seasons, make ever-shorter flights. Snakes vanish.

Bambouseraie d'Anduze

This is unique and extraordinary, and justifies a short excursion outside the strict limits of Provence. Indeed, you might easily think that you've strayed into some green pocket of Laos or Bali, and you need to remind yourself that you are no more than thirty miles or so from Nîmes.

The Bambouseraie de Prafrance, as it is officially called, is a living monument to one man's botanical love affair. Eugène Mazel, having made a fortune importing spices from Asia, spent it—all of it—between 1855 and 1890, perfecting the conditions in which the object of his passion could flourish. What he wanted was a bamboo forest.

He was helped by what was already there: a sheltered bowl of land lined at the bottom with fertile alluvial soil, and a local microclimate that was judged by Mazel to be suitable for bamboo planting on a grand scale. There was, however, a problem. The natural water supply was erratic—weeks or months of drought punctuated by the extravagant downpours of the Provençal monsoon. To correct this, Mazel decided to create an irrigation system that would bring water from the upper reaches of the river Gardon, a few miles from the property. In this way, his precious bamboo would not have to struggle to survive on a rainfall that was at best capricious and at worst nonexistent.

Making adjustments to the climate is an expensive hobby, and Mazel had to dip deep into his fortune. There was also the matter of the care and maintenance of his giant garden, and several dozen full-time gardeners were needed. But Mazel kept the money flowing, and eventually he achieved his dream. He had his *bambouseraie:* not only close to three hundred species of bamboo, but palm trees, banana trees, sequoias, a maze, lotuses, an elaborate water garden, Japanese carp, and an assortment of

exotic plants, all spread over fifteen hectares. I can only hope that he had a few years of enjoyment from it before the money trickled to a stop, which it did in 1890. Mazel had been ruined by his obsession.

During the next few years, the *bambouseraie* was administered by a bank, whose interests, naturally enough, were financial rather than horticultural. It wasn't until 1902 that it came into more sympathetic hands, when Gaston Nègre and his family took over and began the immense task of restoring the property after a twelve-year lapse. Today Monsieur Nègre's granddaughter and her husband are in charge, and they do a formidable job. All those labor-intensive hectares, hundreds of thousands of trees and plants, a palatial nineteenth-century greenhouse, a couple of miles of irrigation channels, and, no matter where you look, not a leaf out of place, not a weed to be seen. Old Mazel would be thrilled.

What strikes the visitor first is size. The bamboo, after all, is a member of the grass family, and it is difficult to imagine a distant cousin of your lawn growing to a height of eighty-five feet, with a trunk thicker than a footballer's thigh. Some species shoot up so fast in their season that an attentive man can watch his bamboo grow as much as a meter taller in the space of twenty-four hours.

The colors are another surprise. As well as the classic dull yellow of Chaplin's cane, there is a range of greens from shiny emerald to a matte camouflage, shades of brown, green with yellow stripes, and a distinguished black that darkens in the sun to a rich ebony. Given this choice, and the huge variety of sizes—from a forest to a hedge to a single feathery plant in a pot—bamboo can just as easily decorate an apartment terrace as a field.

And it is a most restful plant, soothing to the eye and good for the soul.

Walking through the *bambouseraie,* with the light flickering through the tall trunks and with no sound louder than the rustle of a breeze in the leaves, is one of life's truly peaceful moments. A magical place.

Bancaus

Agriculture in Provence is, at the best of times, a hard business. Winters are often severe, summers are always blistering, drought is followed by flood, and the mistral nags away, blowing precious topsoil into your neighbor's vineyard, never to return. If, in addition, your few acres are on a forty-degree slope, it is enough to make all but the most determined abandon the land in favor of an undemanding career in politics.

Clearly, the Provençal *agriculteurs* of old were not only determined but ingenious, and no slope was too steep for them, thanks to the *bancau,* prepared as follows:

First, slice your hillside into giant steps (between waist and chest high), leaving a wide, flat terrace between each step. Against the vertical face of these steps, build retaining walls of dry stone, not forgetting to link one level to the next with a short flight of smaller steps set into the wall. Now plant your terraces with olives, fruit trees, vines, and vegetables. Tend and water for a hundred years or more, and you will have *bancaus* similar to those you see clinging to high ground all over Provence.

It is gardening on a massive scale, at the same time practical and decorative. And it was achieved not with the aid of labor-saving devices like bulldozers but with the horse, the mule, the pickax, the shovel, bare hands, strong backs, and sweat.

Banon

Legend, that marvelously vague and unverifiable form of history, tells us that the noble goat cheese of Banon was greatly loved by the Romans. And no Roman could have loved it more than Emperor Antoninus Pius

(A.D. 86–161), who ate so much of it that he died of terminal indigestion. This is perhaps not something that today's cheese makers care to remember, but it does indicate how difficult it is to stop eating good ripe Banon once you start.

My own introduction to goat cheese was, I'm sure, similar to that of many people who first tried it outside France: a disappointment. In my case, it happened many years ago in London. Things are better now, but in those days the English didn't understand exotic foreign cheeses and treated them all like cheddar, often making them inedible. Thus it was with my first goat cheese—a pallid, sweaty, unyielding substance that tasted bitter and smelled strongly of ammonia.

Nothing could be further from that unlovely lump than the veritable Banon, which is usually—and accurately—described as unctuous. Smooth and soft, it is a cheese that murmurs rather than shouts, and there is an interesting reason for its subtle flavor. Every true Banon must be *plié*—entirely covered in chestnut leaves that are secured with raffia to form a kind of rustic gift-wrapping. To keep the leaves supple and prevent them from flaking, they are soaked before use in wine or in *marc*. This combines with the tannin already in the leaves to give the cheese the taste—creamy but not bland—that the Romans found so much to their liking.

Some vital statistics: each cheese should measure between seventy-five and eighty-five millimeters in diameter and between twenty to thirty millimeters in height. This is the ideal size to be shared by two people, who should be armed with a fresh baguette and a bottle of local wine. For the younger Banon, a white or a light red from Les Baux-en-Provence or the Luberon; for

26

the more mature specimen, something sweeter, like a *muscat* from Beaumes-de-Venise.

A final statistic: on July 24, 2003, Banon was granted an Appellation d'Origine Contrôlée, an accolade reserved for the most distinguished cheeses in France. Emperor Antoninus would have been delighted.

Bastide

Elsewhere in France, a *bastide* is a fortified town; in Provence it is a house. Although less grand than châteaus, *bastides* were built to be inhabited by people rather than by the goats, horses, or sheep that often used to be part of the family in farmhouses and shared the accommodations. Consequently, the rooms in a *bastide* are normally spacious, the ceilings high, the windows large and numerous, and the overall design much more disciplined than the often haphazard style of agricultural architecture. The façade is regular, with symmetrical openings under a hipped roof—not unlike a child's drawing of a house.

As for the setting, there is a wide range of decorative options. If the original owner, back in 1790, was a keen gardener, he might have planted an *allée* of plane trees leading up to the house. There would be a fountain, a *bassin* stocked with carp, a few tasteful touches of wrought iron in the form of balconies and banisters, an assortment of urns, and probably one or two statues. In the distance, his back diligently bent, would be the gardener, clipping box bushes into perfect spheres.

Unusually for France, where everything down to the size of the gravel in your courtyard is officially calibrated, there are no rules governing the use of the word *bastide*. It is up for grabs, and grabbed it frequently is, to lend an air of spurious distinction to small modern houses that have been constructed of salmon-pink concrete. So far, I have not yet seen the ultimate horror—the *bastidette*—but I'm sure it's around somewhere.

Bauxite

Les Baux is the least likely setting one could imagine for a major industrial advance. The village is almost too picturesque to be true, with a history to match: bloodthirsty *seigneurs,* the beastly Raymond de Turenne, troubadours, poets, beautiful women, the Court of Love—this corner of the Alpilles saw them all come and go. And then a decidedly less romantic figure made his contribution to the annals of Les Baux. Pierre Berthier discovered the raw matter of aluminum and named his discovery after the village where he found it. In 1821, bauxite was officially born, and the world could look forward to an aluminum future, complete with space shuttles and beer cans.

The old bauxite quarries have now been turned into the Cathédrale d'Images. This is basically a giant slide show, with a different theme each year, in which enormous images are projected onto the limestone walls. Partly because of this (and partly, no doubt, because of the sublime food at the nearby two-star Oustau de Baumanière), the village has become one of the biggest attractions in France: a million tourists a year, so the statistics say, and in the high season it occasionally feels as though they have all arrived on the same day. It's well worth a visit, nevertheless.

Beaumes-de-Venise

Despite its romantic name, this village north of Carpentras has absolutely nothing to do with the famous city of canals in Italy. The "Venise" here refers to the Comtat Venaissin, the old name for an area roughly the same as today's Vaucluse.

The business of the village is wine. There is a red, and a good honest red it is, too. But the Beaumes-de-Venise more generally known and more widely drunk is the luscious sweet white wine made from the muscat grape. The locals drink it chilled as an *apéritif,* and some of them find the

Anglo-Saxon habit of drinking it with dessert rather quaint. In fact, I have known some enthusiastic Anglo-Saxons who drink it with foie gras, with certain cheeses, with chocolate pudding, as a nightcap, and as a heart starter the following morning, such is the ease with which it slips down.

The people at the Domaine de Durban, just outside the village, make a consistently good *muscat* that regularly receives excellent, if slightly ornate, reviews from wine critics. One of them has written as follows: "The robe is pale gold, the nose light and flowery, with hints of exoticism and fresh lemon. The intensity bursts in the mouth, with notes of roast grape and preserved apricot." Which, I suppose, is just another way of saying that it is indeed a lovely drop.

Belges, Les

It is a sad fact that most of us need, from time to time, a foreigner to ridicule; it improves our sense of self-esteem. The English love to poke fun at the Irish. The Americans (until it became politically incorrect) had themselves in stitches with their Polish jokes. And the French in general— despite already possessing boundless self-esteem—have so many targets that it would be difficult to identify the most popular.

Down in Provence, however, there are two species of foreigner that regularly cause gales of mirth in the village café: the Parisian, whom we shall come to later, and, above all, the Belgian.

Why the poor Belgians should be singled out for this distinction I couldn't say, and so I asked Monsieur Farigoule, who usually advises me on social matters of this sort. "Why do we mock the Belgians?" he said, pausing for emphasis before delivering the punch line. "Because they are Belgian."

He then told me these two jokes—or rather, what he described as jokes:

The French drive on the right side of the road. The British drive on the wrong side of the road. The Belgians drive in the middle of the road.

The correct response to a Parisian waiter who claims to have problems comprehending what you say: "Monsieur, you seem to have difficulty understanding French. Evidently, you are Belgian."

You can see that Farigoule's sense of humor could never be accused of subtlety. But what can you expect from someone who greets every Englishman he meets by saying, with a wink and a nudge, "Aha! My tailor is rich, eh?"

There is a theory about the French sense of humor, and I decided one day to try it out on Farigoule. It is in the form of question and answer.

> Question: Why are the French amused by jokes about the Belgians?
>
> Answer: Because they are the only jokes the French can understand.

This, I must admit, fell flat, and relations between Farigoule and myself went through a sensitive period. The breach was healed, curiously enough, by President Chirac. When he told the world that Britain's most important contribution to agriculture was mad cow disease, Farigoule felt that French superiority in the matter of humorous insults had been reestablished, and we were back on cordial terms again.

Bises et Bisous

Visitors from the north are frequently surprised by the intensely tactile nature of social intercourse in Provence. Most Parisians or Londoners, for instance, are accustomed to conversations that are purely verbal exchanges conducted at arm's length. In Provence, they find various body parts being hugged and squeezed, tweaked and tapped and prodded and occasionally massaged. I have seen men and women retreat from these encounters with alarmed expressions on their faces as they examine themselves for superficial bruises. It takes some time for them to realize that speech without touch, for a Provençal, is like *aioli* without garlic.

Further confusion and surprise are in store when it comes to the obligatory exchange of kisses when meeting friends and acquaintances. The national average in France is one kiss per cheek. This is considered polite, at least in the north. In the south, too, it can be considered polite—but also reserved, cold, even a little snobbish. Three kisses are the popular ration; four are by no means unusual. However, there is a delicate problem here, one that I still haven't solved after several years of trial and error.

The kisser approaches the kissee, his lips at the ready. But ready for what? Two? Three? Four? Too few, and you risk the embarrassment of leaving a proffered cheek unkissed. Too many, and you might find yourself kissing an unsuspecting nose instead of a cheek. The best advice I can offer is to pay very close attention to the turning of the head and kiss accordingly.

Another puzzling question is the gender of the kiss. In the dictionary, you will find the feminine *bise* and the masculine *bisou*. On paper, both mean exactly the same thing. But in practice, surely there must be a difference between giving someone a *bise* or a *bisou*. Probably a subtle change of technique: a more pronounced pursing of the lips, an extra second or two of lingering on the cheek. Only in France would one worry about such things.

Bories

Somebody once counted the *bories* in Provence and arrived at an approximate figure of three thousand. You'll find them dotted around the more isolated parts of the Provençal countryside, where peasants cleared their land of stones. These were used to store their agricultural tools (and even to store themselves during intemperate weather, or when plague threatened the villages). Scholars will tell you that *bories* have a distinctly

Neolithic appearance, similar to the *nuraghi* of Sardinia, but in fact most of them were built no earlier than the eighteenth century.

To call them small huts doesn't begin to do them justice. They are

extraordinary architectural balancing acts, built of dry stone and nothing but dry stone—no mortar, no supporting beams—depending on nothing more than perfect weight distribution and the force of gravity to keep them from collapsing. They come in three basic styles: *en gradin*, with stepped walls and an almost flat roof; *en cône*, the tallest of the three, which resembles the pointed tip of a bullet; and *en ruche*, with the squat profile of a beehive.

In their simple way, they are wonderfully decorative structures, particularly when set in a field of lavender, and I once asked a *maçon* if he would build a *borie*

for me. "A real one?" he asked. "No mortar, no beams, every stone chosen by hand, every stone placed by hand?" He sucked his teeth and considered for a few moments before nodding. Yes, of course it was possible. But because of the highly skilled labor required, not to mention the problem of finding suitable stones, it would probably cost as much to build as a large modern garage. I thought it was ironic that something peasants once used as a toolshed should have become a luxury. My lavender field remains entirely devoted to lavender, without the benefit of a *borie*.

Bouchons Rustiques

One of the joys of driving around the back country of Provence is the relative absence of traffic. There will be the occasional tractor and the odd small van, but a car—particularly a clean car, free of dust and mud and therefore clearly from elsewhere—is sufficiently rare on some of these narrow, pockmarked roads to cause the men working in the fields to look up and take notice. Easing their backs and squinting into the sun, they follow the progress of the car as long as it remains in view before stooping once again over their vines or their melons.

A few peaceful, traffic-free miles like this are enough to make the driver dangerously relaxed. His attention wanders. His eye lingers on the beauties of the countryside, looking to left and right instead of ahead. And when he comes to a bend, he barely slows down; after all, he has the road to himself. This is the moment when disaster nearly strikes, and it is only by the grace of God and a swift foot on the brakes that he is prevented from running into a moving woolly wall.

Sheep—there they are, hundreds of them, blocking the way almost as far as the

eye can see, bleating in alarm, on the verge of mass flight. A sheepdog appears, furious that his orderly and obedient flock is being inconvenienced. In the far distance, over a sea of heaving gray backs, a solitary figure folds his hands over the top of his crook and waits.

The first time this happened to me I panicked and started to reverse the car as fast as I could. The sheep increased their pace and followed; some of the more athletic among them overtook me. The dog's barking became hysterical. The distant shepherd made what I took to be a helpful gesture. Distracted by the living chaos around me, I backed the car into a shallow ditch and stalled.

It took ten minutes or so for the flock to pass. The shepherd brought up the rear, his impassive face the color and texture of cracked leather. He stopped, looked at the car, shook his head, and informed me that I was stuck. I should have stayed where I was, he said. I should have turned off the engine and practiced patience. He shook his head again at the breakneck habits of motorists and moved on.

Moral: When driving in Provence, remember that sheep have the right of way.

Bouffadou

This ingenious gadget originated not in Provence but in the *département* of Lozère, noted for its mountainous countryside and the luxuriant mustaches of its male inhabitants. It was, so we are told, these very mustaches that inspired the invention of the *bouffadou.*

Like many good ideas, it is practical and uncomplicated—a straight pine branch, perhaps thirty inches long, with a hole bored through from one end to the other. The hole transforms the branch into a simplified bellows. Aim into the fireplace, apply your lips to the *bouffadou,* blow down the hole, and *voilà!* The newly lit fire is encouraged; the glowing embers are revived. And it was all done without the slightest risk of setting

fire to your
mustache.
(Alas, there
are no records
of the incidence of
flaming mustaches, but the
existence of the *bouffadou* proves
that they were common enough at one
point.)

Clearly, it was an idea that deserved to
travel far beyond its birthplace in Lozère. It
couldn't have been long before it reached
Provence, where it was refined, improved,
and given a second use.

The Provençal *bouffadou* is made not from pine but from iron. Sophisticated versions have a brass mouthpiece at one end and a sturdy prong at the other. Being iron, it can be thrust into the heart of the fire to rearrange logs before applying another gust of air as required. Thus it became the invaluable tool it is today: half poker, half blower. Every fireplace should have one.

Bouillabaisse

It has been variously described as a stew, a soup of gold, a mystical experience, a magical synthesis, beach food, a divine seduction, or the reason God invented fish. Poetry of the most ornate kind has been written about it. Venus is said to have fed it to her husband, Vulcan, to lull him to sleep so that she could engage in dalliance with Mars. Arguments have raged about the correct ingredients for at least a hundred years and continue to this day. It has its own official charter. *Bouillabaisse* is not a simple dish.

Its origins, however, probably were. Fishermen returning to the small ports along the Mediterranean coast would sort their catch according to type and general condition. Those fish that were considered the least salable were put aside for the fishermen's supper. A fire was lit, a cauldron of water was brought to the boil, the fish were dropped in, and that was that. The name is generally believed to be an abbreviation of *bouillon abaissé*—literally, "broth lowered," or reduced by evaporation.

Those uncomplicated days have long since gone, thanks to the French genius for codifying everything in sight, particularly everything they eat and drink. This eventually affected the fishermen's supper. *Bouillabaisse* was given a formal recipe, or rather a series of recipes, since the inhabitants of several seaside towns—notably Marseille, Toulon, and Antibes—had their own views on what should or should not go into the pot. White wine? Obligatory in one recipe, forbidden in another. Potatoes? Never, says one connoisseur; always, says another. Croutons rubbed with garlic? Absolutely essential or a disgraceful heresy, depending on which expert you listen to (and we must never forget that *everyone* in Provence is an expert).

It took the Marseillais to settle matters, at least to their satisfaction, once and for all. Just as they had appropriated *pastis* to be their very own—*le vrai pastis de Marseille*—they turned their considerable promotional skills to establishing the idea that if you wanted the true, the authentic, the *véritable bouillabaisse,* the place to go was Marseille. Because in Marseille you would find *bouillabaisse* prepared according to the rules and regulations contained in that fishy manifesto, the official Bouillabaisse Charter.

It will come as no surprise to learn that the Charter was concocted by some of Marseille's chefs. In 1980, a group of them got together to lay down the law about *bouillabaisse,* in order, as they said, to protect the innocent man in the street from spurious imitations. The public-spirited chefs defined and described the basic ingredients, the correct recipe, and the way in which *bouillabaisse* should be served. The unwritten but obvious subtext was that anyone misguided enough to eat *bouillabaisse* at a non-Charter establishment would have to make do with a pale imitation of the real thing.

A Charter member, and one of the most famous restaurants in Marseille, is Le Miramar, on the Quai du Port. If you order what they call La Vraie Bouillabaisse Miramar (a variation on La Vraie Bouillabaisse Marseillaise), this is what you'll get: scorpion fish, John Dory, conger eel, weaver fish, anglerfish, sea hen, soup fish, tomatoes, potatoes, onions, garlic (of course), saffron, cumin, fennel, olive oil, parsley, pepper, and salt.

According to tradition, you should be shown the fish before they are cooked, so that you can see how fresh they are. After being cooked, they should be cut up in front of you by your waiter and not hacked to pieces by some inexperienced lad in the kitchen. Then there is the *rouille*, the accompanying sauce, which is similar to *aioli* but spiced up with hot peppers and tinged with saffron; some thin slices of baguette that have been crisped in the oven; and finally, a bottle of white Bandol or white Châteauneauf-du-Pape. Now you have all you need for a long, messy, and delectable feast.

Although the details of *bouillabaisse* recipes are subject to violent and sometimes acrimonious debate, there is one fundamental fact on which everyone from Perpignan to Menton can agree: true *bouillabaisse* can only be made with fish from the Mediterranean. Which is why I was surprised recently when I came across the recipe for something called Creole Bouillabaisse. Surprise turned to dismay when I saw some of the ingredients: shrimp, flour, vegetable oil or margarine, oysters, chicken broth—what have these got to do with *bouillabaisse*? Heaven knows what the chef at Le Miramar would say.

Countries cannot always choose their national symbols, but on the whole France has been lucky. One only has to think of the Eiffel Tower, the baguette, Napoléon, and Brigitte Bardot. There is, however, a macabre addition to this list that you will never see on a postcard, even though it is (or was) uniquely French: the guillotine.

Although the death penalty had existed in France since the Middle Ages, it wasn't until 1791 that any serious attempt was made to abolish it, during a debate in the National Assembly. Results were mixed. Torture was banned, perhaps as a sop to the abolitionists, but the death penalty was retained. And not only that—a method for carrying it out was agreed upon and made into law: *Tout condamné à mort aura la tête tranchée.*

It is, of course, one thing to say that heads must roll and quite another to specify in detail how that should be achieved. But by chance, one of the politicians of the time, Dr. Joseph Guillotin, was also a professor of anatomy. He commissioned a purpose-built machine to do the job of official decapitation, and despite his understandable reluctance to be forever associated with an instrument of death, the machine was named after him.

The guillotine had a long career, and it wasn't finally abolished until 1981. There are still public executioners alive today, and I met one of the last of them, Fernand Meyssonnier, at his home in Fontaine-de-Vaucluse. This is one of the more popular tourist destinations in Provence, renowned for its associations with the fourteenth-century poet Petrarch and the picturesque gush of the river Sorgues as it comes out of a cave at the bottom of a sheer cliff.

It's a small village, and not the kind of place where one can live anonymously. But then Monsieur Meyssonnier is not a man who shrinks from celebrity. He has written a book, *Paroles de bourreau,* in which he describes his life as an executioner (twenty years, two hundred decapitations) and is quite comfortable talking about his work. A stocky man in his early seventies, his appearance gives no hint of his previous career. You could easily imagine him as a farmer, driving his tractor or pruning his vines or hunting. The only clues to his past are displayed in his living room—a small-scale working model of a guillotine and a collection of books and tracts dealing with crime, punishment, and justice.

These subjects are of consuming interest to Monsieur Meyssonnier— you might say they are his hobbies—and he talks at length about them. He is also a great collector of the tools and accessories of punishment. At one time, these were the exhibits in a museum that he opened to the public, but business of late has been disappointingly slow, and everything is now on sale. Should your taste run to fetters and shackles, there is a comprehensive choice, from the simple eighteenth-century iron chain and collar at 30 euros to the much more elaborate two-collar-plus-handcuffs set priced at 1,448 euros. But that's just the beginning. There are branding irons, thumbscrews, a supremely nasty chair with a spiked seat, a hangman's noose autographed by the hangman himself, multilash whips, pincers, a giant pillory, tourniquets, finger crushers, restraints of all shapes and sizes, iron masks, head squeezers, mantraps, and Indian executioners' swords. Price list available on request.

Taking a break from the apparatus of torture, I admired a pair of handsome gray parrots that were peering at us through the bars of their cage next to the model guillotine. Intelligent and patriotic birds they are, too; Monsieur Meyssonnier has trained them to say *"Vive la France"* before breakfast every morning. And then, at some point in the ensuing conversation, he mentioned his birthday. I was rather taken aback to find that it was the same as mine: June 14. As if this weren't enough of a spooky coincidence, our birth sign, Gemini, is the only sign in the zodiac with two heads.

Boutis

As long ago as the fifteenth century, the best-dressed beds in Provence wore the *boutis*—a quilted bedcover, often intricately decorated with designs of flowers, animals, or religious and ancestral symbols. In fact, the first recorded *boutis* appeared in the inventory of the Comtesse d'Avelin at the Château des Baux in 1426. Today more recent versions of the *boutis* are still covering elegant beds and sofas, not just in Provence but all over the world.

It's easy to see why they have been so popular for so long. A *boutis* is a thing of beauty, hand-stitched with the finest needlework, quilted to a satisfying plumpness, thick enough to withstand winter drafts, sturdy enough to survive generations of use. And it was not confined to the bedroom. Sometime between the fifteenth and seventeenth centuries, the fashionable ladies of Provence started wearing quilted skirts, and the more pampered babies of Provence were being swaddled in quilted *petassouns*. (These had a practical advantage as well as being ornamental, providing a water-resistant layer between an incontinent baby and his mother's Sunday-best clothes.)

The undisputed world capital of the *boutis* was Marseille. In 1680, between five thousand and six thousand nimble-fingered women were turning out more than forty thousand quilted items a year, and the *broderie de Marseille* was exported throughout Europe. The more elaborate and colorful fabrics imported from India and known as *les indiennes* were particularly popular with everyone—except, not surprisingly, others in the textile business. Sensing commercial catastrophe, the silk, velvet, and tapestry lobby took their problem to the king, who obliged them with a royal decree banning *les indiennes* in 1686. And then came the plague of 1720, partly transmitted by an infected cargo of cotton. Fifty thousand people died. All imports of cotton were forbidden. Dark days for Marseille and for the *boutis* business.

In time it revived. The white *boutis* became established as the traditional covering for the nuptial bed, and quilted skirts could still be seen in Provence up until the First World War. Now probably the best place to see the very best *boutis* is L'Isle-sur-la-Sorgue, in the shop of Michel Biehn, a collector and dealer of great taste and expertise. If you should ever want to cover your bed with an heirloom, he's your man.

Brandade de Morue

In theory, this should be a creamy and subtle purée of salt cod, olive oil, milk, and garlic, a state of perfection that can only be achieved with patience and proper salt cod (not the rigid planks of dried stockfish that masquerade as the real thing).

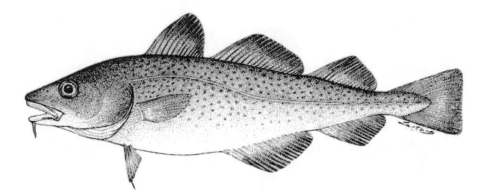

Brandade is not a dish to be rushed. The cod needs to be soaked in cold water for up to forty-eight hours, and the water should be changed at regular intervals during that time. Those of you who are busy or forgetful might want to adopt the desalting technique devised by a certain Monsieur Ramadier, who used to place the salt cod in the cistern of his toilet, thus ensuring that the water was changed with the required regularity, and with very little effort.

The desalted cod should be gently poached until tender (about eight minutes), then filleted and flaked while oil and milk are heating in separate saucepans. Once the oil is very hot, add the cod and beat briskly with a wooden spoon over low heat. Add more oil, alternating with milk, a tablespoon at a time, beating after each tablespoon until the mixture is smooth, and thick enough to hold its shape.

As for the garlic, expert opinion is divided. It can be crushed and stirred in, or a cut clove can be used to rub the bowl, or you can follow the advice of a group of *brandade* enthusiasts in Nîmes and leave it out altogether. "Garlic in the *brandade*," says one of them, "is a crime against gastronomy."

Two variations of the classic recipe are the *brandade du vendredi*, in which the cod is mixed with puréed potato, and *brandade aux truffes*, with the breathtakingly expensive addition of chopped truffles.

Eat with pieces of fried bread.

Bronzettes

Until comparatively recently, a tanned skin was the badge of the serf, the humble toiler who was obliged to work in the fields for his living. The upper reaches of society shielded themselves from the vulgar glare of the sun, stayed in the shade, called for iced sherbet, and cultivated their porcelain complexions.

How things have changed in less than a hundred years. The tan has become something of a status symbol, especially in winter. It is a sign of travel and leisure and affluence, and the previously pale bourgeoisie now jump at the chance to strip off their clothes and change color. As anyone who has seen the human rotisseries around the pools of Provence or on the beaches of the Riviera can tell you, sunbathing is a serious business. For the true enthusiast, not a millimeter of visible skin should be left untanned. I remember once seeing a young woman—already, it seemed to me, sufficiently dusky—applying tanning oil, drop by careful drop, to the crevices between her toes.

Sun worshipping in France started to become fashionable in the 1920s, thanks partly to an American couple, Sara and Gerald Murphy. They would take their houseguests at the Villa America—Ernest Hemingway and F. Scott Fitzgerald among them—to the nearby beach at La Garoupe, to swim and soak up the sun. Their friend Pablo Picasso would often be there in his capacity as sunbather-in-chief, his skin the color of a well-cured cigar. Little by little, season by season, the habit of the *bronzette* took root and flourished.

Today it is still possible to identify some social types and professional occupations by their summer markings. There is the *boulevardier*'s café tan, covering hands, arms, and the lower part of the face (the upper part being protected from the sun by large dark glasses and a Montecristi Panama hat). There is the *gendarme*'s tan: forearms, most of the face, and a V of color from an open-necked shirt. An off-duty *gendarme* can usually be identified by the prominent demarcation line—white above, brown below—on his forehead, caused by the horizontal peak of his official *képi*. There is the peasant's tan (also known as the tractor tan), with a similar band of pale skin across the forehead from wearing a cap, and the colors of the upper body conforming precisely to the shape of his sleeveless vest. And finally, there is the visitor's tan, which will vary from a throbbing scorched pink to a well-established amber, depending on skin type and length of vacation.

43

Every year as summer approaches, the same dire warnings are issued about the damage caused by too much sun: premature wrinkles, pigment blotches, and cancer of the epidermis. And yet the tan seems to retain its popularity, partly as a visible vacation souvenir and partly because most of us look better, or think we do, with honey-colored limbs and faces. One of my earliest French memories is arriving in Provence, fresh from England and pallid as a slug, to find myself surrounded by people glowing with health and sunshine. I took to the sun immediately and have never lost the habit. And I have the wrinkles to prove it.

Bruxelles

A word that evokes strong reactions in Provence, above all among farmers, who suspect that their subsidies are being nibbled away by European Union bureaucrats in the Belgian capital using their prodigal expense accounts to gorge on beer and *moules frites.*

Cacheille

Here is a problem faced by every cheese-loving cook: what to do with the remnants—those chunks, fragments, and dollops of cheese that are too small, too squashed, or generally too disreputable to serve up again. And here is the aromatic, alcoholic solution: *la cacheille,* a venerable Provençal system of recycling.

Any soft or semi-soft cheese will do. Put all the leftovers, with garlic and herbs according to your taste, in a deep pot and knead them until they are blended into one unified mass. Pour in a generous slug of *marc,* and mix thoroughly. Now you have a base, to which you can add more cheese—and always more *marc*—in the weeks and months to come, or even years. There are stories of a legendary *cacheille* that reached the ripe old age of ten on its diet of leftovers and *marc.* And ripe, in fact, is the word that best describes both the smell and the flavor of this dense, tangy, stick-to-the-teeth mixture.

I have known people who grill it on toast to make a fierce Welsh rarebit, one with a kick. But I prefer to eat it straight from the pot, spread on a piece of baguette and helped down by the heaviest red wine in the house.

Calissons d'Aix

Italians may have their *calisone* and Greeks their *kalitsounia,* but as any Provençal will tell you, the most famous member of this particular family is the *calisson,* and the only true *calisson*—"the legitimate king of biscuits"—is made in Aix.

The size of one greedy bite or two more modest nibbles, the *calisson*

d'Aix comes in the shape of a lozenge: a flat, narrow oval with slightly pointed ends. The basic ingredients are almonds, preserved melons, fruit syrup, and sugar, although different *calissoniers* add their own refinements: a touch of orange blossom here, a soupçon of lemon or vanilla extract there. These variations are the only ones permitted; any further tinkering with the traditional recipe and the *calisson* will no longer meet *appellation* requirements. In biscuits as in wine, the rules are strict.

There is no doubt that *calissons* have been in Aix for several centuries, but historical accounts of how they became popular differ, and you can take your pick between romance and religion. Either they were served at the wedding breakfast of Jeanne de Laval and King René in 1473, or at a service commemorating the end of the great plague of 1630. Or, quite possibly, at both.

Since those early days, the *calisson* has developed from a biscuit to an industry, with the rules and regulations that industries accumulate: the almonds used in the recipes must be Mediterranean almonds; there shall be no preservatives or artificial coloring agents; the dimensions must be uniform (although an exception was made for the monster *calisson* of 1988, which weighed in at more than 450 pounds and measured just over twelve feet long by five feet wide—the mother of all tidbits, now enshrined in *Guinness World Records*); and, of course, every *calisson* must be made in Aix.

Given the French fondness for cliques, clubs, societies, associations, brotherhoods, directorates, and official bodies of every possible kind, it is not surprising that the worthy *calissoniers* of Aix got together to form their own organization. This was authorized in 1990 as the Union des Fabricants de Calissons d'Aix, and swiftly awarded its inevitable acronym, UFCA. (They also have an uncompromising motto: "From Aix-en-Provence and nowhere else.") The main purpose of the union is to protect the integrity and reputation of the true *calisson* from attempts by nefarious counterfeiters to pass off an inferior biscuit as the genuine article. And, like so many other protective arrangements in French gastronomy, it provides a guarantee of quality for the consumer.

The rules of consumption, unlike the rules of manufacture, are comfortably loose. You may eat a *calisson* any time you like—with coffee, with tea, with Champagne, or with a glass of musky, sweet Beaumes-de-Venise. Intimate personal moments are also catered for. Should you be involved in the pleasant agonies of courtship, you can buy a special circular box filled with twenty-eight *calissons* arranged in the form of daisy petals, to be plucked one by one while murmuring (between mouthfuls) She loves me . . . she loves me not . . . she loves me. No other biscuit, as far as I know, has ever claimed to be a barometer of passion. But then, there is no other biscuit quite like the *calisson d'Aix*.

Cambrioleurs

Although I have never had any personal dealings with the Provençal burglar, I have always had an interest in unusual or ingenious thefts—the kind that rise above the standard handbag snatching and car poaching. And I find myself actually liking burglars with a sense of humor, such as the legendary Albert Spaggiari. Having successfully robbed a bank in

Nice, he was eventually tracked down and arrested, only to escape by jumping out of the courtroom window. He landed on the roof of a Renault before making his getaway on the back of a motorcycle driven by an accomplice. Little was heard of him after that except for a letter of apology he sent to the owner of the Renault, together with a check to pay for repairing the dent he had made in the roof. He has never been caught.

The country burglar, while not as dramatic as Spaggiari, is not short of his own imaginative techniques. These have been devised to suit rural conditions, and here the uninvited visitor has a great advantage over his urban counterpart: homeowners actually advertise their absence. All over Provence, there are large and well-appointed *résidences secondaires*—second homes that are used for a couple of months in the summer, and for shorter stays at Christmas and Easter. In between visits these houses—many of them conveniently isolated—are empty, and their emptiness is announced for all to see by closed shutters, padlocked gates, or a chain slung across the driveway. Seeing these encouraging signs, our burglar can feel confident that he has weeks, even months, of uninterrupted opportunity.

Given the generous length of the burglary season, it is not surprising that one hears stories of thefts that are more than usually ambitious, time-consuming, and complicated. For example: an entire fitted kitchen, complete with La Cornue cooker; a dozen mature olive trees (they transplant easily); a pair of antique iron gates, together with two supporting stone pillars; several hundred nineteenth-century earthenware roof tiles; statuary, urns, a miniature gazebo—all these items, which one would have thought too firmly anchored or bulky to steal, have been plucked from their legal homes and taken elsewhere.

I have this on the authority of Jacky, who retired from the police some years ago to set up as a security consultant. He has made himself an expert in protective electronic technology, or invisible walls, as he calls them. He can turn your house into a fortress, guarded by tremblers, sensors, flashing lights, roof sirens—just about everything you could imagine short of lethal laser beams, although he would dearly love to include those in his repertoire. He is also able, thanks to his old police connections, to keep himself up to date about new developments in burglar methodology. Here is one of his recent favorites.

We had been talking about a magnificent property not far from Aix, which was well known in the area for the enthusiastic viciousness of its guard dogs, two large Dobermans who had the run of the grounds at night. Despite them, however, the property had been burgled. And not a sound had come from the dogs, who were unharmed and in good health the following morning. How had this been achieved? Drugging the dogs was out of the question; they had been trained to accept food and water only from members of the household. Investigation showed that they hadn't been locked up or shot with tranquilizing darts—although they did seem a little sleepy and more amiable than usual. The police had run up against a dead end. It was a complete mystery.

It remained unsolved until the burglars were caught trying to fence some of the jewelry they had stolen. Under interrogation, the secret came out. Together with the normal tools of their trade—gloves, glass cutters, skeleton keys, and all the rest—the burglars had brought along two bitches in heat. These were released and quickly found by the Dobermans. While the dogs were enjoying what was described as a *bon moment* in the bushes, the burglars entered the house and did what they had come to do.

In the face of criminals who pay such careful attention to detail, what is the prudent property owner to do? I put the question to Jacky, whose best advice was to stay at home, preferably with a shotgun.

Canadairs

For most of us, forest fires are images seen on television; disturbing, even shocking, but reassuringly far away. In Provence they are closer to home, a horribly predictable part of every summer.

Fires are caused by a combination of drought, strong winds, and human carelessness—or worse. Many are deliberately started by pyromaniacs, driven by their perverse urge to see beautiful countryside in flames. Whatever the cause and whoever the culprit, the sight of pillars of dark smoke against the deep blue sky is enough to cause a flutter of panic in the chest, and the instinctive raising of a finger in the air to check the direction of the wind.

The first time I saw smoke from a forest fire, it must have been a dozen miles away from the house. Some other poor wretch's catastrophe, I thought, and went back to work. Not long afterward, I heard the dogs whining and looked out of the window to see fine flakes of ash falling in the courtyard, like pale gray snow. The wind had shifted, and the fire had advanced—still not close enough to see flames, but no longer at a comfortable distance. It was then that I saw the Canadairs.

There were four of them: red-and-yellow, heavy-bellied twin-engine planes, lumbering overhead in the direction of the smoke with their cargo of water or flame retardant. (I later learned that the average time between a fire being reported and takeoff is less than fifteen minutes.) The pilots are known as firemen of the sky, or water bombardiers, and in my opinion they all deserve medals for exceptional skill and bravery. As you will see, it is a job that demands both, in large measures.

The idea of aerial firefighting began in Canada and America during the early 1950s, when tests showed that water dropped from a plane in flight was not dispersed by wind on the way down, but landed in one more-or-less concentrated mass; in other words, a liquid bomb that could be aimed at the flames. News of the tests spread across the Atlantic, and a French *préfet*, Francis Arrighi, managed to convince his colleagues in government to establish a fleet of planes equipped to deal with the fires that swept through the forests of the south each year.

To begin with, the fleet was barely a fleet: two Catalinas and a team of eight men. Forty years have passed since then. There are now twenty-eight aircraft—many of which you can see during the summer, lined up

and ready to go, at Marseille's Marignane airport—and the team has grown to 148: administrative staff, service engineers, specialized mechanics, and navigators. And then there are the pilots.

This is not an easy club to join. Applicants are normally at least forty years old and must have twelve years of professional experience, three thousand hours of flying time, and a current IFR qualification (a degree in instrument flying, one step below the qualification required by top airline pilots). For every hundred pilots who apply, only one is accepted, and he must begin on the bottom rung of the training ladder. First, a year of initiation, watching and learning; then a year as copilot of a Canadair, followed by seven to ten years as solo pilot of one of the smaller Tracker planes. The final promotion is to *commandant de bord* of a Canadair, a distinction not often achieved below the age of fifty.

The new *commandant de bord* is in charge of a curious hybrid: part aircraft, part pelican, part bucket; an odd but extremely effective combination, specifically designed to pick up water from one place and deposit it on another *without stopping at any time during the process*. This is how it happens.

The plane approaches the water at about 110 miles per hour, reducing speed to about 90 before touching down on the surface. At this point, the Canadair is neither flying nor floating, but hydroplaning, the fuselage maintained at an angle of seven degrees to keep the wings from being damaged by waves or swell. The speed drops to 70, and the twin scoops in the plane's belly are opened, gathering water at the rate of 1,100 pounds a second, with the pilot making continuous adjustments to the controls to avoid a nosedive and to compensate for the rapidly increasing weight. In twelve seconds the tanks are full, with just over six thousand liters of water. The pilot pushes the speed up to 90, and the Canadair lifts off. Now comes the really dangerous part.

The worst fires are always during periods when the mistral is blowing—often with gusts of at least 80 miles an hour. This alone is enough to make low-level flying more than usually hazardous, even when crossing flat countryside. But in Provence, unfortunately for the pilot, the countryside is far from flat. There are hills, there are cliffs and mountains, there are wickedly narrow and deep valleys. When these are on fire, the air currents coming up from the ground are hot, turbulent, and changeable, while at the same time short-range visibility is reduced to nothing but a thick fog of smoke. It is under these conditions that the Canadair must make an accurate drop where the water will do the most good. Not just once, but time after time; sometimes, day after day.

Eventually, I suppose, the pilots must become used to their work, even knowing that a tiny error of judgment could end either in drowning or incineration. But admirable as they all are, one pilot in particular stands out. Maurice Levaillant, in the course of his career, made an astonishing 12,356 drops, a world record that is now included in that bible of amazing achievements, *Guinness World Records.*

If recent history is any guide, there will be forest fires again this year, probably dozens of them. One hopes that there will always be men like Levaillant who are prepared to fight them for us.

Cartier-Bresson

We all know Henri Cartier-Bresson's work, those world-famous images that made him one of the most celebrated photographers of the twentieth century. But I wonder if much attention has ever been paid to one of his last photographs. It was taken in the 1990s, some years after he had given up photography to concentrate on his painting and drawing, and it took a squabble in Provence to bring him out of his retirement.

Montjustin is a small village off the N100 road that leads up from Apt to Haute Provence. As in most villages, the inhabitants normally tolerate the whims of their neighbors in the interests of a quiet life. Occasionally, however, someone will commit an act of such unspeakable wickedness that the entire village is obliged to rise up and respond. This was the situation in Montjustin.

One of the residents (if I remember correctly, an Englishman) had constructed a low stone wall to mark the boundary of his property. It was a well-built, even attractive wall; a wall that, so one would have thought, couldn't possibly offend a single soul. But one would have been wrong. It was quickly noticed that part of the new wall cut across a pathway that had been used by villagers since time began, blocking their comings and goings. Clearly, it was a serious matter, demanding prompt action.

The press was alerted, and a reporter—or, more likely, an investigative journalist—from the local paper, *La Provence*, was sent to the scene. But to do his report full justice, it was considered vital to have a photograph of the offending wall. By chance, there was an illustrious ex-photographer in the village. How he was persuaded to pick up his camera again I don't know, but in the copy of *La Provence* that features the story there is a photograph—a simple photograph, such as you or I might have taken—of a house with a low stone wall in front of it. And alongside the photograph is the photographer's credit, which reads: Henri Cartier-Bresson.

Caviar d'Aubergine

The *aubergine,* or eggplant, is thought to have originated in India before setting off on its travels through the Balkans, the Middle East, and the Mediterranean, gathering recipes along the way. One of these was *caviar d'aubergine,* or poor man's caviar—so called because the *aubergine* seeds, when looked at with an uncritical eye, resemble the eggs of the virgin sturgeon. It is a dish that has been described as typically Jewish, typically Bulgarian, typically Greek, and probably typical of half a dozen other national cuisines as well. However, the Provençaux, not slow in recognizing a good thing when they taste it, have not only adopted it but have rechristened it as "a classic from Provence."

It is best eaten in the summer, and best grilled on a barbecue, which imparts a wonderfully smoky flavor. Never, ever forget to prick your *aubergine* with a fork before cooking; the unpricked *aubergine* has a disconcerting habit of exploding, splattering the cook and ruining the dish. Otherwise, the initial preparation is straightforward. Grill the *aubergine* until the skin turns black and blistered and the inside becomes really soft, which you can judge by pressing the *aubergine* with the back of a fork. Scoop out the flesh; drain and press out the juices. Then chop and mash the flesh into a purée. You are now ready to choose your refinements.

These can be as simple or as elaborate as you want. The basic recipe calls for olive oil (3 tablespoons for every 500 grams of *aubergine*), a little salt, and some lemon juice. That's all. For the Provençal version, add black olives, parsley, garlic, and savory. If your taste runs to something more ambitious, there are dozens of possibilities—tomatoes, onions, dill, star anise, mint, yogurt, peppers, basil, thyme, goat cheese, and ground coriander are just a few. There is even a recipe that uses black truffle juice, which is hardly what you'd expect to find in a poor man's caviar. But the principle is clear enough: *caviar d'aubergine* is a marvelously flexible appetizer. Spread it on fresh bread or toast, and raise your glass in memory of the Arab imam who, when he tasted his wife's *aubergine* recipe, fainted with delight. No cook could ask for greater praise.

Cézanne

"When you've been born there, that's it. Nothing else will do." That was Paul Cézanne speaking about Provence, words that might have been a blueprint for his work and for his life. He was born in Aix in 1839 and died there in 1906. In his later years he left Provence as little as possible, and missed it when he did. Forty-six of his sixty-six years were spent there.

It is difficult to imagine that a man widely recognized as an inspiration to other eminent artists—and once called "the greatest painter ever"—received little attention and less praise in his hometown. And yet the people of Aix either ignored him or reviled him as a primitive dauber. Cézanne, like artists everywhere, did not take kindly to criticism, as the following short but pungent exchange shows. All too often, critics have the advantage of being insulated from their victims, but not this time. Cézanne happened one day to be standing behind a gentleman who was making loud and offensive comments about one of his paintings. Tapping his critic on the shoulder, the artist was heard to say: "Monsieur, I shit on you." It must have been a most satisfactory moment in the great man's day.

Cézanne was fascinated above all by Mont Sainte-Victoire, the 3,300-foot-high mountain east of Aix, and painted it at least sixty times, trying, as he said, "to get it right." For all his fascination, though, he never took his canvas and easel and brushes up to the summit, which I have always thought a pity. It would have been wonderful to see his version of that long, lofty view toward Marseille and the Mediterranean.

He died a painter's death. Working through a rainstorm near his studio at Les Lauves, he collapsed, brush in hand. According to legend, he was placed on a wagon piled with canvases, and spent his final moments surrounded by art.

Chapelier Mouret

Living as we do in the age of the baseball cap, it is rare and refreshing to discover a genuine hatter—one that provides a generous selection of elegant and practical hats not only for ladies and gentlemen but for shepherds, farmers, amateur aviators, adventurers, jungle explorers, and

nostalgic crooners. Mouret is just such an establishment, and has been for more than 140 years.

Little has changed *chez* Mouret, a classified *monument historique,* since it opened its doors in 1860. The address—20 rue des Marchands, Avignon—is the same. The wooden façade is the same, simple and classic. The interior, decorated in the style of Louis XVI, is the same, with moldings, mirrors, and a ceiling wrinkled and veined like an old man's face. However, the passage of time has seen some adjustments to the eight thousand items of merchandise normally available. Naturally, old favorites have been retained, but several novelties have been introduced.

There is, for instance, the aviator's bonnet, identical in every way to the model worn by Antoine de Saint-Exupéry and the Red Baron. It is a snug-fitting creation made from supple leather, lined with ultra-fine felt, and guaranteed to keep the head warm in the chilliest of cockpits; or indeed when bicycling in cold weather, on winter walks with the dog, or skiing.

To deal with the other end of the temperature scale, there is the *sola topi,* or *casque colonial véritable,* a triumph of air-conditioning for the head. The interior is lined with cork, which provides excellent natural insulation against the hammerlike rays of the tropical sun. Ventilation holes on each side of the helmet allow a flow of air to circulate around the skull, and the brim—extended at the back to protect the nape of the neck—is lined in a soothing shade of green cotton drill. In the days when mad dogs and Englishmen went out in the midday sun, this is the hat they (the Englishmen) used to wear.

It is only fair to say that the *casque colonial véritable* has lost ground in recent years to the *chapeau véritable* Indiana Jones, the *chapeau* Western and the Stetson *style aventurier*. These models all offer a useful advantage to the busy adventurer: they can be soaked, pummeled, folded, squashed, rolled, and sat on without suffering any visible ill effects.

Of course, there is also the beret, made in Oloron-Sainte-Marie, the beret capital of the world; the wide-brimmed black felt, as worn by Frédéric Mistral; the Pagnolesque *casquette marseillaise;* the straw boater made famous by Maurice Chevalier; the lavender pickers' *capeline* (a straw hat the size of a small cartwheel); genuine Panamas in several different styles; and a selection of fashionable hats for social occasions. In fact, just about the only form of headgear you won't find here, thank God, is the *casquette véritable de baseball.*

Chasseurs

For wild boar, rabbits, thrushes, and game of all descriptions, life in Provence took a distinct turn for the worse toward the end of the eighteenth century. Before 1789, hunting was a privilege reserved for aristocrats, and while they may have been a bloodthirsty bunch, at least there weren't many of them.

The Revolution changed everything. Aristocrats became an endangered species, and in the spirit of democracy, hunting was thrown open to the general public. Not surprisingly, since it promised food as well as sport, hunting quickly became one of the common man's most jealously guarded rights. Ever since then, the edible inhabitants of the forest have been looking back over their shoulders with increased apprehension.

They were quite right to do so. As the centuries passed, more efficient weapons were invented, with high-powered rifles and pump-action shotguns replacing the harquebus and the musket. At the same time, the population of hunters increased, with the inevitable result that the amount of game diminished.

One development that might have redressed the balance between hunter and hunted was the curious and much disputed appearance of a new breed of pig: half-wild, half-domestic. Many hunters insist that this is a myth perpetuated by journalists in search of material during the slow news days of summer, which is quite possible. At any rate, I have been unable to discover the man or men behind this bizarre experiment in genetic engineering. The most common story is that widespread fires in the Var some years ago reduced the *sanglier* (wild boar) population to such an extent that domestic pigs were set loose in the forest to make up the numbers. After that, the mathematics of procreation took over: the female *sanglier* gives birth once a year, normally to a litter of two or three. The female domestic *cochon* gives birth twice a year, normally to larger litters of six or eight. Put the two together, and you have the *cochonglier*—not the same as a genuine wild boar, of course, but with the great advantage, to a hunter, of being plentiful. I am told that they never cross the border between the Var and the neighboring *département* of the Vaucluse, and so cannot be officially confirmed as a true Provençal oddity. On the other hand, I have yet to hear of a pig that could read a map.

Cochongliers apart, the hunting season is short and strictly enforced. In Provence, it normally starts on the second Sunday of September and ends, depending on species, on November 30 (partridge), December 25 (hare), or January 11 (rabbit, pheasant, deer, *sanglier*). The opening weekend of the season starts, usually very early in the morning, with an extended burst of pandemonium. The hunting dogs are delighted to be given the freedom of the forest after spending the previous nine months confined to kennels, and their delight can be heard several kilometers away. They are in full song, and they bark continuously—a chorus of mournful groans and hoots that sounds like a group of rather bad amateur bassoonists tuning up. Accompaniment is provided by the clanking of their *clochettes*—the bells attached to their collars—the shouts, whistles, and curses of their owners, and sporadic bursts of gunfire. Any game that isn't stone deaf immediately retreats to a more tranquil part of the Luberon.

The hooting and the shooting, however, continue until just before noon, when there is a pause while the hunters go home to refresh themselves. Sometimes their dogs go with them. Sometimes they don't; intoxicated by strange and wonderful scents, they choose liberty over lunch, and they can be heard, clanking and barking, well into the afternoon. Eventually, hoarse and thirsty, they come down from the hills in search of water, and after several years we are now used to the sight of a group of exhausted hounds drinking from the *bassin* in front of our house. We telephone their owners, who come to pick them up. So ends the first day of the season.

As autumn turns to winter, the early morning fusillades are noticeably fewer, possibly because the temperatures don't encourage long rambles in the cold fields, possibly because most of the game has long since gone. Even so, one can usually find a few hardy and optimistic souls lurking in the undergrowth, "taking their guns for a walk," as they say. It can be a most disconcerting experience to come across one of them—a motionless figure behind a bush, clad in camouflage, and armed to the teeth. This is especially unnerving at twilight, when the thrushes return to the forest after feeding in the vines. At that time of day, a hunter waiting in the trees as little as fifteen feet away can be invisible; only the sound of his gun, going off, it seems, in your ear, tells you that he's there. I have often thought of wearing a *clochette* myself, for safety's sake, when going for a walk. I don't think I could ever be mistaken for a thrush, or even a *sanglier,* but you never know.

Exploring the Provençal countryside, you will occasionally come across stern notices telling you that the *propriété* through which you are walking is *privée,* or that the *chasse* is *gardée.* These warnings are largely ignored, which may have prompted the owner of an isolated stretch of land north of Apt to resort to stronger language. Trespassers Will Be Shot, reads his notice, and Survivors Will Be Prosecuted.

I was interested in the legality of this extreme form of discouragement, and so I asked a local expert in hunting matters for his opinion. He told me it was probably quite justified, but only as long as the trespassers were moving—a bird on the wing, as it were. It is considered very unsporting to shoot them while they're standing still.

Chèvre

Grass is in short supply in Provence, and so are cows, who prefer the lush pastures farther north. Goats, however, can thrive on the most curious and meager rations: sunflower leaves and melon skins, clumps of thyme and savory, geraniums and thistles, and indeed almost anything they might come across in an unprotected garden or on the dry, rocky slopes of Provençal hills. From this unpromising diet comes that most delicate and versatile of cheeses: *chèvre*.

People living around the Mediterranean basin were eating *chèvre* ten thousand years before Christ (the Romans considered it more digestible than either sheep or cow cheese), and Ulysses never left home without it. By the Middle Ages, it was sufficiently well known and well thought of to be used as a substitute for cash. Today there are altogether about a hundred different varieties of *chèvre* produced in France, mainly from areas south of the Loire.

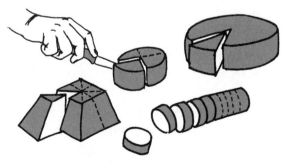

In a generous moment, a Provençal might admit that

most of these are excellent, although he will be quick to add that they are not *quite* as excellent as the *chèvres* of Provence. Probably the best-known of these is Banon (q.v.), but there are at least two others that no cheese connoisseur should miss.

The first is Brousse du Rove, from an area a few miles west of Marseille. This is goat's cheese at its most fresh—light, white, and creamy, without even the trace of a rind. It can be eaten sweet, with fruit and sugar; or savory, with herbs and a sprinkling of salt. I have found that it goes equally well with chopped sun-dried tomatoes or with roasted figs and honey. Thus the real enthusiast can have Brousse du Rove at the beginning and the end of the meal.

The second is the *picodon* of Valréas; a round cheese, just under an inch thick, with a diameter of about two and a half inches. It is white, as all goat's cheeses are (unlike cow's milk, goat's milk contains no carotene), and has a thin rind. The flavor varies with age—mild when young, stronger when kept for a few weeks; either dry, in olive oil, or in *eau-de-vie*. A particularly good cooking cheese, lightly grilled with salad or barbecued *en brochette,* the *picodon* is the big brother of the *crottin* and a cousin of the other members of the goat cheese family shown on the previous page—the *briques, bûches,* and *pyramides.*

Research into any subject can sometimes lead to unexpected jewels of information, and so it was with goat cheese. I was astonished and impressed to discover that the male goat can copulate up to forty times a day. It is true that each encounter only lasts for two seconds or so, but one has to admire the stamina and optimism involved.

Chiens Truffiers

Here is a well-loved and often-told story that illustrates the importance and value of a good truffle hound.

Once upon a time, a truffle poacher was caught in the act by the owner of the land on which he was poaching. The poacher had brought his wife with him that night, anticipating a good haul. But it was not to be. Suddenly, after an hour or two of fruitful poaching, the two of them, together with their dog, found themselves trapped in the glare of the owner's flashlight. Escape was discouraged by the owner, who had his shotgun trained on them. And since this was not the first time his truffles had been stolen, he was in no mood to be merciful.

Under questioning (with some persuasive jabs of the shotgun), the poacher admitted that he had visited this particular piece of land many times before and had taken kilos of truffles, worth a small fortune. The owner said nothing. The only sound, in the still of the night, was the click of the shotgun's hammer as it was cocked. The poacher felt that it was time to negotiate.

There is money at home, he told the owner; cash, a lifetime's savings. A just and appropriate reimbursement can surely be arranged.

The owner reflected for a few moments and then came to his decision: the poacher would be allowed to go home and pick up 100,000 francs—

the sum he had calculated all those stolen truffles would have fetched in Carpentras market. To guarantee the poacher's return with the money, the owner would hold his wife as hostage. So it was agreed.

But of course, the poacher never did come back and was never seen again in the region. (Although there were rumors that he'd been spotted in Périgueux.) History doesn't relate what happened to the unfortunate woman stranded in the middle of the night with an armed and increasingly angry man, but general opinion about the story is clear and unanimous. The owner had made a fundamental mistake. Had he kept the dog instead of the wife as hostage, the poacher would undoubtedly have returned with the money, since a good truffle dog is literally worth his weight in gold.

Traditionally, the truffle hunter's working partner had always been a pig, but this method of hunting was very often plagued by two serious technical problems. The first was that many pigs are extremely fond of the taste of truffles, and are determined to eat what they find. Which brings us directly to the second problem: a healthy adult pig can easily weigh 350 pounds, and if you have ever tried to dispute the ownership of a truffle with an obstinate opponent weighing 350 pounds, you will understand why the smaller, lighter, and more tractable dog has taken over as the truffle hunter's best friend. (Dogs are more portable, too; in a car, for instance, the ratio can be as much as six or seven to one over the pig.)

The breed is not important. Any intelligent dog can be trained for the work, although there is a school of logical thought that says short-legged dogs perform better, as nature has provided them with noses that are closer to the ground. So dachshunds, terriers, and low-slung mongrels are always good choices. As for training methodology, one must remember that the aim is to teach the dog to find the truffle without damaging it. Therefore, it is essential to follow a training regime that rewards discovery rather than carefree excavation. And here one could do no better than follow the system invented and perfected by Jean-Marie Rocchia, the truffle guru of Aix.

For the *système* Rocchia, one needs great patience, a fresh truffle, and a new, odor-neutral sock. Placing the truffle in the sock, you knot the end so that the truffle can't come out. Give this powerfully perfumed toy to your puppy, throwing it for him to chase and bring back. When he does, make him drop it by bribing him with a treat, such as a small piece of cheese. Repeat twenty times a day for a week. During subsequent weeks, the dog is restrained while the sock is thrown farther and farther away, but always in view. Each time the dog is released and fetches the sock, he is rewarded. The final stage is to hide the sock from view, first indoors and later outside, so that the dog has to use his sense of smell to find it. (Since even truffles lose their perfume eventually, the training truffle should be replaced at least once a week.)

I have only sketched out the bare bones of the program, but you can see the theory behind it, and the results speak for themselves. Monsieur Rocchia has trained a dozen of his own dogs using the sock method, and many others for friends—one of whom became a professional truffle dog trainer. There can be no more distinguished credential than that.

Cigales

It is the official insect of Provence, and you see its likeness everywhere—on pottery, plates, glasses, fabric, stamps, and postcards; carved in wood, formed in wrought iron, commemorated in chocolate, pressed out in plastic. All this despite the fact that the *cigale* is not a particularly handsome creature—more like a large armor-plated fly than anything else. But one should never judge an instrument by its looks, and the *cigale* is celebrated not for what you see, but for what you hear, because it makes the sound of summer.

The usual descriptions of that sound—the song of the sun, the symphony of heat, the orchestra of Provence—are perhaps more fanciful than accurate. *Cigales* in full cry make a repetitive, jagged sound, somewhere between a chirp and a squeak, a faintly metallic, scratchy chorus. One of my English friends, hearing it for the first time, said it reminded him of light machinery in need of adjustment and a drop of oil. There is no question, however, that it is instantly evocative of long, hot, dry days—days of blinding light and bare feet and chilled *rosé*. (The same friend came to like the sound so much that he obtained a recording of it. This he plays through outdoor speakers hidden behind the bushes in his usually cool, usually damp London garden, mystifying his neighbors and his cat.)

The *cigale* is an audible thermometer. You won't hear a peep out of it until the temperature reaches 72 degrees. At this point, as if activated by a switch, it begins to perform; or rather, *he* begins to perform. The female never makes a sound, a fact pointed out by the ancient misogynist Xénarque of Rhodes, who came to the conclusion that *"cigales* are happy because the females are mute." What he didn't mention is that the male sings entirely for the benefit of the female. He is anxious to attract her so that the two of them can get together and start a family—but not just a modest affair with one or two offspring. A successful union usually produces between three and four hundred eggs.

The *appel nuptial,* as it has been delicately described, is a far cry from merely rubbing various body parts together and hoping for the best, in the primitive fashion of less musically accomplished insects. The *cigale*'s love call is made through a complex system involving membranes that are made to vibrate by the contraction and release of an abdominal muscle. The resulting sound is amplified by the abdomen, sometimes with ear-splitting results: there is an Australian *cigale* whose romantic signals have been measured at 158 decibels—approximately the same noise level as an exploding grenade. Mind you, distances are vast in Australia, so perhaps the high volume is essential.

Assuming that all has gone well in the *cigale*'s hunt for a mate, the eggs laid by the female spend anything from three to six years underground. This is considerably longer than the adult's life span of only a few weeks, and it seems an excessive period of preparation for such a brief moment of joy. However, that's the way it has been for at least two million years, so *cigales* must be used to it by now.

The day they fall silent always takes me by surprise. The sun is still shining, the air feels as warm as it did the day before. But the sound of summer has gone, and when I go to tap the thermometer in the courtyard, sure enough the temperature has dropped below 72 degrees. It's a turning point in the year, one of the first hints of autumn.

Climat

It has often been said that by far the most popular conversational topic of the English is the weather, and in a country where all four seasons have been known to occur within twenty-four hours, that is probably not surprising. What did surprise me, though, was to find that the men and women of Provence are equally weather-sensitive, and their response to climatic idiosyncrasies is much more pronounced. Not for them the English attitude to the climate, which is to grin and bear it. If the Provençaux should suffer more than two consecutive days of damp weather, they become morose, huddling in bars and counting the raindrops that slide down the window. A winter that drags on past mid-February brings talk of a new ice age. (A mild, short winter is also a cause for deep concern, since it won't have been cold enough to kill noxious insects. These will come back to torment us later in the year.) A brisk wind from the north provokes attacks of mild dementia. And a particularly dry summer brings out flocks of Provençal pessimists, who will tell you to expect everything from forest fires to plagues of bionic locusts because of the drought.

In their defense, it is only fair to say that the climate is often dramatic and can be brutal. Statistics, for once, tell a reasonably accurate story. The coldest recorded temperature in Marseille was 3 degrees Fahrenheit, during the *vague de froid* of 1956 that killed thousands of normally frost-proof olive trees. The highest official temperature was recorded in Orange: 109 degrees in August 2003—hot enough, so they said, to fry the proverbial egg on the pavement, and certainly hot enough to qualify for the place of honor in the *canicule*. These are the dog days of stupefying heat that take their name from the principal star in the constellation known as Sirius, or Le Grand Chien. And, since nothing in France can escape precise definition, we find that the *canicule* has its very own official timetable: from July 24 until August 24. (This is interrupted by the traditional storm of August 15, but not for long. The *canicule* shakes itself dry and comes back, sometimes hotter than ever.)

As if extremes of temperature weren't enough to try a man's patience, there is also the problem of rainfall that is not only wildly erratic, but surprisingly copious. The average rainfall of Carpentras, at 656.9 millimeters per year, is more than in that famously moist city, London, which receives an average of 583.6 millimeters per year. The big difference is in how the rain chooses to fall. In England, it is a more or less regular pattern throughout the year, and the water is delivered in reasonably sized drops. In Provence, it arrives in short, infrequent, but violent torrents, as though God were tossing it down from giant buckets. The volume and weight of water are such that a morning's rain can flatten a field of wheat, drown a vineyard, or flood an entire village. During 1992, for example, the village of Entrechaux, near Vaison-la-Romaine, received 300 millimeters of rain in twenty-four hours.

But the clouds rarely stay for long, and nothing gets rid of them more quickly than the mistral, one of the world's famous winds. It blows, on average, between 100 and 150 days a year, almost always, it seems, for two or three days at a time, and occasionally with a force that can send café tables flying. It is, in some ways, a most exasperating wind. Doors, windows, and shutters creak and slam; roof tiles are dislodged and hurtle to the ground; eating outdoors is impossible, unless you are adept at catching airborne food that has been sucked from your plate; and there is the constant, enervating moan of the wind as it swirls around the house looking for a way to get in.

All that can be forgiven. A day of mistral scrubs the sky, leaving it that deep, implausible, cloudless blue of a crudely printed postcard; and at night it burnishes the stars so that they stand out with an almost surreal clarity. The air is clean and dry, with no trace of humidity, the light brilliant enough to encourage the most amateur of amateur artists to put brush to canvas.

In fact, it is the light—the absence of gray—that I have found to be the single most addictive quality of the Provençal climate. No matter what the season, to walk out of the house and into a sparkling morning, when the entire countryside looks as though it has been polished, lifts the spirit. One feels optimistic and healthy. As the people in the village will tell you on such a day, "*On est bien ici.*"

Collet Marseillais

The original *collet* was a poacher's snare, a loop of wire set to tighten around the neck of the unfortunate rabbit or hare. The prey has now changed, and a different kind of poacher is at work. His victims have two legs, and the tool of his trade is what is known as the *collet marseillais.*

It is at the same time a simple yet sophisticated scam, usually practiced on weekends, and it works like this. You insert your credit card into the cash machine outside a bank and press all the appropriate buttons. Nothing comes out. No cash—and even worse, no card. However, there is a friendly stranger waiting behind you for his turn. He tells you that this often happens with these unreliable machines, and cards are always getting stuck. Try tapping in your personal identification number once again, he says. That usually works. This time, unfortunately, it doesn't, and as it is a Sunday, the bank is closed. All you can do, he tells you, is to come back on Monday, when someone at the bank will be able to extract your card.

Not wanting to call up, cancel the card, and go through the tedious business of getting a replacement, you decide to take the advice of the friendly stranger. You thank him and go on your way.

Alas, when you do come back the following day, your card has already been extracted, not by the bank, but by the friendly stranger once the coast was clear. Not only that. Unnoticed by you, he had looked over your shoulder and memorized your PIN. And now he has had the use of your card for a most agreeable twenty-four hours—withdrawing cash, dining out, shopping energetically, and generally having a whale of a time, as you will see when your next statement arrives.

When this happened to me, I couldn't help but admire the audacity and the technical ingenuity required to make this scheme work. I was later told that the idea of inserting fine wire into the slot of the machine to block the card was a local invention. And so, although I'm sure it's something that happens all over this wicked world, in Provence poor old Marseille gets the blame.

Conduite à la Provençale

There is a noticeable difference between Provençal cars and the sleek, highly polished machines that come down each summer from Paris, Germany, and Britain. The local vehicles—or many of them—bear scars: a crushed side mirror (the automotive equivalent of a boxer's cauliflower ear), a rumpled bumper, a smashed rear light, scrapes fore and aft, missing hubcaps, the occasional dangling exhaust pipe. These are wounds honorably earned on the battlefields of narrow roads and cramped parking areas, and the visiting motorist would be well advised to give a wide berth to cars that appear to have been in the wars. They are not to be trifled with.

It is not that the Provençal driver is any less capable or more aggressive than other drivers, just that he is impatient, in a hurry and extremely optimistic when it comes to judging parking opportunities. He takes plea-sure in squeezing into spots that less adventurous drivers might avoid, and if he misjudges the space by an inch or so—well, what are bumpers for if not for bumping? In fact, he has a certain view of what a car should be, which has a direct effect on its appearance. Also, his technique at the wheel is often hampered by a physical handicap. We shall come to that later.

But first, how does he see his car? Not as an extension of his personal-ity or an expression of his wealth, status, and virility, but as a box on wheels. It is not supposed to attract admiring glances from strangers or envious stares from the neighbors. It is supposed to transport its contents from one place to the next, preferably with minimal upkeep. In other words, it is a functional object, and as long as it functions, why fuss with it? A dent here or a scrape there won't interfere with the car's ability to do its job, so there is no need to go to the trouble and expense of cosmetic surgery. (Unless, of course, it can be proved that the dent was another driver's fault and that he will have to pay for any repairs, in

which case fixing the dent becomes an urgent priority.) It is this practical attitude toward personal transport that partly accounts for the disheveled appearance of so many cars and small vans. But only partly.

The other factor, equally important, is that the Provençal driver's physical equipment is lacking in one important respect. For some reason, nature has given him only two hands, clearly not enough to steer a car, smoke a cigarette, and have a conversation at the same time. Whether that conversation is by phone or with the passenger next to him, it cannot possibly be conducted without the battery of hand gestures that are the obligatory aids to verbal communication in Provence. This can occasionally lead to moments of diminished control at the wheel, but in the absence of a third hand, what's to be done? One ominous possibility: the authorities, encouraged by the success of the recent crackdown on drinking and driving, could turn their attention to the intoxicating effects of a spirited argument. Penalties for driving a car while under the influence of conversation may be closer than we think.

Cours Mirabeau

This was once the most fashionable address in Aix. The Comte de Mirabeau married the aristocratic Émilie de Covet-Marignane at number 12 (and had the street named after him in 1876). The unfortunate Angélique Pulchérie de Castellane-Saint-Juers was murdered at number 10. And Cézanne grew up at number 55, where his father had a hat shop before he became a banker.

Straight and beautifully proportioned, it follows da Vinci's rule to "let the street be as wide as the height of the houses." It is protected from the summer heat by a canopy of dappled shade formed by tall rows of plane trees. There is elegant architecture on either side. There are fountains in the center. It is not surprising that it has been called the most satisfying street in France, and despite the eyesores of modern shop fronts, it retains, overall, a marvelously pleasing and graceful appearance.

The Cours was laid out between 1649 and 1651 on the site of the town's medieval ramparts, and it reflects the architect's obsessive fondness for the number four or its multiples. The street is 440 meters long, and 42 meters wide; 44 plane trees were planted at equal, 10-meter intervals; there are four fountains. And yet, as you stroll from one end to the other, there is no sense of being in the middle of a strict mathematical design. The trees help to soften the straight lines, and the pavements are saved from neatness by the sprawl of the cafés.

But that's only on the north side. It appears as though some form of commercial segregation is in force on the Cours Mirabeau, and you won't find anything as cheap and cheerful as a cup of coffee on the other side of the street. This—the shady side, appropriately enough—is now the haunt of lawyers, banks, and real estate agents, a smart *pâtisserie,* and the Tribunal de Commerce building, guarded by two heroically muscled statues holding up a balcony over the doorway.

The fountains range from the grandiose to the charming, by way of the therapeutic. First and biggest, at the western end of the street, is La Rotonde, a truly monumental affair: 39 feet high, and a *bassin* with a diameter of 105 feet. Even so, there's not much room to spare, since the inhabitants take up most of the space. In the center, we find the statues of Justice, Commerce, Agriculture, and the Arts, clearly not on speaking terms, since each faces in a different direction. Romping around the *bassin* is a small zoo of lions, dolphins, and swans, these last ridden by angels with the apprehensive expressions that anyone who has ever tried to ride a swan will understand. And keeping them all cool, a constant gush of water from the river Verdon. (I have often wondered how sculptors choose their subjects for these fountains. Lions and dolphins are always well represented, but the occasional donkey, polar bear, octopus, frog, seal, or even rabbit would be welcome.)

Moving up the street, we come to La Fontaine des Neuf Canons, once a bar for sheep and goats. The flocks coming over from Arles would stop for a drink before continuing their journey, which is why the edge of the *bassin* is so low to the ground, a feature still appreciated by thirsty short-legged dogs in summer.

For hot, or at least warm water, there is La Fontaine d'Eau Chaude, shaggy with moss, and delivering a continuous supply of water naturally heated to 64 degrees Fahrenheit. This is thermal water, of the kind that attracted the Romans back in the days when Aix was known as Aquae Sextiae, and its remedial qualities were impressive. It was said to encourage fertility in women, to cure goiter, and to reduce the painful swellings of the king's evil, scrofula.

I decided to take a dose myself. Not knowing quite what to expect, I dipped my hand in this miraculous fluid and then drank. The temperature was about the same as that of a tepid bath. The taste, which I had expected to be reassuringly foul in the way of all potent medicines, was a disappointment: no fizz, no sulfurous reek, no hint of subterranean alchemy. Just warm, flat, apparently unremarkable water. Although having said that, I have checked myself regularly ever since for signs of the king's evil and have tested negative. So perhaps it really does work.

Finally, at the top end of the Cours, is La Fontaine du Roi René, a handsome memorial to a man well loved by posterity. It was *le bon roi René* who introduced the turkey, the silkworm, and the muscat grape to Provence. He also supported the arts and was by all accounts a thoroughly enlightened king. (And an extremely generous uncle; in his will he left Provence—all of it—to his nephew Charles.) He stands above his fountain, a pile of books at his feet, a scepter in one hand, a bunch of grapes in the other, looking down the length of the Cours through the green tunnel of trees. It's one of the best views in Aix; a view, as the locals like to tell you, fit for a good king.

Daube à la Provençale

The weather is seldom included in any recipe or listed on any menu, and yet its contribution to the enjoyment of food is enormous. This is a fact often overlooked in cities, where people spend most of their time indoors and where air-conditioning and heating provide a more-or-less constant interior climate. In the country, however, things are different. A friend who lives in Paris is convinced that there is actually *more* weather in the country than in town; or if not more, then he is certainly more aware of it when he comes to visit us. Wind, rain, sun, snow—elements of passing interest that he usually observes through closed windows or in televised weather reports—are suddenly presented to him face-to-face, in the raw. He admits that these natural intrusions affect his appetite, which he claims tends to decrease as the temperature rises. (Although for his birthday lunch, he invariably insists on having *cassoulet,* not the most suitable dish for mid-August in Provence.)

In the days before the freezer and global food distribution made almost everything available throughout the year, our diet was very much tied to climate. Strawberries at Christmas or pheasant in June were impossible treats. We ate according to the seasons. We waited for the first asparagus and endured summers without truffles, and anticipation made them taste all the better.

Although today Provence is well enough served with freezers and supermarkets, seasonal eating is, for me, still the best way to eat: light in spring and summer, heavier in autumn and winter. I find it odd that *daube à la provençale* is often served by local restaurants during the summer (like that other old standby, *pieds et paquets,* a nourishing mixture of sheep's feet and tripe), because I always think of *daube* as cold weather food, solid and comforting, to be served when the wind begins to bite and the kitchen fire is roaring.

Daube starts with beef, cut into chunks and marinated in red wine for up to three days. On that, most cooks agree. Where they differ is in the details; every cook in Provence seems to have a personal recipe, and my wife is no exception. Here is her *daube,* and very good it is too.

Serves 6–8

4 1/2 pounds of beef, cut into 2-inch cubes

For the marinade

1 bottle of the best red wine you can spare
3 slivers of orange peel (without the pith)
20 peppercorns
6 juniper berries
a pinch of ground cloves
a pinch of cinnamon (optional)
2 large cloves of garlic (peeled)
a few sprigs of parsley & thyme tied together with
    2 bay leaves
1 tablespoon of olive oil

The rest of the ingredients for the daube:

2 tablespoons olive oil
7 oz of chopped smoked bacon
3 tablespoons plain flour
salt and black pepper
1 large onion, roughly chopped
2 large carrots, peeled and sliced
14 oz can of crushed tomatoes

1. Using a large glass or ceramic mixing bowl, combine the ingredients for the marinade and add the beef. Cover with plastic film and refrigerate for forty-eight hours, turning it now and again until the meat is nicely blackened.

2. Preheat the oven to 350°. Heat a tablespoon of olive oil in a sauté pan and sauté the chopped bacon. Remove and keep to one side. Remove the beef from the marinade (reserve the marinade), dry it, and toss it in seasoned flour. Add the remaining olive oil to the pan and heat. Add the beef to the hot oil. (Do this in small batches to keep the oil hot enough to sear but not cook the meat.) Keep turning until the beef is sealed, then remove with a slotted spoon and put it on a large plate. Now sauté the onions and carrots in the same pan. Remove and place them in a cast iron casserole, or an earthenware *daubière,* with the bacon.

3. Put all the beef back into the sauté pan with its juices. Add the marinade and heat to just below boiling point. Now turn the beef and the marinade into the casserole with the vegetables and bacon. Add the can of crushed tomatoes and mix thoroughly. Season well with pepper. Cover the meat with a piece of greaseproof paper and put on the lid.

4. Place the casserole in the oven at 350° for thirty minutes, then turn down the temperature to 325° and cook for at least three and a half to four more hours until the beef can be cut with a spoon.

5. The *daube* should rest for at least 24 hours before eating. Refrigerate when cool.

6. Preheat the oven to 300°. Take the *daube* from the refrigerator and remove any fat from the top. (Once the fat is removed, the *daube* may also be frozen.) At this point you may add, according to taste, chopped olives, partially cooked button onions, more cooked chopped bacon, lightly cooked sliced porcini mushrooms, a good dollop of mustard, or some *tapenade*—there are endless variations. Reheat gently for about 2 hours. Serve with boiled or mashed potatoes or pasta.

Serious *daube*-makers should consider keeping a pot—a dedicated *daubière*—just for this one dish. In Provence, a *daubière* is traditionally a deep, dark earthenware pot, and in the best kitchens it is never washed after use. Instead, it is dried over a hotplate or a flame, turning the remains of the sauce into a veneer, or fine crust, which impregnates the earthenware. Thus, the ghost of the old *daube* adds to the flavor of *daubes* to come, an evolutionary process that fills some ultra-hygienic cooks with alarm. Accustomed to spotless stainless steel, their instinct on seeing a well-seasoned *daubière* is to scrub it—a tragedy.

Dégustations

From time to time, even in Provence, the sun goes in, the clouds gather, and the light is reduced to a sullen Parisian gray. It is on days such as this that house guests, deprived of their hours of lolling by the pool, tend to fidget and become restive. "What do you *do* when it's like this?" they ask.

I used to suggest reading, until a marked lack of enthusiasm in response taught me that our visitors wanted something else; something more active, more Provençal, more typical of their vacation—something, in other words, that they couldn't do at home.

There followed a period when taking tours of other people's houses was the preferred distraction on a dull day. The excuse was that these properties were being inspected with a view to purchase, and local real estate agents, optimists to a man, were naturally delighted to meet prospective clients. Unfortunately, on returning home to real life, the idea of buying a place in the sun would be either postponed or abandoned—except by the agents, who would continue to bombard us with details of properties that we absolutely had to see on our friends' behalf, so perfect were they in every way. The final straw was someone whom we were assured had serious intentions. He said he was looking for the ruins of a small, secluded hamlet to restore. Eventually, after searching for three months, we located one. We called him in London with the good news,

only to find that he'd completely forgotten about his Provençal hamlet and had bought a house in Wiltshire.

Wiser and more cautious now, I think I have discovered the solution to the problem of what to do with guests on a gray day: the *dégustation* or, better still, several *dégustations*. We are fortunate enough to live in an area rich in vines and winemakers. The wines of Côtes du Luberon, Côtes du Ventoux, and Coteaux d'Aix-en-Provence are virtually on the doorstep, and the treasures of the Rhône valley—Condrieu, Hermitage, Rasteau, and many more—are an easy drive away. Within this great choice are various levels of quality and price, from the *vins de table* and small local wines found in the *caves coopératives* to the elegant vintages of Châteauneuf. More than enough, at any rate, to satisfy most tastes and wallets.

A tour of the vineyards offers aesthetic and social rewards, as well as the alcoholic bonus. Well-kept vines are always a pleasure to look at, and the architecture and gardens of even the most minor châteaux are often fascinating. (Obviously, there will be occasions when tastings are conducted in a garage rather than a baronial basement, but variety is part of the charm of these expeditions.)

Over the years, I have found that men and women who make wine are, almost without exception, extremely congenial people. They are, after all, in the hospitality business, and the simple act of pouring a glass of wine for a stranger is the most pleasant of welcomes. From there, it is only a short step to conversation. In some cases, this can eventually lead to friendship; at the very least, you can be sure of an educational and sociable half hour. As for the wines you will sample—peering at the robe, inhaling the bouquet, swallowing or spitting according to choice—they might be fruity and mild-mannered or dense and dark and velvety, but they will rarely be without interest.

Three or four tastings will fit comfortably into an afternoon. Our experience has been that guests return to the house docile and mellow, with many bottles in the car, all thoughts of bad weather forgotten. But it is absolutely essential that one of the group—a teetotaler or someone with selfless restraint—does all the driving and none of the drinking. There was a time, I'm told, when the alcoholic limit for drivers in Provence was an *apéritif*, half a bottle of wine, and a *digestif*. This indulgence no longer applies.

Desserts, Les Treize

The unsuspecting glutton, licking his lips at the thought of thirteen desserts, would be surprised and possibly a little disappointed to find this traditional Provençal treat laid out on the table. Instead of the modern Technicolored and sugary extravaganza of ice creams, meringues, cakes, pies, tarts, and chocolate in every conceivable form, our glutton would see a more sober display, with not a *crème brûlée* or *profiterole* in sight.

This is the final course of the *gros souper*, the most important meal of the Provençal year, eaten on Christmas Eve. But while it might be *gros*, it certainly isn't *gras*. Meat is not on the menu. The first course is fish, usually cod, with perhaps some *aioli* and snails, a savory prelude to the main gastronomic event of the evening.

Symbolic of Jesus and the twelve apostles, the thirteen desserts consist mainly of fruit and nuts. A typical selection would be chosen from fresh fruits, such as apple, pear, orange, and pomegranate, and dried fruits and nuts, such as hazelnuts, walnuts, figs, dates, pistachios, and currants. (These are called the *mendiants*, because their colors resemble those of the habits worn by certain orders of monks.) Then there should be two kinds of nougat, white and black, fruit pâtés, preserved fruits, jams, and finally, *la pompe*. Its full name is *pompe à l'huile*, also called *gibassier*—a flat bread made with olive oil, orange water, and sugar, to be dipped in sweet wine before eating.

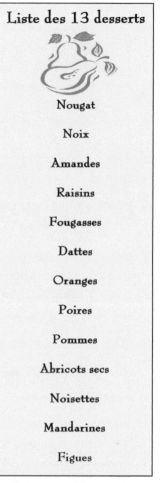

Liste des 13 desserts

Nougat

Noix

Amandes

Raisins

Fougasses

Dattes

Oranges

Poires

Pommes

Abricots secs

Noisettes

Mandarines

Figues

Dictons

Classic French, as practiced and preserved by the immortals of the Académie Française, is without doubt a thing of beauty and a joy to listen to. But I have to admit to a great fondness for the less formal language overheard on the streets, in cafés, and wherever ordinary mortals gather. It may not be grammatically sound or even in the best of taste, but it can often be colorful, funny, and occasionally wise. Above all, I like the odd sayings and unusual words that are particular to a specific region, and Provence has more than its fair share of these. Here are some of my favorites.

Bon avocat, mauvais voisin. Good lawyer, bad neighbor. A sentiment that is sure to find universal acceptance. I am reminded of the lawyer on a yacht who fell overboard in shark-infested waters, only to survive without a scratch. When asked how it was that the sharks had left him alone, he replied: "Professional courtesy."

Parler pointu. To speak with an affected or curious (that is, not Provençal) accent.

C'est un vrai cul cousu. Someone who has suffered the misfortune of being born without a sense of humor or the ability to relax, and is thus a bit of a wet blanket socially. In northern France he would probably be called a *pisse-vinaigre;* in America, a tightass.

Donner un coup de pied à l'armoire. A maneuver that is carried out on those occasions when you want to look your best, since a well-aimed kick to the armoire is known to be helpful when selecting your finest and most flattering clothes.

Se toucher les cinq sardines. To shake hands.

Partir comme un pet. To leave with uncommon speed, as swift as a fart in a hurry.

Bon pour le cinquante-quatre. A phrase that originated in Marseille, where the old number 54 streetcar used to stop at the hospital specializing in mental disorders. A man thought of as being completely mad—a man who has the poor judgment to disagree with your point of view, for instance—can therefore be said to qualify for a seat on the 54.

Pomme d'amour. When the tomato arrived in Europe from the Aztecs of South America sometime in the sixteenth century, it was thought to have aphrodisiac qualities. Naturally, it needed a suitably romantic name, and it was known as the apple of love long before it was rechristened as the plain old tomato. A distinction still exists, according to my local vegetable expert. "In the north, they grow tomatoes," she told me. "In Provence, we grow *pommes d'amour.*"

Maigre comme un stoquefiche. Truly skinny, like a strip of dried fish.

Tafanari. A Provençal word used to describe the bottom, especially if it is a bottom of significant proportions. A really substantial and curvaceous *tafanari* is sometimes compared to the triumphal arch of the monumental Porte d'Aix in Marseille. An alternative would be to say *"il a le cul comme cent limaces,"* a picturesque description even though a backside the size of a hundred slugs is not easily imagined.

Sourd comme un toupin. Deaf as one of the all-purpose terra-cotta pots found in old Provençal kitchens. Farther north, the description would be "deaf as a pot."

Retourner les chaussettes is to die. I have been unable to discover why socks have been chosen for this sad euphemism. Why not boots, waistcoat, corset, or hat? Perhaps it has something to do with the cold feet that accompany death.

Le Bon Dieu endormi. Should a man have a stroke of luck that is totally undeserved, his envious neighbors will put it down to the fact that God was fast asleep at the time. (Should the stroke of luck occur to you, of course, it is because God was watching over you.)

La terre couvre les fautes des médecins. This is similar in its sentiments to the Anglo-Saxon saying "The operation was a success. Unfortunately, the patient died." It seems that doctors, like lawyers, must endure defamation as an everyday part of the job.

Finally, *stinginess.* Someone who is reluctant to reach for his wallet is said to have *"des oursins dans les poches,"* or sea urchins in his pockets. A more dedicated skinflint would be *"généreux comme une noix serrée,"* or as generous as a crushed nut. And as for the ultimate miser: *"s'il me vendait des oeufs, je croirai qu'il à enlevé les jaunes,*" or, if he were to sell me some eggs, he'd take out the yolks first.

A word of warning here. Some of these phrases should be used with caution. It is always best to know someone well before insulting him.

Divin Marquis, Le

Lacoste is one of several much-photographed hill villages between Cavaillon and Apt. There are wonderful views across the valley toward the northern slopes of the Luberon, steep cobbled streets, charming houses, and a handsome bell tower. Picturesque nooks abound. There is also a quarry just outside the village, conveniently placed for those who need limestone pillars, turrets, or triumphal arches for their *résidences secondaires.* But without doubt, Lacoste's main claim to fame is that Donatien Alphonse François, the Marquis de Sade, spent an important part of his life there, in the château that dominates the village.

Dating from the eleventh century, the château eventually passed from the Simiane family to the Sades in 1710. Nearly sixty years later, Donatien Alphonse inherited it from his father, and it couldn't have come at a better time. The young marquis was getting himself into all kinds of trouble in Paris, and Lacoste provided a bolt-hole, somewhere he could escape the attentions of lawyers and the scandalized parents of the maidens he was so fond of ravishing.

Not unlike today's refugees who leave the city for a quieter life in Provence, de Sade saw plenty of room for improvement in his country home and decided to do a little refurbishing. Thanks largely to his wife's money, he transformed the château into what was described as an "*aimable édifice*" of forty-two rooms with a private chapel and a private theater, where he used to put on his own theatrical works. One can imagine the casting sessions.

De Sade's rural idyll came to an end in 1778, when he was imprisoned on a variety of charges. These included poisoning a prostitute, doling out "aphrodisiac bonbons" to unsuspecting servant girls, and worse. And yet, despite his enthusiastic debauchery, he is today referred to, more often than not, as the divine marquis.

This puzzled me. Of all the adjectives you might use to describe de Sade and his life, *divine* is hardly one that springs immediately to mind. Research took me first to the faculty of letters at the University of Paris. There, the helpful Dr. Laurence Campa pointed out that Le Divin Marquis was the title used by the poet Guillaume Apollinaire in 1909 in his introduction to an anthology of de Sade's writings. Dr. Campa also said, however, that it was quite likely that it had existed before.

More research, this time into a few of de Sade's titles, revealed another clue. In *The 120 Days of Sodom* and *Philosophy in the Boudoir*, in *Juliette* and *Justine*, the word *divin* crops up again and again and again, from the most divine of *derrières* to divine pleasure, divine incest, and a wide range of other divine activities and body parts. It was clearly one of de Sade's favorite adjectives; perhaps it rubbed off on the author.

And what became of his château? Parts of it still stand, giving Lacoste its distinctive skyline, but it is no more than an architectural skeleton, gaunt and rather grim. It was burned in the Revolution and ransacked by the locals, who carried away stones to use for more modest buildings. What they left now belongs to Pierre Cardin.

Drailles

Anyone who walks regularly across the hills and through the forests of Provence will from time to time come across evidence of rural traffic—

overgrown but still recognizable paths, apparently going from nowhere to nowhere. These are *drailles,* once the routes used by flocks of sheep and goats on their annual exodus to escape the heat of the plains and pass the summer in the higher, cooler pastures of Haute Provence.

The seemingly aimless, twisting, looping course followed by some of these paths is due partly to the contours of the land, and partly to ancient boundaries. The grand *seigneurs* of Provence were not the kind of people to take kindly to invaders who might eat everything in sight, and penalties for trespass could be savage; indeed, deadly. Consequently, the prudent shepherd made sure his flock never drifted into forbidden territory.

At times, this must have been a nightmare. An account from June 1753 records with great precision that a flock of 15,809 animals crossed the Durance River on their way to summer pastures. One wonders how those counting the sheep managed to stay awake, and how on earth this enormous living mass was persuaded not to stray off the beaten track.

For flocks of this size there was, of course, a system. A team of shepherds, working under the command of a *bayle,* the shepherd-in-chief, would be stationed at intervals along the length of the flock. Sheep were split into groups of thirty, with the thirtieth sheep in each group wearing a *clochette* to facilitate the counting. And so the clanking, unwieldy procession would start off, more or less neatly grouped. It's hard to say whether this formation would survive the entire trip, and even more difficult to know what would have been done if the recount on arrival came to only 15,808.

Dumas et Ses Melons

The melons of Cavaillon are perhaps the most highly esteemed melons in France. They "charm the throat and cool the belly," according to one poetic admirer, and he wasn't the only literary gentleman to appreciate their juicy virtues. Alexandre Dumas, a writer whose prodigious output was interrupted from time to time by the need to eat, had such a passion for them that in 1864 he struck a deal with the mayor of Cavaillon: books for melons. Dumas had heard that the Cavaillon library couldn't afford to buy his books, so he made a gift to the town of the 194 volumes that he had so far written. But this was just a start; more, many more, were promised—hundreds more, in fact. In return, all he asked for was a modest life annuity of a dozen melons every year. These were duly sent to him until his death in 1870.

But what about the books? The last 135 years have seen two world wars and countless upheavals. Had the Dumas collection survived? Was it arranged under glass, preserved in an attic, or hidden in the private library of a local melon baron? A call to the Bibliothèque Municipale in Cavaillon revealed that the books—or those that had survived—were still safe and sound in the archives, and could be inspected on request. And so, one bright October morning, I presented myself to Madame Maignan, who is responsible for the archives, and who had brought the books out from their resting place for me to have a look.

There were fifty-four of them altogether, carefully arranged in a large cardboard box. As I leaned over the box, I was aware of the smell of old books, a faint musty perfume that reminded me of rainy afternoons during my childhood spent reading old dog-eared volumes discovered in the attic.

Madame Maignan explained that the Dumas books were not expensive editions, but *livres de poche,* the nineteenth-century equivalent of today's mass-market paperbacks. Even at a glance, I could see that they put modern paperbacks to shame. All of them had sturdy board covers; the pages were stitched together, rather than glued; and many of them had their spines bound in leather, with the titles embossed in faded gold lettering. Not surprisingly, all of them were what a book dealer would describe as "slightly foxed," showing signs of old age: mottled, gently undulating pages, tinged with brown at the edges and brittle to the touch. Even so, it was a collection any book lover would covet.

The mayor of Cavaillon at the time, Monsieur Guis, was clearly conscious of the need to give Dumas's books the respect they deserved. Neatly pasted inside the front cover of every volume were printed instructions to readers, urging them to treat the books kindly. *Do not fold the pages. Do not write in the margins. Ask the librarian for a bookmark.* Unfortunately, he omitted to say *Do not keep this book,* because over the years the great majority of the original collection never made it back to the library.

Dumas once said that "history is a nail on which I hang my stories," and he is often credited as the inventor of the historical novel (he wrote more than six hundred of them). But that was by no means all he wrote, as the list in each of his books shows. His titles take up an entire closely printed page. *The Count of Monte Cristo* and *The Three Musketeers* are there, of course, together with *La Dame de volupté, Les Frères corses,* and *Les Mohicans de Paris.* But after finishing a novel, Dumas would often reward himself with a trip abroad, and he could never resist writing about his experiences; Switzerland, Sinai, a voyage from Paris to Cádiz, and life in the desert were all subjects for more books. He seemed to enjoy Florence enormously, writing not only *Une Année à Florence* but also *Une Nuit à Florence.* And then there was the *Grand Dictionnaire de cuisine.* How he found the time and energy to be this productive, heaven knows; I like to think the melons helped.

Eau-de-Vie

As grapes make their long and sometimes traumatic journey from vine to wine, they are subjected to the attentions of a device called the *égrappoir*, which rips off the stalks and splits open the grapes before they travel on to the storage vat. Periods of maceration and fermentation follow, as well as a crushing encounter with the *pressoir*. But eventually, the youthful wine is drained off, leaving a thick, pulpy, almost solid residue of grape skins and pips: this is *marc*. It is not a pretty sight, and it's difficult to imagine that it could be used for anything other than fertilizer. But there is still some juice left in it, and once this is distilled it becomes *eau-de-vie*, or more precisely, *eau-de-vie de marc*.

Not surprisingly, the chance to make something intoxicating out of leftovers from the grape harvest was, for many peasant farmers, far too good to pass up. True, one needed an alembic that could distill the *marc* and transform it into *eau-de-vie*, but if you didn't have your own, there was always the *alambic ambulant*. This was a kind of alcoholic wheelbarrow that used to make its way from farm to farm, distilling as it went, and undoubtedly leaving a trail of smiling faces behind it.

Many farmers had private alembics, and some still do; but only for decorative purposes, so they will tell you, and not—*certainly* not—for personal use. The reason they are at pains to make this distinction dates back to 1916, the year the government, sensing an untapped source of revenue, moved into the distillation business and passed a law restricting distillation to registered public enterprises, such as cooperative associations. In this way, the tax man could keep his avaricious eye on every distilled drop. The *alambic ambulant* was eventually pensioned off, and there was no further need—officially, at least—for a man to keep an alembic in his outhouse.

Despite its less than elegant origins, the *marc* family has a few aristocratic branches, among them *marc de Champagne, marc de Bourgogne,* and *marc de Châteauneuf.* There is a lesser-known country cousin: *marc de Provence,* and I have a small glass of it in front of me as I write. It is a robust beverage: 50 percent alcohol, stronger than brandy, whiskey, or gin. The liquid is pale, pale gold in color and very slightly oily, giving the surface a slick sheen. The taste is a series of sensations of diminishing strength. First, there is an involuntary gasp as the first jolt of *marc* hits the palate, followed by a glow in the throat, then a warm, lingering finish that spreads through the upper body. You get the distinct impression that nothing, however solid, could prevent a mouthful of *marc* from reaching its destination in the lower reaches of your stomach. Its power of penetration explains why *marc* is often used to punctuate a long, heavy meal, the theory being that a couple of nips taken between courses will make a *trou,* helping to clear the way for the courses to come. I have tried this, and it works.

Marc has other uses, too. Should you suffer a scratch, a sting, or a bite, it is a powerful external disinfectant. And I am told by a lady in the village that it does a wonderful job of cleaning greasy windows.

Écrivains

As a source of inspiration, Provence has been more than generous to artists. The glittering light, the honey-colored villages, the ostentatious sunsets, the olive groves and regiments of plane trees—these and much more have been sketched and etched, painted, watercolored, and photographed, exposed in art galleries and commemorated in large and opulent books.

Writers, although they don't receive the instant accolade of having

their work hung on a collector's wall, seem to have been equally inspired. Here is a short but illustrious list: Frédéric Mistral, Alphonse Daudet (to the left), Henri Bosco, Jean Giono, Marcel Pagnol, Ford Madox Ford, Albert Camus, René Char, and Lawrence Durrell. All of them found something in Provence that helped them to overcome the writer's daily problem: that daunting confrontation with the blank page.

What was it? There are probably as many different theories as there are authors. Personally, I wouldn't dream of trying to pinpoint exactly what has inspired others, particularly writers of such distinction. But in general terms, it's not difficult to see why Provence is such a rich source of encouragement for anyone blessed—or cursed—with the urge to write.

First, there is the vast hoard of Provençal history, with more than two thousand years' worth of stories and myths: bloodthirsty, romantic, tragic, comic, or bizarre. There were great battles, such as the victory of the Roman general Marius a hundred years before Christ, in which 200,000 Teutons were slaughtered and left where they fell in the fields to the east of Aix, an area later known by the grisly name of Les Pourrières, or "the rotting fields." There have been great love stories (in between outbreaks of more bloodshed) from the medieval times when the Courts of Love flourished in Les Baux. Great surges in piety, art, and crime occurred between 1309 and 1377, a period when the papacy was based in Avignon, attracting such unsavory hangers-on that the town was described by

Petrarch as a "thoroughfare of vice, the sewers of the earth." Looking back over the centuries, there is enough material for hundreds of new books, even though hundreds have already been written.

It is a commonly held belief that writers spend their days looking inward, inspecting their imagination or searching for their muse, and of course that is partly true. There are times, however, when even the most diligent writer tires of the interior landscape and needs a breath of air from the outside world, a change of mental pace, and a little stimulus for the creative juices. Provence can provide this like nowhere else I know.

It takes several different forms, and the first of these is nature. There have been many days when I have found the process of writing to be more than usually difficult. The words ground out with such effort die on the page like so many flattened insects, and I don't seem to be able to reach the end of a sentence without tripping over the punctuation. It's not writer's block exactly, but a kind of ennui. Luckily, there is a cure: two or three hours of walking in the hills, where, most of the time, I have the countryside to myself. The happy combination of exercise, sunshine, solitude, and glorious scenery has such a tonic effect that I can come back to work and attack the alphabet again, if not with confidence, at least with renewed optimism.

For more lively inspiration there is the café, a paradise for observers and eavesdroppers. I doubt that it is in the Provençal personality to speak quietly, except when talking about income tax. Almost all other subjects, from minor ailments to the charms of the girl behind the bar, are discussed at full volume, loudly enough to be heard three or four tables away. Stories, village feuds, the perfidy of neighbors, the price of melons, the antics of foreigners, the politics of the mayor—the café is a human reference library for anyone interested in the details of Provençal life. And there is an ever-changing visual accompaniment, since conversations are decorated with nods, winks, shrugs, moues, and expressions of astonishment or outrage, often with minor explosions of even more dramatic body language. This, too, is helpful to a writer, as mannerisms of all kinds can be stolen from their owners and attached to fictional characters. So a couple of hours in the café, pretending to read the newspaper, is always time well spent.

There is also the advantage of distance, which provides a comfortable layer of insulation. Provence is a long way from publishers. An impatient editor based in New York, London, or Paris cannot just drop in to check whether the day's words have actually been written. E-mail, for those, unlike me, who have it, is much easier to ignore than a knock on the door; so are faxes. And telephones can be turned off, leaving the writer in Provence to exercise his talent for procrastination in peace.

Finally, the opportunities for enjoyment disguised as work are almost limitless. The quest for inspiration has taken me to wine *caves,* to truffle hunts, to olive oil mills, to frog festivals and snail farms, to hidden chapels and grand châteaux, to *boules* tournaments, stone quarries, cemeteries, topless beaches, eccentric museums, and, I must admit, to many, many restaurants. Some may call this wanton self-indulgence. I call it research, and an abiding pleasure it is, too.

Eh Bè, Hè Beh, Beh Oui, Etc.

When I first arrived in Provence, one of the phrases in the local lexicon of shorthand that perplexed me for months was *eh bè,* or perhaps *hè beh.* I heard it every day, sometimes abbreviated to *bè* and sometimes elongated to *hè beh oui.* What did it mean? What was an *hè beh?* Although it seemed to crop up every five minutes in daily speech, I never saw it written down. And so when I consulted the dictionary, it was on the rather fuzzy basis of phonetics. I started with *aibay,* then *heybay,* then *ébay,* not realizing then that the phrase was two separate words. The dictionary failed to help.

Illumination finally came, as it so often does, during the course of a conversation in a café. On hearing the third *hè beh,* of the morning, I asked for it to be spelled out, which it duly was, accents and all, on the back of a beer mat. My instructor, one of the café waiters, then translated it for me.

93

Hè is the Provençal version of *hein*, which is used in the rest of France as an all-purpose interjection or as an audible question mark (as in: "So you liked the snail soufflé, *hein*?"). As for *beh*, it is simply the abbreviation of *bien*, and has more or less the same vague but convenient range of uses. Depending on inflection, it can add a hint of certainty, hesitation, surprise, or resignation to a sentence. This is not to say that it has replaced *bien*, which is frequently heard although differently pronounced, *bieng* being preferred in Provence to the clipped northern version.

Escargots

You will not be surprised to hear that the French currently hold the world record for snail consumption, at approximately twenty-five thousand tons per year. So great is the demand that many tons are imported—from Turkey, Greece, Hungary, Taiwan, and Indonesia—and it amazes me that a country that prides itself on all things gastronomic should allow this to happen. Why isn't there a Snail Marketing Board, dedicated to achieving national self-sufficiency in snails, with reproduction encouraged by government subsidy? Where are the snail tycoons, second only to chefs or soccer players in national esteem? What ever happened to plans for that exciting annual promotion: *L'Escargot Nouveau est arrivé*?

Maybe one day we shall see some progress in these areas. Meanwhile, the good news is that the homegrown French snail, at least in two regions, is thriving. In Burgundy, there is *Helix pomatia*, or *gros blanc*, a meaty creature, the largest snail you are likely to see. And in Provence, there is *Helix aspersa* Müller, smaller and, many say, tastier than its Burgundian cousin. The Provençal snail is commonly known as the *petit gris* (despite being brown in color), and has been a local delicacy for thousands of years. Archaeological excavations around Forcalquier, in Haute-Provence, revealed what are reckoned to be mesolithic snail farms dating back to 11,000 years B.C.

After this promising early start, snails continued to keep their place on the menu through the years until the sixteenth century, when they went into a long decline, disappearing from cookbooks, recipes, and restaurants. There is no explanation for this except for the theory that snails came to be regarded as food for the poor (as oysters once were in England), and thus not acceptable at more refined tables. Whatever the reason, there was a period of about two hundred years when no self-respecting gourmet would be seen dead with a snail on his plate.

It wasn't until around the middle of the nineteenth century that the snail enjoyed a renaissance, mainly at the *brasseries* that were becoming more and more fashionable in Paris. Often, the snails were served *à la provençale,* with a stuffing of garlic, parsley, and butter. The same recipe was good enough to be adopted later by the Burgundians. Showing not a trace of shame, the rascals changed the name to *escargots à la bourguignonne.* The Provençaux responded by tinkering with their original recipe, adding tiny cubes of ham, crushed anchovy, and puréed sorrel. The war of the sauces continues. Even today, it is unwise to interfere in an argument between Burgundian and Provençal snail fanciers.

Since its triumph in Paris, the snail has never looked back, and it has much to recommend it. Being naturally bite-size, it is convenient to eat. It keeps well, without any particular maintenance, and as proof there is the story of Monsieur Locard, who kept a bucket of snails in his wardrobe (God knows why) for eighteen months before eating them. And from a nutritional point of view, the snail is a very healthful food, low in fat and rich in nitrogen. As for the taste, be guided by this simple rule: it is the sauce that makes the snail. Without sauce, the snail, as with many kinds of fish, is bland—unless it has been raised on a diet that includes thyme and other herbs.

I was intrigued by the idea of a naturally preseasoned snail, born and bred, like Sisteron lambs, among the wealth of herbs that grow in Provence. Would it be noticeably more tasty? Could it do without sauce, making it even more of a conve-

nience food? And then, driving out of the village of Cadenet one cold December day, I thought I was about to find the answers to my questions. On the side of the road was a sign directing passersby to a narrow stony track, at the end of which they would find a snail farm.

I should have known it would be closed. It was winter, when the snail is not at his most active, saving his strength for the period between May and August, when he eats voraciously and reproduces like a hero. The farm would not reopen until spring. I made a note to come back.

But when I did, all hopes of naturally preseasoned snails were dashed. The farm had been sold, and so far there is no sign that the new owner plans to go into the snail breeding business. This is a great shame, as it helps to leave the door open to businessmen whose snails—and whose ethics—are not what they should be. I refer here to the infamous practice of buying empty French snail shells, inserting inferior foreign snails (smothered in an overenthusiastic garlic sauce), and passing them off as homegrown delicacies. It is high time somebody in Brussels was alerted to this scandal. Surely, among the teeming multitudes of bureaucrats, there must be a minister with snails in his portfolio.

Espigaou

The *espigaou* can be one of the few unpleasant aspects of the Provençal countryside, and every visiting dog (and owner) should watch out for it. During the summer, as the heat builds up and the fields become more and more dry, seed heads fall from the grasses onto the ground. These are small, barbed, and sharply pointed—perfectly shaped to penetrate the tender skin in between a dog's claws. When this happens, it is no more painful than a pinprick, and most dogs don't notice it. It's only later, after a few hours, that the trouble starts. The *espigaou* works its way up into the paw and disappears, leaving only the tiniest of punctures in the flesh. The dog begins to limp. The paw, and sometimes the lower part of the leg, swells up. But the mystified owner, looking for the cause of the problem, can see nothing.

The cure for this is a visit to the vet, who will have to anesthetize the dog and remove the *espigaou* surgically. Prevention is preferable, and not difficult: a foot inspection after each walk. If your dog is one of the shaggy varieties, shaving his feet is also a good idea.

Estrangers

Until the second half of the twentieth century, the march of progress in Provence was largely confined to the coast and major towns. The backcountry remained remote, unfamiliar to all but the most adventurous tourist. Narrow roads made travel slow; sparse road signs made it uncertain and frequently mysterious. Life for the inhabitants of isolated villages and hamlets was much as it had been for generations. Strangers were rare, and often regarded with considerable suspicion.

It was quite normal for people to live their lives and die within a few kilometers of where they had been born. Their travels would take them no farther than the nearest market town or to a neighboring village for a wedding or a funeral. Under the iron laws of inheritance, property passed from parents to their children, and then on to their children, often provoking (as it still does today) furious family squabbles. Nevertheless, families tended to stay, if not together, then in the same commune.

Despite all that has changed, the stranger—or, to give him his Provençal title, *l'estranger*—is still a marked man, and he is not necessarily foreign. I have heard the people of Roussillon, on the north side of the Luberon, described as *estrangers* by the people of Cucuron, on the south side of the Luberon. The distance separating the two villages is no more than thirty kilometers. Sometimes it doesn't even take thirty kilometers to make *estrangers*. Let's say, for example, that you live on the plain. Three kilometers away there is a hamlet perched on a hill. Living up there, you might think, are neighbors; not cheek by jowl, perhaps, but neighbors just the same. Far from it. They are *"les gens du haut."* And while that label might sound unfriendly, it seems almost cozy when compared with the two brusque initials that are attached to any passerby with an unknown face. He is an E.P., or *estranger provençal*.

From this you can see that there are degrees of strangeness, depending on the provenance of the stranger. Extreme foreigners, those cloaked in an exoticism that comes from living in a completely different world, are usually identified by race, such as Parisians. But unlike the English, who delight in giving derogatory nicknames to foreigners, the Provençaux— most of the time—resist the temptation to insult visitors, content to call a Belgian a Belgian and a German a German. (Although, very occasionally, you will hear an Englishman described as a *rosbif*.)

As families disperse, village tribes die out, and the global population becomes ever more mobile, I suppose it is inevitable that one day the *estranger* will become extinct. My mentor Monsieur Farigoule, who studies these things closely, is convinced that one day our eminent leaders (whom he calls *"nos amis les cons a Bruxelles"*) will condemn the word as being discriminatory. Meanwhile, as he says, we should continue to take pleasure in treating the inhabitants of neighboring villages with a healthy dose of traditional suspicion.

Été

Not yet noon. Temperature in the mid-eighties and rising. Summer has set in. Fresh figs for breakfast, warm from the sun. Dogs asleep in the shade. The summer hubbub of languages on the café terrace: whinnies from the British, barks from the Germans, mutters from the Dutch. Short but glorious displays of roses. Fields of many colors—striped with lavender, gilded with sunflowers, beige with wheat, bottle-green with vines. Swimming in the dark. The scent of burning rosemary on the barbecue. Air like a hot, dry bandage. You sometimes wish the sun would take a day off.

Étoilés

One of the many delights of exploring France is that the traveling stomach is so well served. Wherever you go, you are seldom very far from a decent meal, and with minimal research you can be sure of finding it. Indeed, there are dozens of guides to help you. Many of these, unfortunately, try to combine flights of literary fancy with gastronomic information, and so the hungry reader, avid for facts, is obliged to plow through passages of purple prose before reaching the *plat du jour*. It is for this reason that I have come to prefer the laconic recommendations of that plump red classic, the Michelin guide, now in its 106th year.

More than nine thousand hotels and restaurants are currently listed in it, with admirable concision and an almost total lack of exclamation marks. Opinions, when given, are brief, and the editorial tone of the guide is restrained, practical, and devoid of exaggeration. It comes as something of a surprise, therefore, to find that the appearance each year of this staid volume provokes such a ruckus in the national press. Conflicting opinions are hurled back and forth, excuses and recriminations fly, reputations are made or tarnished—and all because of the curious little emblem that is an internationally recognized symbol of outstanding performance in the kitchen: the Michelin star.

It looks nothing like a star, more like an overweight rosette or a stylized macaroon, and macaroon is how it is often referred to in gastronomic circles. (Although eminent chefs are always known as *étoilés,* rather than *macaronés,* presumably for reasons of professional dignity. It wouldn't do to be described as a bun.) Whatever you call it, the star is a great distinction: the cause of celebration when awarded, gloom and even despair when taken away.

Traditionally, stars have twinkled at their brightest in and around Paris, with a healthy scattering down through Burgundy to Lyon, and on the Côte d'Azur. Until fairly recently, Provence was known more for its sturdy *aioli* and even more solid *pieds et paquets* than for the kind of refined and imaginative dishes that bring tears of joy to a Michelin inspector's eyes and stars to the chef. But this has changed.

Looking through the latest edition of the guide, I counted up the number of stars allocated to Haute-Provence, the Vaucluse, and the Bouches-du-Rhône. Even though I had been aware, in a general way, of the improvement in standards over the past few years, I found the numbers surprising and impressive: twenty-four stars, shared among twenty restaurants.

My ambition is to visit all twenty of them. So far, I've managed nine, which in research terms could be called a statistically significant sample—enough, at any rate, to draw a couple of conclusions.

The first and most obvious is that we in Provence are spoiled by the climate, which allows us to eat out of doors for several months a year, from May to mid-October, often earlier and later. Although I'm writing this in the winter, the memories of summer are still vivid. Hot sun, cool shade, linen tablecloths dappled with light: the terrace of La Fenière, between Lourmarin and Cadenet; the vast courtyard of the Hôtel d'Europe, in Avignon; the walled garden of Le Moulin, in Lourmarin; the smaller, more intimate garden of La Petite Maison, in Cucuron. There is something very special about eating beautiful food, beautifully presented, in the open air. Does everything taste better? It seems to.

And it certainly affects the atmosphere. One reservation I have about the Michelin system is that the award of a star can sometimes encourage a little too much reverence, turning what should be an enjoyable experience into a solemn ritual. Recommendations are murmured, almost whispered. Your food arrives enshrined under a silver dome. The ingredients are recited in the tones of a priest administering a blessing. Throughout the restaurant, hush replaces conversation.

This doesn't seem to happen when you're eating in a garden instead of a room. Customers, sommeliers, and waiters are more at ease. Clothes are more casual. Laughter can be heard. The occasional dog can be seen under a table, nose twitching and eyes rolling upward in the hope that something—a crust, a rosy sliver of lamb, a mouthful of cheese—will fall his way. The mood is more like that of a luxurious, highly civilized picnic than a serious restaurant.

Winter eventually comes, of course, and we have to move indoors and do without the advantages of sunshine and fresh air. Even so, I have found that our local Michelin-starred establishments are noticeably more relaxed than their counterparts farther north—due, I'm sure, to the Provençal character, which is not comfortable with excessive formality. I'm happy to say that this is only a half-proven theory at the moment. I still have another eleven restaurants to check.

Ex-Voto

O, hear us when we cry to Thee
For those in peril on the sea

—William Whiting, 1825–78

The fishermen and sailors of the past, with only centimeters of wood and a few strips of canvas between them and eternity, probably had more brushes with death and disaster than any other group of civilians. Each year, inevitably, had its tragedies. But each year also had its miraculous escapes, and these were often celebrated by ex-votos.

The full Latin version is *ex-voto suscepto.* A rough translation would be "the consequence of a vow made," and one can imagine the vows that were made by desperate seamen clinging to the wreckage and hoping against hope for supernatural help. For the lucky survivors, the ex-voto was a tangible way of giving thanks and thereby honoring their vow, and it is a tradition that still exists. In fact, it has developed and expanded over the years to include those in peril in the air and on the road; plane crashes, car and motorcycle accidents have been added to the original storms and shipwrecks. To see them all, ancient and modern, gathered together in one fascinating collection, take a deep breath and climb the hill to the basilica of Notre Dame de la Garde in Marseille.

Notre Dame is locally known as La Bonne Mère, and her golden statue, nearly ten meters high, stands on the top of the tower, looking out over the best view in Marseille: the rooftops of the city, the Vieux Port, the Mediterranean, the Frioul islands and the Château d'If. The basilica, even by the sometimes overdecorated standards of religious architecture, is a remarkably ornamental piece of work. There are massive domes inlaid with mosaics, columns of red and pink marble ringed with gilded bronze, a gold cornice decorated with precious stones, a tabernacle with a silver

STEAMER OBBIA MARSEILLE
Compagnie GYP - FABRE.

LE 4 DÉCEMBRE 1901 DANS L'OCÉAN INDIEN
DÉSEMPARÉ ET ASSAILLI PAR UN ÉPOUVANTABLE CYCLONE
RECONNAISSANT A NOTRE-DAME DE LA-GARDE
POUR NOUS AVOIR SAUVÉS.
Commandant A. J. Mattei.
783

gilt door—all this, and a bell in the tower that weighs eight tons. (The bell is called Marie Joséphine; the clapper is called Bertrand. Make of that what you will.)

In the midst of such elaborate splendor, the ex-votos provide welcome touches of humanity. There are no rules about the form an ex-voto should take. It is a personal expression of thanks and might be an effigy made from tin or wax, a painted scene, a collage of objects, a plaque, a mosaic— anything that tells all or part of the story of an escape from catastrophe.

As you would expect in a seaside church, there are literally hundreds of ex-votos showing scenes of ships in various forms of distress, mostly painted in the somber colors of a Force 10 gale. Some vessels are sinking by the stern, some by the bow. Masts are shattered, sails are in tatters. Sky-high waves are poised to smash down on terrified passengers, some clutching top hats, as they face their last moments on unprotected decks. And yet, thanks to La Bonne Mère, at least a handful of fortunate souls featured in these paintings must have survived.

Others, possibly not as artistic, expressed their gratitude in less dramatic form, and shipwrecks are probably outnumbered by the engraved marble tablets that cover long stretches of the basilica walls. Simple, and not much bigger than postcards, their messages are usually brief— "*Merci*" or "*Merci Bonne Mère*" are common, sometimes without even a name or any details, although I did notice three tablets from the same family, each with a different date.

With the passing of the years, ex-votos have taken more modern and sometimes more creative forms. Framed medals and miniature anchors compete for wall space with life belts, a soldier's helmet from World War I, a sailor's cap complete with scarlet pom-pom, and the pennant of General de Monsabert, commemorating the liberation of Marseille from the Nazis in August 1944. And everywhere—hanging from the ceiling, displayed in glass cases—scale models of yachts, brigs, three-masters, steamboats, packets, schooners, and several types of aircraft. A model of the *Mayflower* is there, for reasons that aren't immediately obvious; tugboats, a P&O cargo vessel, a tiny Peugeot 206. Finally, lest we forget one of the most perilous forms of modern transport, there is a plaque announcing that La Bonne Mère is the *patronne* of all motorcyclists.

It is a most extraordinary display—part museum, part art gallery, part shrine. It is also a history lesson, and a reminder that the Mediterranean, which we normally imagine to be as smooth and as blue as a postcard, has its darker side: turbulent, destructive, and lethal. I left the basilica with a profound sense of gratitude that I had never been tempted to run away to sea.

Fanny

I always think of Fanny as one of the great heroines of Provençal mythology, up there with Petrarch's Laura and Mistral's Mireille. It may seem like a heretical grouping, but my excuse for doing so is that Fanny, in sporting circles at least, is perhaps even more celebrated than the others, and still very much with us; her name is invoked wherever the game of *boules* is played.

Like many mythical heroines, Fanny's origins are a little murky. One version has it that she was a *boules* groupie in Lyon—the kind of girl whom today you might see hanging around soccer players. Another is that she was a café waitress in Isère. The Provençal version, which is naturally the one I take as gospel, is that she worked in a bar overlooking the *boulodrome* in La Ciotat, where *pétanque* (q.v.) was invented.

Boules players may disagree about Fanny's history, but they are unanimous about her place in the sport: she is there to provide comfort and solace to any player who loses by the humiliating score of 13–0. As to the delicate question of exactly what form the comfort and solace should take, a kiss is the generally accepted consolation prize. But where? Originally, the cheek was the target area. Over the years, however, the focus of the kiss changed—encouraged, so the story goes, by a deliberate wardrobe malfunction that left Fanny's *derrière* exposed. You can guess the rest.

Fanny is remembered today in *boules* terminology: *faire Fanny, baiser Fanny,* or *embrasser Fanny,* all of which mean a 13–0 loss. And her *derrière* has been commemorated at sporting bars throughout Provence in the form of statuettes and wall sculptures, each awaiting the loser's kiss. Like so many other things in life, consolation ain't what it used to be.

Félibrige

The definitive nail in the coffin of the Provençal dialect was hammered in when it was officially decided that French should be the only legal language in France. Until then, Provençal had been one of the seven major dialects of the Occitan language and was widely spoken in the south. This must have been a source of considerable frustration to government bureaucrats in Paris, who couldn't understand a word of it; neither could Provençal speakers understand the bureaucrats. It was an untidy state of affairs, and one that interfered with the authorities' passion for centralization. Where was the satisfaction in issuing laws and edicts that could not be understood by a large part of the southern population? It was like singing to the deaf. And so the decision was made—ratified by a decree in 1793—that Provençal could not be used in schools, government, the press, or the military. It had to be French.

But it takes time to kill a language, and Provençal managed to survive. It passed in the natural way from one generation to the next, encouraged, I suspect, by a healthy dislike of being told what to do by a bunch of busybodies in Paris (a sentiment that still exists today, most strongly in Marseille). And then, in 1854, Provençal received its most celebrated boost: Frédéric Mistral and six other poets got together and formed a literary movement to "safeguard indefinitely for Provence its language." Mistral's name for the movement was the Félibrige, and its members were Félibres—a word taken from Provençal folklore.

The Félibrige was a brave attempt, and it was enormously helped when Mistral was awarded the Nobel Prize for Literature in 1904. But despite that, the safeguarding of Provençal was a lost cause, perhaps because it was nostalgic rather than contemporary; in practical terms, its usefulness had passed. It also had the law of the land against it, and poetry is seldom a match for politics.

Today it is rare to hear Provençal spoken except by octogenarians living in the most remote parts of Provence. Otherwise, it is used on certain ceremonial occasions, like the truffle Mass at Richerenches, and at the annual gatherings of traditional societies. Some Provençal words have managed to edge their way into the French language—*santon, cabanon, jarre,* and *pistou**, for instance—but for the most visible traces of the old tongue you often need look no farther than your nearest Provençal village.

Having succeeded in eliminating the dialect from everyday speech, the bureaucracy has now, in its infinite wisdom, permitted it to creep back, in the form of the original Provençal place-names. These can be seen featured on handsome signs that appear at the entrance to an increasing number of villages, as if they had been twinned with their older selves. Thus Ménerbes is now also officially announced as Menerbo; Richerenches is also Richarencho; Aix is also Aix en Prouvenco; Lauris is also Lauri; and Vaugines is also Vau-Gino.

This is all very well as far as it goes, but why stop at village names? Why not apply those wonderful rolling Provençal vowels—those *oun*s, *aou*s, *uio*s, *ieou*s and *ai*s—to other areas where the public needs to be informed or directed? Let us take the humble *toilettes publiques* as an

---

*Clay figurine; stone hut; large earthenware pot; and basil, garlic, and olive oil sauce, respectively.

example. How much more poetic it would be if this invaluable facility were known by its Provençal name, *le cagadou*. The same principle could be extended throughout the village: the parking area, the *mairie*, the church, the fountain, the café—all of these useful but rather prosaic labels would benefit from a touch of old world linguistic charm. It would be a pleasant reminder of the Félibrige, with the added advantage of being incomprehensible to Parisians.

Fer Forgé

For centuries, when man and beast did the work that tractors do today, every village in Provence worth the name had its own forge. Horses and donkeys needed shoes, farmers needed tools, staircases needed balustrades, fireplaces needed grates, doors needed bolts—and the village *forgeron*, half technician, half artist, made them all.

Les Forges du Luberon

Ferronnerie Michel

tél./fax atelier :
04.90.68.38.97
port. 06.09.97.42.98

You would be lucky to find the village forge today. It is now more than likely to be a gas station, with the *forgeron* long since gone to his rest. But I am happy to say that his spiritual descendant, the *ferronnier*, is still very much with us. Our local man of iron, Olivier, has his atelier outside the village, where he has room to spread himself and his massive works in progress: the half-finished double gates, the sheep-sized barbecue, the outdoor dining table long enough to seat a regiment, the skeleton of a twenty-meter trellis. There they are, to be hosed down from time to time until they have acquired the patina of rust that, when treated and waxed, will make them look as though they were made by Olivier's great-grandfather.

Inside the atelier, there is the sizzle of sparks and the smell of red-hot iron, and a scattering of intricately worked oddments—iron curled and pointed, rounded or flattened, twisted like barley sugar; clusters of iron grapes and tendrils of iron vines; iron pineapples and iron acorns—a seemingly haphazard collection. And yet, to the *ferronnier* at least, it all makes sense. These fragments are the finishing touches and will eventually decorate the larger pieces that are waiting outside.

A good *ferronnier* not only creates but restores. Not long ago, we were shown the remains of what we were told was a nineteenth-century *gloriette,* or pergola. To my ignorant eye it was a mess, a shambles of iron rods and curlicues collapsed in a heap on the ground. To the *ferronnier,* it was—or could be—an elegant addition to our garden. He took the shambles away and sorted through it, discovering in the process that several pieces were missing. He replaced them, matching exactly not only the size and form of the existing ironwork, but also the uneven, slightly pockmarked finish. The *gloriette* is in the garden today, and it is impossible to tell where the old ends and the new begins.

For me, the greatest charm of a *ferronnier*'s work is not his technical skill, or even the originality of his designs, but something he would probably consider a slight fault. I love the tiny imperfections—the odd wrinkle in the iron, the faint mark of a hammer, the surface that is not quite smooth, the angle that is not quite true. You will see them only if you look very closely. And the reason I like them is that they have been made by a man and not by a machine.

Fêtes Votives

Such is the abundance of saints in the French calendar, from Alphonse to Zita, that every village in Provence, no matter how small, has its own particular patron saint. And according to custom, the saint's day is marked by a celebration—the *fête votive*—which is an opportunity for all the villagers to forget their debts and differences, to eat and drink and dance together, and to give themselves over to what anthropologists, with their gift for the sonorous phrase, have called "social cohesion."

The *fête votive* is a delightful idea, but it is no longer quite what it used to be. Saints' days are not observed quite as rigidly as they were, perhaps because the influence of religion is less strong. Or perhaps it's just the weather. Let us say the patron saint of the village is Cédric. His day, January 7, happens to fall in the season of hibernation, when, if there is any social cohesion at all, it takes place indoors. The hours of daylight are limited, and temperatures are often below freezing—not the best conditions for making merry in the streets. Would Saint Cédric object if the villagers postponed the celebration until spring or summer? Surely not.

Another reason for the fair-weather *fête* is that villages, too, are not what they used to be. At one time, the inhabitants of most villages would have been born locally and would have spent their lives more or less attached to their roots. In a more mobile society, that's no longer the case. People leave. Instead of marrying the boy next door, the baker's daughter marries a young man from Clermont-Ferrand and goes to live there. Instead of working on the land, the farmer's son gets a job with Eurocopter in Marseille and goes to live there. Instead of staying in his large old village house, the retired *notaire* moves to an apartment in Aix. Little by little, the native-born population of the village shrinks.

Former inhabitants are replaced, but they are replaced by foreigners—that is, anyone coming from outside a thirty-mile radius. These newcomers are very often part-time villagers, using their *résidences secondaires* only during the summer. The annual party, if it is to be well attended, needs to take place when they can join in. And so there has been a basic change to the *fête votive* itself. What was once an almost private occasion purely for the enjoyment of the long-established inhabitants now includes "outsiders" and their friends; the more the merrier, since a successful *fête* is generally regarded to be good for the morale and the economy of the village.

So much so that there is an element of competition among villages to put on a show that will pull in the crowds. Pocket circuses and traveling fairgrounds, fireworks displays, local rock groups, prize-laden *tombolas*, stands selling wines and cheeses, *boules* tournaments—and, if the organizational abilities of the village run to it, my favorite attraction, the communal dinner.

Ideally, this is held outside. There are lights in the plane trees, long trestle tables in the square, a small makeshift stage and an area left free for dancing. You sit wherever there's a place, which could be next to the mayor or between a German couple and a Swedish family. Glasses are filled and introductions are made, sometimes despite the fact that there is a significant language problem. (This, you will find, becomes less of a problem as the evening wears on and the wine takes hold.) On the menu there may be *aioli*, pizza, paella, or a sizzling array of barbecued meats. With their feet firmly under the table, the revelers fortify themselves for the energetic activities ahead.

At this stage, the rock band is silent, the members of the group attending to their thirst, flexing their leather trousers, and putting the final touches to their stick-on tattoos. Dinner music is provided by another group, virtuosos of the accordion, playing a selection of old favorites, and inevitably, there is a *paso doble*. Ah, the *paso doble*. Here is the signal for some of the more mature couples to take to the dance floor and demonstrate their swoops and twirls, little fingers cocked, heads snapping from side to side as they glide carefully around the children and dogs that have strayed away from the tables. Younger spectators eye one another and wait, impatient for the throb of drums and guitars.

Eventually, once the plates are empty, eating gives way to table-hopping. The ladies of the village compare fashion notes, passing judgment on *le look* displayed by one or two of the female strangers: the height of their heels, the brevity of their skirts, the plunge of their *décolletés*. Their husbands wisely avoid comment, discussing instead OM's prospects for the next soccer season or the state of their vines. Meanwhile, preceded by a series of electronic burps and squawks as they tune the amplifier, the rockers attack their first number, putting a stop to any conversation in the vicinity of the stage.

And so the evening goes on, noisy and good-natured, the way a party should be. It may not be the traditional *fête* of fifty or sixty years ago, when the villagers themselves provided the entertainment and everybody knew everybody else. And it certainly has little to do with Saint Cédric or any other patron saint. Even so, it's a fine way to spend a summer's night and to celebrate one's good luck at being here, in the warmth and laughter of Provence.

Fontaines

It is hard to think of a modern equivalent. The fountain, in its heyday, served not only as a source of clean, fresh water, but as an active social center. It was the place to meet some of your neighbors (and undoubtedly to discuss the doings and character of those others who weren't present), catch up on the price of olive oil and wheat, flirt or exchange insults with passersby, gossip, loiter, cool off in the summer, and generally pass the time agreeably while performing a daily chore. And it was a daily chore, because those were the days when water storage was primitive, a cistern was a luxury, and the contents of the cistern were, more often than not, stagnant and undrinkable. So the fountain was a vital part of Provençal village life until well into the twentieth century, often having its very own municipal employee, the *fontainier,* who was responsible for looking after it.

The style of the fountain frequently reflected the wealth and artistic ambitions of the commune. In Saignon, for instance, the fountain is a marvelously elaborate affair sculpted by the eminent Monsieur Sollier. Rising

from the hexagonal base is a column supporting a small but ornate
bassin, and rising from the *bassin* is
a statue of a young woman decant-
ing a stone torrent from her water
jar. Not bad for a village of fewer
than a thousand inhabitants. Other
towns and villages often used their
fountains to commemorate past
events of local importance, which
is why I was intrigued to discover
that in Forcalquier, the Fontaine
Saint-Michel is decorated with
what looks very much like an
erotic carving. Sadly, it is not
known whether this is historically
accurate, or whether the sculptor
was simply doodling in stone
while waiting for inspiration.

You can see more modest decorative flourishes—some bizarre, some
ingenious, some with a nice sense of humor—applied to the business end
of the fountain, that point at which the water appears. It gushes from the
mouths of angels, devils, and nymphs; gargoyles and swans; dolphins and
lions; and from innumerable human faces. If the water has been allowed to
dribble down a stone chin for a couple of centuries, there will often be a
luxuriant mossy beard. On other faces, the water is projected through a
short iron tube sticking out of the mouth. It resembles a dripping cigar and
looks rather incongruous between a cherub's lips.

At the height of a Provençal summer, the plash of water and the glint
and ripple of sunshine on its surface are magnets for overheated tourists.
Perhaps for the benefit of such an audience there is the occasional message, chiseled somewhere on the fountain. One from Clovis Hugues, the

enfant terrible of Ménerbes, reads: *"C'est l'eau, qui nous donna le vin"*—It's water that gives us wine. Another, from an anonymous Provençal: *"Eici l'aigo es d'or"*—Here, water is gold. And finally, no doubt from a modern descendant of the old *fontainier,* a less poetic thought: *"The water is not to be used for washing your car."*

Fruit Confit

It is one of the more obscure and unlikely groupings in Provençal history: those two brothers in piety, Pope Clement VI and Pope Urban V, and the far from pious Marquis de Sade. What could they possibly have had in common?

The answer is a sweet tooth. All three of them were partial to crystallized fruit, and ever since the fourteenth century, there has been no better place to get this sugary treat than the town of Apt, the self-proclaimed Capitale Mondiale du Fruit Confit. It started with a handful of families, their cauldrons, and a few cherries, figs, and apricots that had been sun-ripened in the surrounding fields. Little by little it turned into an industry, and by the end of the nineteenth century, there were ten factories in Apt employing eight hundred people and producing 165,000 kilos of fruit a year.

These numbers have now dropped far below what they used to be, probably because of the huge increase in competition from other kinds of confectionery. Someone looking for a sugar fix today has an almost unlimited choice, from doctored breakfast cereals to ice cream, from chocolate to chewing gum. But luckily for the artisans of Apt, there are those who prefer a natural flavor to an artificial additive, and for these connoisseurs of sweetness there is nothing quite like traditionally cooked, lavishly coated, gloriously sticky crystallized fruit.

If not quite an art, the crystallization of fruit is certainly an advanced skill, and one that requires time, patience, and great attention to detail. In theory, the process is simple: water contained in the fruit is replaced, through osmosis, by sugar, which preserves the fruit. When done correctly, the result is sweet and firm, retaining the shape, color, and flavor of the original. Doing it correctly is where the skill and patience come in.

The fruit is plunged briefly into boiling water and left to cool before being immersed again, this time in syrup. After boiling for three to four minutes, the syrup is drained off and the fruit cools once more. This is repeated as many as a dozen times, increasing the concentration of sugar in the syrup gradually each time. (It is the gradual increase that allows the fruit to keep its shape and stay tender; too much sugar too soon would shrivel and toughen the flesh.) After this series of syrup baths, which can take anything from weeks to months depending on the fruit, there is a final drying session lasting several days in very gentle heat. As you can see, it is not something to be attempted at home by an impatient amateur cook.

Of the remaining *confiseurs* in Apt, the largest is Kerry Aptunion, an industrial enterprise just outside the center of town. One of the oldest independent firms is the Maison Léopold Marliagues, established in 1873, still run by the founding family and still doing things the old-fashioned way, even down to recycling cherry stalks, which are rotted down to make compost, and cherry pits, which are burned as fuel to heat the greenhouses.

As with everything edible in France, there are some fine points to be kept in mind when tasting. "One does not go from an apricot to a lemon and then back to a fig." Perish the thought; there is a certain order that should be observed. You start with the more subtle tastes—apricots, plums, figs, pineapple, melon—before moving on to the citrus fruits. This will allow you to experience *"un véritable crescendo de saveurs."* Something that cannot be said for presweetened corn flakes.

G

The letter that adds a Provençal twang to words that misguided purists seem to think should end in *n*. Thus we find, among many others, *bieng* and *paing, ving* and *copaing, raising* and *fing* (otherwise known as well, bread, wine, friend, grape, and end). It only takes a few years of hearing words spoken with this extra resonance before other forms of pronunciation, without the single-letter suffix, sound incomplete and rather strange. Locally, anyone who suffers from this particular speech defect is said to *parler pointu*, or to speak like a Parisian.

Gaulage

This is an act of violence committed against a tree, during which the branches are beaten with a stick to make the fruit fall off. A harvesting technique that probably predates the invention of the ladder, *gaulage* is still practiced in the wilder parts of Provence, and very picturesque it is, too. A net or a tarpaulin is spread around the base of the tree to catch the fruit, and then the merry tree beaters go at it, thrashing fruit and walnut trees to within an inch of their lives. It is, so I'm told, a cathartic experience, an excellent opportunity to let off steam with only minimal risk of injury, although there is the occasional case of temporary blindness caused by a direct hit in the eye from a rogue apricot. But on the whole it is a charming, if slightly noisy, method of gathering your fruit and nuts.

Gaulage was also used on olive trees until progress intervened with the invention of the tree comb, a device that resembles a miniature garden rake with a short handle. The comb's teeth are made of flexible plastic that is kind to both olive and tree, and the process of drawing the comb through the branches is remarkably efficient. Olives fall like showers of plump green raindrops, their complexions unblemished. It seemed to me the ideal way of stripping a tree of its fruit—gentle, effective, and quiet. But I had reckoned without the Provençal fondness for gadgets, preferably loud gadgets. (I think the liking for noise often starts at a young age with a boy's first Mobylette, which, with the muffler removed, can be made to sound like a baby Ferrari.)

I was made aware of the latest comb developments last November. Frédéric, the young man who nurses our olives, had arrived with his team to start picking, normally two or three days of tranquil activity. This time it was different. Even from far away, I could hear a regular clacking sound, as if two pieces of wood were being slapped together, a sound that would undoubtedly drive you mad if you heard too much of it. Coming over the brow of the hill, I could see Frédéric standing by a tree with what appeared to be a fishing rod, its end hidden in the higher branches. Seeing me coming, he flicked a switch, the clacking stopped, and he stepped away from the tree to show me his new pride and joy: *le peigne mécanique,* or mechanical comb. As I quickly learned, it was not only *mécanique* but also *téléscopique,* with the comb on a long adjustable stem that provided access to the highest olives without need of a ladder. It was quicker than combing by hand, equally kind to olives, convenient, and modern—and it made that infinitely satisfying *clack-clack-clack.* No doubt about it: a triumph of olive-picking technology, twenty-first century *gaulage,* complete with noise. I have to say I hate it.

Génoise

Traditionally, houses in Provence, with their thick walls and small windows, were built to stay cool in summer and keep out the chill of the mistral in winter. But very rarely were they built with an eye for the rainy day; and rain in Provence, when it comes, is often excessive, gushing down with sufficient force to wash away or damage almost everything in

its path. While the roof of a house bears the worst of the downpour, the unprotected façade suffers too. So do lintels and shutters. And anyone poking his nose out of the front door gets instantly drenched.

Or so it was until the eighteenth century, when Italian *maçons*, looking for work, came to Provence. They brought with them the *génoise*, a stylish solution to the problem of dripping walls and water-warped shutters. They added extra tiles to the edges of the roof, thus extending the roof line all around the house by twenty inches or so, and forming eaves. In this way, rainwater was diverted so that it fell a comfortable distance away from walls, windows, and doors. Not a complete waterproofing technique, perhaps, but certainly a great improvement on what had been done before.

The overhang of the roof was supported from below by the *génoise*—stepped rows of curved tiles built out from the wall, their hollow spaces packed with plaster or cement. The number of rows was—and probably still is—an indication of affluence and social standing. Two rows for a modest *bastide*, three for something a little more elaborate, and in exceptional cases of wealth and architectural grandeur, four. Visually, the effect is sober but decorative, an elegant transition between roof and house.

But alert observers of the *génoise* will have noticed recently that imitations have been sprouting from all kinds of unlikely houses. Owners of villas and Provençal haciendas of very recent construction have adopted this eighteenth-century classic, with one important omission: they have left the tiles of the *génoise* hollow, avoiding the expense of hand-packing each tile with plaster. The result is unfortunate, since it gives a jagged, unfinished look to the roofline and invites derogatory comments from architectural purists, who love to mutter about faux Provençal trimmings.

Gestes

As anyone who has spent more than five minutes in a village bar will tell you, the Provençal is a gregarious, garrulous fellow. Not for him the extended silence or the terse exchange; nor will he normally restrict himself to one meager word when ten will do. I think it would be true to say that he has no problem communicating verbally. However, words alone, he feels, are often not enough. From time to time there is the need for extra emphasis, some physical punctuation, or a soupçon of drama. And so he finds it necessary to decorate his conversations with a second vocabulary, one of gestures.

Some of these might be familiar to you, as pale versions of them can be seen in other parts of France. But only in Provence will you find them executed with such relish, or with such careful attention to detail. Even a shrug, probably the most common of Gallic spasms, is more intricate and impressive when carried out by a Provençal. The conventional shrug is nothing more than a swift twitch of the shoulders; the Provençal shrug brings in the jaw (which must be thrust forward as the mouth is turned down), the eyebrows (which must rise to their upper limit), and the hands (which must be spread out, palms upward, as the shoulders are raised)— not forgetting the sound effects (a forceful exhalation of air between pursed lips) to bring the performance to a satisfactory finale.

Second to the shrug in popularity is that signal of opposition and reproof, the index finger. In its simplest manifestation, held up at eye level, it acts as a silent interruption; it is impossible to ignore and can stop a conversation in midsentence. To express disagreement, it is wagged back and forth in the manner of a metronome. To express violent disagreement, or to put particular emphasis on a point of view held by the owner of the finger, it is used to peck at the chest of the opponent like an irate bird. Small it may be, that nagging finger, but effective it most certainly is.

Now we come to the hand that wavers, where two similar gestures have two quite separate meanings. The first is to indicate a lack of precise information when answering a question, such as, what is the melon crop going to be like this year? The answer, whether good or bad, will be qualified by the hand. Held in front of the body, palm down at elbow level, the hand performs a gentle rocking motion, as if to acknowledge the degree of uncertainty that exists when forecasting anything that involves nature. (This is often accompanied by the demi-shrug, in which just one shoulder moves upward.) A subtle variation is used when replying to a more personal question that includes a specific time, such as, when do you think you can come and unblock the septic tank? This is awkward, since the Provençal has an innate dislike of being pinned down by times and dates. And so the answer, whether it be this afternoon or next Thursday, will be given with an unspoken disclaimer. The hand, this time more discreetly positioned lower down and close to the thigh, can be seen to tremble for a few revealing seconds. Seeing this, the student of hand language will know at once that the date given is almost certainly subject to postponement. I once made the mistake of pointing this out to our *maçon,* and even now, years later, he keeps both hands in his pockets when talking about delivery dates.

On an altogether more visible level is the gesture for which there is no polite translation, although once seen there is little doubt about its meaning. In its most uninhibited form, one fist is clenched, the arm swings out and upward, and the other hand is applied, with an audible smack, to the biceps. This, of course, is possible only if you have adequate space for the considerable freedom of movement required. However, the gesture can be adapted to suit cramped circumstances as well. Staying close to the body at all times, the left hand is brought forward and upward as the right hand comes across to land with a firm clip on the wrist. And in extreme conditions, when there is a barely room to breathe, the same maneuver can be carried out using only the index finger of each hand. This may not be quite as gratifying as the full-blown insult, but it is better than nothing; after all, it's the thought that counts.

Gibassier

Seen next to the iced and sugary perfection of the other *gâteaux* on the baker's shelf, the *gibassier* looks as though it has been in a fight. Its profile is a little squashed, its form a little irregular, its surface torn by deep gashes. You might easily pass over it in favor of something smooth and chocolate-coated and visibly more glamorous. But this would be a pity, because the *gibassier* has a sweetness all its own.

It is disc-shaped and plump, like a very well upholstered pancake, and its flavor comes from a mixture of sugar, olive oil, orange flower water, and the zest of orange peel; light, subtle, and distinctive. Thanks to the olive oil in the recipe, it is sometimes known as a *pompe à l'huile*. Should you see something similar that is described merely as a *pompe*, you should know that it is probably not the real thing, but has been made with butter instead of oil, and may well con-

tain all kinds of unauthorized ingredients like raisins, aniseed, preserved fruit, chopped almonds, and heaven knows what else. Delicious though this may be, it is not a true *gibassier,* but a more voluptuous relative.

Gibier d'Été

I remember the first time I heard the phrase. I was sitting outside the village café one morning in July, watching the heat shimmer up from the cobblestones, when a group of people came down the street. They were tourists. Their bright new clothes were crisp, their skins were going through that pink period before the tan sets in, their sunglasses were fashionably impenetrable.

The waiter put my coffee on the table and looked up to inspect them. *"Voilà,"* he said with a nod, *"le gibier d'été."*

Tourists are given many labels, not all of them complimentary, but this was the first time I had heard them compared to wild game, and it set me thinking. There are definite similarities: tourists tend to move around in small flocks, their migration patterns are seasonal, they can be startled into flight if treated inhospitably, and they cluster in particular spots for nourishment. But I can't think of any other species that even comes close to them in terms of numbers.

In 2003, the most recent year for which detailed statistics are available, the three *départements* of Provence received very nearly 16 million tourists. Of these, 2.6 million went to Haute-Provence, 4.4 million to the Vaucluse, and 8.8 million to the Bouches-du-Rhône. And although there were some early arrivals at Easter and some stragglers at Christmas, the vast majority came during the summer.

For some, this will make horrifying reading. There is a strong element of snobbery attached to travel, and we all have acquaintances who would feel insulted if they were to be described as tourists. They see themselves as mobile citizens of the world—civilized, sophisticated, considerate, enlightened, a blessing upon their chosen destinations. It is the hoi polloi who are tourists. *They* are the ones who clog up the roads, strip the shelves of the *boulangerie* bare, monopolize the restaurants, litter the countryside, and generally turn peace into chaos.

On the whole, Provence doesn't make that distinction. Tourists of all kinds and from all countries are generally treated with courtesy and good humor, and not just because they spend money. Most Provençaux are proud of the region and pleased that it has become a magnet for so many visitors. And, like any other hosts, they hope their summer guests will take pleasant memories home with them.

But what do you do with 16 million extra bodies every year? Occasionally, I must admit, the July and August invasion seems overwhelming. The better-known villages of the Luberon—Gordes, Bonnieux, Ménerbes, Roussillon—teem with what are sometimes called the swallows of summer: English, American, German, Swedish, Dutch. The weekly markets, particularly in Apt and Lourmarin, become so congested that you can easily find yourself putting the cheese you've just bought into someone else's basket. Supplies of *rosé* in the cafés run dangerously low. Parking is an exercise in frustration.

And yet this can be avoided, either by doing all your errands in the cool of the morning before ten o'clock or by heading for the hills. From most towns or villages, a twenty-minute drive will take you to open, beautiful countryside. Here, you will find no sign of the unattractive monuments to mass tourism: no condominiums, no theme parks, no three-hundred-room hotels—and very few people. Vast areas of Provence, even in July and August, stay empty. Silence, which has become an endangered commodity in the modern world, is still available. There is room to breathe and the air is clear. And the summer millions seem far, far away.

Hannibal

One of the earlier visitors to Provence, and almost certainly the first to bring his own elephants, Hannibal unfortunately failed to provide us with a detailed record of his travels. We are told that he came through the Pyrenees with sixty thousand infantry, nine thousand cavalry, and thirty-seven elephants. We are told that he followed the line of the coast before turning north toward Avignon. And, of course, we know that he crossed the Alps into Italy before causing havoc among the Romans. But where exactly did he cross the Rhône? Where did he turn east toward Italy? Which alpine pass did he use? These and many other questions have been the subjects of speculation, disagreement, and argument among generations of historians, probably started by Livy and Polybius more than two thousand years ago. However, one thing is agreed: it is beyond dispute that Hannibal and his elephants made their way through parts of Provence.

In trying to establish the exact route they took, I found little help from reference sources. They were more concerned with the crossing of the Alps, a wonderfully dramatic business involving "natives, springing from their place of concealment, leaping into the fray, hurling missiles, rolling down rocks from the heights above." Compare this with Livy's passing mention of the march through Provence: "Hannibal advanced toward the Alps mainly through open country, and reached the foothills without encountering any opposition from the local tribes." Not nearly as exciting.

Even today, Provence has a great deal of open country, and there must have been considerably more of it in Hannibal's time. Where does one start looking? The most likely bet seemed to be the small village of Montfaucon, not far from Châteauneuf-du-Pape. Here, there is an area known as Pas d'Hannibal, or Hannibal's Footstep—a reminder that this is where the great warrior is supposed to have crossed the Rhône. Much encouraged, I thought I was beginning to make progress. And then I made the mistake of mentioning what I'd learned to Monsieur Farigoule.

I have had several intellectual encounters with Farigoule over the years and have always come off second best. He presents his opinions so emphatically, and with such

Lioux

a wealth of supporting evidence, that I am invariably persuaded, probably wrongly, that he knows what he's talking about. The Hannibal exchange ran true to form. While he admitted that Hannibal must have crossed the Rhône, Farigoule was not convinced that he crossed it at Montfaucon. This would be at odds with the Farigoule theory of Hannibal's detour into the Luberon, which, as he told me with great satisfaction, very few historians had spotted. Not Livy, and definitely not Polybius. No; it took a scholar with intimate local knowledge and a gift for detective work to put two and two together and make five (my words, not his).

I was then treated to the full-length Farigoule theory, complete with erudite asides and many unflattering references to historians past and present. I will give you the gist.

Hannibal had lost his way. This was not surprising, since he was in unfamiliar territory, and the compass wasn't going to be invented for another fourteen hundred years or so. Having crossed the Rhône, he was wandering around the countryside south of Avignon, keeping his eyes open for anything resembling an Alp. One clear morning, he saw in the distance a mountain range—perhaps not quite Alpine, but high enough to look promising. Closer inspection convinced him that he was approaching the foothills of the Alps, and Italy must therefore be just over the horizon. Crying "Onward to Rome!" and gathering his elephants about him, he pressed on until dusk, when he stopped to spend the night near the village of Lioux.

Here I should say that I have often been to Lioux—a pleasant, tiny village with, at most, two hundred inhabitants—and have never seen a Rue Hannibal, a Place Hannibal, a Hannibal statue, or any memorial that might suggest a historic visitor. I said as much to Farigoule, who looked at me with the expression of tolerant despair that he reserves for the hopelessly ignorant. Had I not seen the emblem of the village? The blue elephant? A creature that even I must know is not native to Provence? Where else could the good people of Lioux have seen an elephant if not with Hannibal?

Fairly flimsy evidence, you will say, and you would be right. But you have never heard Monsieur Farigoule in full cry. And I cannot deny the fact that the elephant really is the symbol of Lioux. Nobody knows why; at least, nobody except Farigoule.

Herbes de Provence

In Britain, the *h* is pronounced. In the United States it is silent, often prompting unkind British remarks about curious American pronunciation. In fact, it was only in the nineteenth century that the British tacked on the hard *h*, presumably to avoid being taken for London Cockneys (who have a careless habit of dropping their aitches). Americans continue to use the original pronunciation, *à la française*.

However you pronounce them, *herbes de Provence* are famous. They are evocative of sunny hillsides and simple meals eaten outdoors. They travel well, since they don't have to be used fresh; indeed, they have a shelf life of months, even years, keeping much of their scent and flavor when dry. This makes them popular with owners of *épiceries*, delicatessens, specialty shops, food boutiques, market stalls, and souvenir stands. I have seen them on sale at airports and *autoroute* gas stations, in the Harrods food halls and in fragrant corners of Fauchon; in tiny earthenware pots, glass jars, linen pouches, and patterned sachets. Sometimes, the contents have been reduced by the extended passage of time to not much more than dust, and bear little resemblance, either in taste or smell, to the real thing. And quite often, alas, they were not the real thing to begin with.

The majority of aromatic plants sold in France—one estimate is as high as 80 percent—come from elsewhere. Turkish bay, Egyptian marjoram, Moroccan and Spanish thyme, and Spanish rosemary have been transformed, by miracles of unscrupulous packaging, into *herbes de Provence*. Naturally enough, the *herboristes* of Provence have taken this very badly, and have fought back. November 28, 2003, saw the introduction of the Label Rouge, a legal guarantee of provenance and quality not unlike the *appellation* system used for wines. Apart from the obvious requirement of Provençal origin, there is a specific recipe, or mixture, to be followed: 19 percent thyme, 26 percent rosemary, 3 percent basil, 26 percent oregano, and 26 percent savory (although which of the more than twenty different types of savory is not specified). This blend has the approval of the official palate, and providing it carries the red label, you can be sure you're getting the genuine article.

But as always in Provence where food is concerned, there is heated disagreement. Many cooks would never be caught mixing their herbs, preferring to use a particular herb for a particular dish: rosemary for lamb, juniper for game and beef, sage for pork and potatoes, fennel for fish, thyme for rabbit and grilled meats, tarragon for chicken and veal, bay for fish and beef, basil for tomatoes and *soupe au pistou*, savory for cheeses. One Provençal cookbook includes the marvelously snooty phrase, "Mixing herbs is out of the question."

Personally, I am a mixer. When grilling, I find that a sprinkling of assorted herbs makes any kind of flesh—fish, fowl, or meat—taste better. As if that weren't heresy enough, I keep by the barbecue a sack full of clippings from our rosemary hedges, and I throw handfuls of these straight onto the coals no matter what is being cooked. They smell wonderful, and they bring back memories of a visit some years ago to a pretentious food emporium on the far reaches of Long Island. There I found twiglets of rosemary, no longer than my little finger and individually wrapped in cellophane, on sale at $1.50 per twiglet. It probably wasn't even Provençal rosemary, either.

While many herbs are normally confined to the kitchen, they stray from time to time into the medicine cabinet. *Millepertuis,* or St. John's wort, when mixed with oil, is a classic old salve that relieves the pain of burns. Oregano, used neat, is a powerful natural disinfectant and is said to have helped people survive the plague. Extract of rosemary is good for the scalp and for indigestion. Wild thyme fights persistent coughs and asthma. Basil soothes gastric pains. Juniper helps to lessen the twinges of rheumatism. Savory, in an unlikely combination of virtues, boosts the libido and cures diarrhea. There are herbal cures, it seems, for just about everything—except for that much-loved French ailment, hypochondria.

Hiboux et Hérons

If there were a prize for the most bumptious and visible bird in Provence, it would have to go to that black-and-white scavenger, the magpie. Even during the hunting season, when most prudent birds head for the comparative safety of Aix or Avignon, you see magpies everywhere. They gather in the middle of the road, bickering over the remains of a squashed field mouse. They lurk by the side of garbage containers in case some putrid delicacy has escaped from a plastic sack. They haunt the vineyards, hoping to find some small, well-rotted corpse. And I assume that it is this, their toxic diet, that keeps them safe from the hunter's gun. I have yet to find a cookbook that includes a recipe for magpie, for the very good reason that your first mouthful would probably be your last. Death or disgust would make a second bite out of the question.

Curiously enough, we rarely see magpies close to the house. I have been told that this is because they don't care to trespass on owl territory, and *hiboux* we most certainly have. In complete contrast to the magpie, the owl is a bird that is normally heard but not seen, and on summer nights, when darkness has finally fallen, we often hear the voice of our resident owl—*hoo-hoo, hoo-hoo*—coming from the plane tree in the courtyard. It is a clean, cool sound, and usually very soothing. One warm night, however, there was a more urgent, agitated note to it: *hoo! hoo! hoo!* And not only that; the hooting was on the move, coming from different parts of the garden. We put it down to the panic brought on by courtship, and thought no more of it until the next morning, when we discovered the visitor in the kitchen.

He was standing on the floor, beneath a window we had left ajar. He was about the size of a beer can, with large yellow eyes and a pair of small, jaunty ears: a baby owl. His mother had obviously mislaid him the night before, and what we had heard were the maternal hoots of a concerned parent. But what should we do with him? Rustle up a few worms or a dead vole for his breakfast? Put him back in the plane tree? Supposing he fell? Could he fly, or had he somehow climbed into the kitchen? Much of the morning was spent under his impassive gaze, trying to work out how we could return him to the bosom of his family.

We decided to leave him on a low stone ledge in the shady part of the courtyard—a safe spot where any observant mother would see him at once. From time to time we would look out of the window, and he would look back at us with those unblinking yellow eyes. Once we thought he'd gone, only to find that he had clambered into a flowerpot and settled himself among the geraniums. There was no sign or sound of mother. We began to think we might have to adopt him, and considered calling the vet for advice about bringing up orphan owls. But at some point during the afternoon, his mother must have come to the rescue and taken him back home, and that night we could tell that all was well. The hooting had returned to the plane tree and resumed its normal serene rhythm.

I later found out that our young visitor was an example of the *moyen-duc* branch of the owl family, and we hope that when he's grown up he'll stay with us. That is more than I can say for our other frequent flyer, who often drops in for breakfast when he thinks nobody's looking: the *héron cendré*. He usually comes very early in the morning, just as the sun is rising, presumably when he thinks the goldfish in the *bassin* will still be drowsy and not yet alert. He stands on the edge of the *bassin*, stretching his neck downward as he peers into the water. Seen from behind, he resembles a lanky, myopic man searching for a small object that he's dropped. He is completely motionless until a careless fish comes within range. Then he strikes. His neck seems to extend by a few extra centimeters and his beak goes in like an arrow, making no more than a ripple in the water before coming up, if he's lucky, with a squirming victim.

Should I leave him undisturbed, I'm sure he will begin to treat the *bassin* as his personal sushi bar and will no doubt graduate from goldfish to the bigger and more expensive carp. This I would like to prevent, and luckily I can count on our dogs to help. There is nothing they like better than to menace a trespasser, and they have discovered that the heron is not only harmless (to them) but satisfyingly timid; one bark and he takes off, great wings flapping and spindly legs dangling as he flies low across the field, a prehistoric vision, with the dogs in hot but hopeless pursuit.

Hier

You will find in Provence two opposing views of the recent past: romantic or practical, and each is commonly expressed through the medium of real estate.

Supporters of the romantic school are usually younger, quite affluent couples who have just arrived from one or another of the northern European cities. They are addicted to yesterday and would like their old farmhouse in Provence to remain, as far as possible, "authentic." Tiny windows, low ceilings, uneven floors, lethally steep stairs, eccentric plumbing, flapping roof tiles, smoking chimneys—these are seen not as severe drawbacks, but as charming relief from the sterile efficiencies of a city apartment. Country living, in all its quaint novelty.

Their house guests come and go, trying to make allowances for what they are asked to endure. They are startled but uncomplaining when they find they are sharing their bedroom with a bat. They survive multiple concussions when they fail to stoop as they pass through doorways made for medieval-sized people. They grapple, tight-lipped, with the intricacies of a lavatory that is twice their age and an antique kitchen stove that has been unwisely rescued from the scrap heap. And yet, far from being apologetic, their hosts seem to take great pride in these obstacles to a civilized existence. Clearly, they revel in the joys of what they call the simple life.

Meanwhile, the previous owners of the farmhouse, an elderly couple who have spent their lives in Provence, are counting their blessings. Having sold at a very good price, they have moved into a small modern villa with double-glazed windows, electric central heating, and a fully equipped kitchen, the *cuisine américaine* of their dreams. They are not addicted to yesterday; they remember it all too well. They remember, as children, having to use the outside privy when the mistral threatened to blow them off the seat; the logistical challenge of getting enough hot water for a bath, one bucket at a time; the winter-long chill of stone floors; the leaks in the roof; the whistle of wind through ill-fitting windows; the daily drudgery of life. Charming? Forget it.

Somewhere between these two extremes are those irritatingly perfect houses you see in magazines, monuments to a certain kind of taste, usually a mixture of period architecture and twenty-first-century comforts: a converted nunnery, perhaps, with an indoor swimming pool. My theory is that nobody actually lives in these extraordinary establishments. They are there only to be photographed. They show no convincing signs of being inhabited; certainly not by couples with children, dogs, or friends with the normal share of untidy habits. Stylists and photographers may spend the odd night there, but they leave no trace.

I was once allowed to see such a place, in the company of the previous owners, a farmer and his wife. We had been invited to inspect the changes that had been made to a vast old *bergerie,* converted at enormous cost into the Provençal equivalent of a Manhattan loft. All went well until we were shown an area off the sitting room that had been transformed into a media complex where, so our hosts said, they were planning to spend many a cozy winter evening watching television and listening to music. We were all suitably impressed by the gleaming array of high-tech gadgets. But something else caught the eye of the farmer's wife. One would never recognize it, she said to the new owner, as the room where Uncle Bruno committed suicide. Haven't those flagstones cleaned up nicely?

Hiver

Unpicked almonds, black on leafless branches. Clipped vines poking twisted fingers through the bare brown earth. Winter sunsets, livid and panoramic, followed by a low and bloody moon. Steam rising from a horse's back. Fields white with flowering wild *roquette*. Gorse bushes bright with acid yellow tips, and a single optimistic violet blossom on a clump of rosemary. Distant feathers of smoke, ruler-straight in the still air. A transparent skin of ice on the moss around the fountain. The pop of gunshots in the morning and at twilight. Moans and howls and the clanking of bells from the hunters' dogs. Frozen earth crunching underfoot. The cough of a tractor starting up. Cedar logs spitting in the chimney. The hush of a countryside soundproofed by snow. Smells of the season: chilled air flavored with wood smoke; the thick, almost rotten whiff of the first truffle; the oily essence of olives being pressed. The last snow of winter, no more than a sprinkle of icing on the tops of the hills.

Huile d'Olives

We normally pay a price for our pleasures, and it is rare in life to find something enjoyable that doesn't sooner or later cause obesity, shortness of breath, cirrhosis of the liver, heartburn, joint pain, dental cavities, gout, or palpitations. But now it can be revealed: after careful consideration of more than two thousand years' worth of evidence, doctors and scientists agree that daily doses of olive oil are good for you.

Not only is it free of LDL (the bad cholesterol), but it can help to increase levels of HDL (the good cholesterol). It is beneficial for the digestion, smoothing the passage of what the French so delicately describe as the *transit intestinal*. It contains vitamin E and oleic acid, which aid bone growth. And, if you accept the claims handed down from past generations, it can prevent dandruff, dry skin, wrinkles, constipation, and high blood pressure. There is a special bonus for drinkers. Two spoonfuls of olive oil, taken before you reach for the bottle, will coat the stomach, reduce the effects of alcohol, and thus minimize the chances of a hangover. (This I know to be true.)

Only about 3 percent of olive oil produced around the Mediterranean basin comes from Provence. However, local oil men have made a deliber-

"LA JOLIE MIREILLE"

HUILE D'OLIVES PURE OLIVE
PURE OIL

COREN JEUNE
SALON (Provence)
(FRANCE)

ate choice in favor of quality rather than quantity, and Provençal oil is, I think, every bit as good as its more famous counterpart from Tuscany. Here it is only fair to declare a personal interest, as I am myself one of the world's smallest oil producers. Growing on the land around our house we have some two hundred trees, and the oil that comes from them tastes—to me, the fond and biased proprietor—like liquid sunshine.

The harvest begins some time after the middle of November, when the tiny *cailletiers* are ready. During the weeks leading up to Christmas, our other varieties, *aglandau* and *picholine,* are picked, combed, or shaken from the trees and taken off to the mill for pressing. This used to be a picturesque process—giant millstones or cone-shaped rollers, wooden hoppers, enormous circular filters made from hemp—and one could watch each step of the journey from olive to oil. Now you are more likely to find a streamlined arrangement of stainless steel; the washed olives go in at one end, oil comes out of the other, and you don't see anything in between. Less romantic but more hygienic.

It takes approximately five kilos of olives to make one liter of oil, and oil from the first cold pressing, to which no heat or chemicals have been applied, is a completely pure product (unlike vegetable oils, which contain toxins and must be treated before they are fit for human consumption). But there is purity and purity, and we now come to the interesting notion of degrees of virginity. Almost all first-cold-pressed oils are classified as virgin. But among these, some can be said to have reached the apogee, the very pinnacle of virginity, and are proudly described as extra virgin.

The first time I saw these words, they were on a bottle of olive oil from Lucca. *Extra virgine*—the more I looked at the phrase, the more unlikely it became. Surely virginity was a particular physical condition, a straightforward matter that required no verbal qualification. How could anything be extra virgin? If that were possible, could someone be extra pregnant? Extra dead? And so, knowing no better, I dismissed *extra virgine* as nothing more than romantic hyperbole, the kind of thing an Italian waiter would murmur in the ear of a pretty customer while attending to her salad dressing.

Of course, I was wrong. There are, in fact, three degrees of virginity, dictated by the percentage of fatty acids in the oil. Less than 1 percent, and the oil can be legitimately described as *vierge extra;* more than 1 percent but less than 1.5 percent places the oil in the *vierge fine* category; anything above this, up to 3.5 percent, and the oil becomes *vierge ordinaire*. But since it is impolite to describe any virgin as ordinary, you will never see the word *ordinaire* on any self-respecting bottle of oil; just *vierge*.

Like wine, olive oil should be stored in a cool, dark place (ideally, a cellar rather than a refrigerator). Unlike wine, it doesn't improve with age but tastes best immediately after pressing. As for tasting methods, the simpler the better. Corsicans will tell you to pour a few drops of oil onto the palm of one hand, dip your finger into the miniature puddle, and lick the finger. Or tear off a piece of fresh baguette, make an indentation in the bread with your thumb, fill the indentation with oil, sniff, sip, and finish up by eating the bread. It's also very good drizzled over a warm slice of steamed potato. And, following the advice of an extremely old gentleman in Haute-Provence, I have also developed the habit of drinking a jigger of oil every morning on an empty stomach before breakfast. He told me that this would add twenty-five years to my life.

In cooking, there are enough recipes using olive oil to fill a library of books—everything from mayonnaise to ice cream, with hundreds of dishes in between. Most remarkably, I have never heard of anyone suffering from an excess of olive oil in the diet. The diet police, search for alarming symptoms though they might, have so far been unable to come up with any credible reason why we shouldn't all consume as much olive oil as we want, whenever we want. For once, it seems, you cannot have too much of a good thing.

If, Château d'

It all started in 1516, when King François I had just defeated the troops of the Duke of Milan at Marignan. Looking around for some rest and recreation after the battle, as conquerors do, he decided to pay a visit to Marseille, which was close by.

His first surprise was to find Marseille unguarded, even in those warlike times, against attack by sea. But while nothing was yet in place to stop an enemy fleet, King François noticed that there was a perfect potential barricade right in front of the port and almost within cannon shot—the tiny, uninhabited island of If. With the addition of a fort and a battery of heavy artillery, this scrap of rock could easily be transformed into Marseille's first line of defense. Suiting the action to the thought, the king summoned his personal galley and set off to inspect the site.

Here he came face-to-face with his second surprise. He found that the island was not entirely uninhabited. There was a single extraordinary resident, grazing contentedly on what little grass had managed to grow in such harsh and unpromising conditions: an adult rhinoceros, slightly travel-weary but otherwise in good health.

In those generous days, heads of state liked to exchange impressive gifts, the more unusual the better. Thus it was that the maharaja of Gujarat, after racking his brains to think of something suitable to give to Emmanuel the Magnificent, the king of Portugal, had sent him a rhinoceros. Emmanuel, no doubt impressed but perhaps unsure of what to do with a domestic pet the size of a tank, decided in turn to impress the pope. He dispatched the rhinoceros to Rome, with a stopover on the island of If to allow his gift to recover from the rigors of his voyage.

The rhinoceros was sent on, and construction of the fort began. It took fifteen years to complete—a timetable that makes today's Provençal builders look like greased lightning—and when it was done, it was a fortress deluxe, with all the trimmings: three towers, a dungeon, cells offering varying degrees of discomfort, and a garrison of sixty men. At last the inhabitants of Marseille could rest easy in their beds, knowing that they were protected by the most up-to-date military installation. But ironically, times had changed over fifteen years, and the fortress now found itself with everything except an enemy. Nobody wanted to invade Marseille, at least for the moment. The troops of the garrison admired the view and twiddled their thumbs.

Not for long. There is always, in an open and democratic society, a need for somewhere secure to lock people up, and where better than this convenient little island? Three hundred meters long, 180 meters wide, and completely surrounded by water, it was the ideal spot. And so the château was converted into the Alcatraz of its day—an escape-proof prison for pilferers, vagabonds, incorrigibles, good-for-nothings, dissenters, troublemakers, and anyone else who fell afoul of the authorities. One poor wretch, a Monsieur de Niozelles, was given six years solitary for failing to take off his hat in the presence of Louis XIV.

There were two types of accommodation. Those in economy class couldn't expect much more than bare floors and walls and the most frugal rations. Wealthier detainees could pass their confinement à la pistole; they paid for their comforts, which included better food and furnished rooms (each with a sea view), and were generally treated in a civilized fashion. Mirabeau, for example, when imprisoned at the request of his exasperated father, might even have felt a twinge of regret when his six-month stay came to an end. He had made friends with the commandant-general of the prison and had seduced the young lady in charge of the canteen. Others were less fortunate, particularly the 3,500 Protestants waiting to be sent off for service in the galleys. Many died before they could be sent off to sea.

The most famous prisoner never existed. Edmond Dantès, the Count of Monte Cristo, was sentenced by his creator, Alexandre Dumas, to fourteen years. He escaped by impersonating a corpse—hiding in a body bag that was thrown into the sea—before swimming five kilometers to the shore. This is commemorated each year by the Défi Monte-Cristo, a race from the Château d'If to the Prado beach. (In 2004, there were four hundred swimmers, and the winning time was 54 minutes, 10 seconds.) Dumas's story also inspired twenty-three movies and a minor adjustment to the Château d'If's architecture. Visitors will find a cell specially made for Dantès, complete with a real hole through which his fictitious body escaped. And since anything is possible in fiction, perhaps he was smoking one of the cigars that were named after him in Havana, where his story was a great favorite among the cigar factory workers.

It seems incongruous that a place with such a grim history should have such a glorious setting. Prisoners had to suffer the additional punishment of being able to see the most dazzling view of Marseille, and there is no better way to arrive in the heart of the city than by boat. Coming into the Vieux Port from the Château d'If, you see it all as it should be seen: the huge statue of the Virgin on the belfry of Notre Dame de la Garde, gilded and gleaming on a hill in the distance; what was once the finest private residence in Marseille, the Pharo, Empress Eugénie's seaside home; the great forts of Saint-Jean and Saint-Nicholas; and beyond them, yachts and boats of all sizes, hundreds of them, tethered neatly in row after row, acres of floating real estate. It's quite a sight, nicely set off by the scale of the buildings around the quay, which are relatively low and pleasantly shabby. The temptation to build thirty-story concrete boxes has been resisted, and the overall look of the port is probably not much different from Dumas's day. I can imagine him sitting outside one of the cafés, glass at his elbow, dashing off a quick novel before lunchtime.

Inconnus, Les Petits

This is a term favored by gentlemen who specialize in the restoration of old Provençal properties. Architects and masons use it endlessly, electricians use it frequently, and even painters, when all other excuses fall on deaf ears, have been known to take refuge behind it. And why? Because it is the ultimate escape clause, at the same time vague and all-embracing, equally effective whether applied to time or money. In its essence, it is the transfer of blame to an earlier generation of workmen, now conveniently dead. Here's what happens.

The first thing to understand is that an old house will not be equipped with anything as modern as a set of wiring diagrams—that is, if electricity has actually been installed. Nor will there be a useful map that shows where pipes and drains and culverts have been concealed. To that extent, the entire house is an *inconnu*. All you know for certain is what you can see: the flagstone floors, the beamed ceilings, the thick and seemingly solid walls.

Reassured by their substantial appearance, you decide to pierce some openings—one or two extra windows, a couple of arches to allow access from one room to another, nothing too drastic. Or so you think. The first enthusiastic attack is launched on the walls with a jackhammer. But abruptly, work stops. The first *petit inconnu* has been discovered. The wall is not as solid as it looks. It has been *mal fait* by some scoundrel back in the eighteenth century. The center has been filled in with sand and small rubble, and if threatened again by the jackhammer, the whole wall will almost certainly collapse, thus putting the handsome ceiling at risk.

Speaking of the handsome ceiling, how is it that nobody has so far spotted those sinister traces of woodworm in the beams? Or the permanently moist patch—there, where the plaster is flaking off—in the kitchen? And what is that curious, unpleasant smell? One by one, the *petits* and often not so *petits inconnus* are brought to your attention, each time with a sympathetic shrug. You ask how much they will cost to fix and how long that will take. Again the shrug. Impossible to say. That's the trouble with *inconnus*. One never knows. It is not long before the original estimate is no more than a pleasant memory, a fraction of the eventual cost. And any thoughts of completing the work by spring have given way to tentative hopes of completing by Christmas.

Then there are the minor *inconnus* that have more to do with natural causes than with structural defects. A hornets' nest has been found under the roof tiles, and work has to stop until the fire brigade's hornet team can come to the rescue. The root system of an ancient plane tree has penetrated the septic tank. Bats have taken up residence in an old ventilation shaft. Or, the most disagreeable surprise of all, there is the goat legacy.

It was at one time quite common for goats to be sheltered at night during the winter, either in an outbuilding or in the main house itself. As one would expect from confined goats, they leave traces of their stay on the floor. Also, they rub themselves against the walls, forming an invisible coating of natural oils on the stone or plaster. When subjected to this for two or three decades, floors and walls become thoroughly impregnated with *eau de chèvre*, and short of demolition and rebuilding, there is no effective remedy. Cleaning with high-pressure hoses, dosing with bleach, sanding down the surfaces, covering with coat after coat of paint—nothing works. There is always a souvenir in the air. That is why you should always trust your nose when looking at old properties; because, very often, what you smell is what you get.

Initiales

For reasons presumably to do with fashion and status, we have allowed our clothes and accessories to be invaded by other people's initials. The *G*s and *C*s of Gucci and Chanel, the *D*s of Dior, the *F*s of Fendi, the *LV*s of Louis Vuitton—they're everywhere, like an expensive rash, and they

seem to be getting bigger, gaudier, and ever more conspicuous. If they continue to spread and grow, the smarter streets of Paris and New York will no longer be populated by men and women dressed with varying degrees of elegance, but by alphabets on legs. A dreadful prospect.

It is therefore with a sense of relief that I turn to the more discreet days of the nineteenth century in Provence, a time when initials knew their place, their function, and their owners. This was the golden age of the monogram. It was gracefully executed by hand, art rather than advertising, and you would find it on wrought-iron gates, on cast-iron fire backs, on sheets and pillowcases, on shirts and dresses, on napkins and handkerchiefs, even on dish towels. It was often beautiful and sometimes very subtle; white on white was a particular favorite for linen, with the raised initials as satisfying under the fingertips as an embossed visiting card.

The function of those initials was very simple: to announce and establish ownership, which has for centuries been a Provençal preoccupation. It started with water and land—two popular subjects for dispute even today—and spread to everything else. By the time the passion for initials had reached its peak, very little was allowed to escape the proprietor's mark. Buckets for carrying water, *cageots* for gathering grapes and olives, ladders for picking cherries, bread boards, crockery, silverware, tombstones—had it been possible to monogram fields and wells, no doubt that would have happened, too.

Today the best selection of initialed relics in Provence is probably to be found on the stands and boutiques of the linen dealers who come each weekend to the market at Isle-sur-la-Sorgue. Much of what they have is well worn and too fragile to be used for anything except ornament, but the monogram can add a certain flourish to a cushion or decorate the cover of a family scrapbook. And occasionally you will come across a fine pair of unused nineteenth-century sheets, still in their original folds and tied with ribbon, woven from that heavy linen-and-cotton mixture called *métis*. This is sturdy stuff, made to withstand the brutal washing techniques of the old days, tough enough to be handed down from one generation to the next. If you're lucky, and if the initials so carefully stitched into the linen happen to match your own, you can enjoy for the next fifty years or so the very private pleasure of sleeping between personalized sheets.

Insectes

Apart from the *cigale*—and possibly the Camargue mosquito, that large and villainous beast—the insects of Provence receive very little attention. Yet the insect population is impressive, both in its size and its diversity. In the Luberon alone there are more than sixteen thousand different species; that's 50 percent of all the species to be found in the whole of France. It's true that one would have to be a dedicated insectophile to become excited at the prospect of meeting fifty-three different kinds of ant. But where else nowadays offers you the chance to wander across hills that are home to two thousand kinds of butterfly? If many of the other species are invisible, at least to us, it is still good to have them around. After all, it is insects that provide food for the birds that provide us with music.

Jardins

In the winter, temperatures often drop to below 20 degrees. In the summer, they often rise to 90 degrees or higher. It is not uncommon to have weeks on end without rain. Soil types vary from clay to sand to earth to limestone chunks, occasionally all on the same patch of land. These are conditions to break a gardener's heart.

And yet there have always been gardens of a sort in Provence. Not, in the early days, those aesthetic masterpieces—with their elaborate plantations and carefully framed vistas—of the classic château park, but *useful* gardens, productive gardens, gardens that worked for a living. Normally, these were close to the house, irrigated (with luck) by a spring, fertilized by natural resources, and dedicated to the cultivation of food. This would probably have been a mixture of beans, onions, leeks, cabbages, lentils, spinach, various kinds of salad greens, and, of course, garlic. A decorative garden was out of the question; who had the time—or, even more precious, the water—to waste on anything as frivolous as a flower bed? And lawns? Lawns were unknown, and so was the concept of the pleasure garden, except to a privileged few.

These were the owners of the large estates, the *grands seigneurs*. They had the necessary money, water, and manpower, and in the interludes between fighting one another they wanted to enjoy a view of something more elegant than rocks and scrub from the windows of their châteaux. And so, as early as the sixteenth century, Provence began to see the creation of gardens that were designed for the eye instead of the stomach. Terraces were laid out, ornamental trees planted, fountains installed, arches and balustrades built, statues strategically placed. This was just the beginning.

During the next three hundred years, the green thumb left its mark on Provence from Manosque to Marseille, from the hanging gardens of Ansouis to the botanical park of Fonscolombe. There are gardens *à la française*, strict and symmetrical; there are herb gardens and flower gardens; labyrinths and grottoes; parterres, topiary, and endless alleys of plane trees; lakes, cascades, canals, *bassins*—the variety of ways in which nature has been sculpted, coaxed, or disciplined is quite extraordinary. And what about the *potager*, the simple vegetable garden of the old days? Has it been able to survive among this ornamental splendor? Well, yes. It still exists, although more as a hobby than as a necessity, and it's now very much an also-ran. Today, when a man invites you to see his garden, it won't be to marvel at his leeks but to admire his roses.

Ironically, it's quite possible that these will have been supplied by an ancestor of the horticultural pioneers who grew vegetables outside their back door many years ago. As times and tastes changed and decorative gardens became more popular, who was better placed to supply them than the peasant? He had the land, the knowledge, and the talent to make things grow. If he were to replace vegetables with plants and flowers (and, eventually, with trees), he could set up in business as a professional gardener. This he did, and you will find that many of the big *pépinières* in Provence are businesses that have been in the family for generations.

Their success in recent years owes a great deal to that powerful and expensive human urge, impatience. As we know, impatience and gardening are not natural allies. But what is a man to do when he wants to create a garden from scratch that he can enjoy in his own lifetime? He's not going to wait for twenty-five years while his saplings grow into trees and his plants become established. Not when he can go to his *pépiniériste* and find twenty-foot cypresses, hundred-year-old olive trees, oleanders as tall as a man, box bushes already clipped into spheres and cones, lavender plants the size of giant hedgehogs, thickets of roses—an instant garden, ready to be transported and installed at the drop of a check. As one *pépiniériste* said to me, watching what looked like a small forest being driven off on one of his trucks: "No doubt about it. We've come a long way from cabbages."

Jarres

In the beginning, there was earthenware. The Provençaux stored their seeds and oil and water in it, they cooked in it, they ate off it, and if by some mischance they broke it, they could easily replace it. There was no shortage of clay or potters.

Then earthenware was pushed aside by progress in the form of mass-produced glass, stainless steel, aluminum, and plastic. But, as so often happens, the passing of a century or two had the magical effect of elevating the status of everyday articles, and the humble pot, once purely functional, became a decorative item. Earthenware, providing it was sufficiently elderly, moved out of the kitchen and storeroom to take its place, artfully spotlighted, in the antiques dealer's boutique. The *jarre* is a good example.

This is without question a cut above a mere round pot, both in size and finish. Usually about thirty inches high, it is gently nipped in at the top before curving outward to form a circular lip. The glaze applied to the interior has often been allowed to dribble in a picturesque fashion around the outside of the lip, making an irregular frieze that contrasts with the color and texture of the earthenware. It's an understated but very attractive effect. If it appeals to you, it can be yours for a few hundred euros, probably more money than the potter who made it ever dreamed of.

Jarres are very much in vogue as ornamental additions to lawns and terraces, or dotted around swimming pools, often with a tumble of geraniums spilling over the top. Their disadvantage, which is a source of expensive grief to those unaccustomed to earthenware and Provençal winters, is that they suffer from frostbite. They flake, they crack, sometimes they split. But no doubt someone, somewhere, is working on a twenty-first-century *jarre*, made from the very finest fiberglass.

Julien, Le Pont

Every time I see this small, perfectly preserved bridge, I find it difficult to believe that it is 2,300 years old. I find it even more difficult to think of anything built in the twentieth century that will still be standing, let alone useful, two thousand years from now.

It was the special genius of the Romans to combine function, elegance, and durability in everything they constructed. There were, of course, many Roman buildings that didn't last, but these were usually victims of centuries of deliberate destruction and pilferage. (Stealing the stones to build your house has traditionally been a popular form of economy in Provence.) But the surviving structures—the aqueducts and amphitheaters and arches and bridges—are numerous enough to show what magnificent work the Romans could do when they weren't marching off to conquer the barbarian hordes.

Le Pont Julien is just off the main N100 road that leads from Apt to Cavaillon. It was built to give travelers on the Domitian Way, once a link between Italy and Spain, a means of crossing the river Calavon. As bridges go, it's not very long, measuring a little less than fifty-five yards. But it has wonderful proportions. The span is made up of three arches that are mounted on two piers. With typical Roman attention to detail, these have been pierced to allow the passage of floodwater, although I have yet to find anyone who can remember the last time the Calavon flooded. In fact, the bridge deserves an altogether more vigorous river. Whatever it might once have been, the Calavon today is little more than a stream.

Never mind. Le Pont Julien is still there, and it still does duty as a bridge, solid enough to support an assortment of machinery that the early Romans could never have imagined: Renaults, Citroëns, Peugeots, trailers, probably the odd overweight truck that has lost its way—they all cross the Calavon every day, quite possibly unaware that what saves them from plunging into the river is two-thousand-year-old technology.

NOTE: Since those words were written the conservation authorities, mindful that not even Roman construction lasts forever, have restricted the bridge's use to pedestrians. You can now cross the Calavon on foot without fear of being run over.

Kaki

The origins of the kaki, a juicy member of the persimmon family, are generally agreed to have been in China. Its means of emigration—how it made its great leaps to other continents and countries—are subject to debate wherever kaki fanciers gather. Some will tell you that it first left the Far East with Commodore Perry, who introduced it to California in 1856. Nonsense, say others; it was to be found in Virginia in the early seventeenth century, where it was described by the traveler William Strachey as "somewhat luscious." A little later, it came to Europe, possibly brought back by Sir Joseph Banks, the botanist who sailed around the world with Captain Cook. What is indisputable is that, by one route or other, the kaki came to Provence and settled in well.

It is a fruit that doesn't conform to a single shape. There are round kakis, conical kakis, flattened kakis, kakis with smooth skin, and kakis with pronounced indentations. The colors vary from red to a yellowy orange, and, off the tree, they look like beefy, larger-than-life tomatoes. Degrees of sweetness vary, but normally the sugar content is high, with a healthy dose of vitamin C; they are delicious when eaten fresh.

But it is the sight of a kaki tree in winter that makes it such a distinctive and memorable fruit. At a time when much of the countryside is drab and bare, the kaki tree stands out as though it had been artificially lit. The branches are completely leafless, but the fruit is still there. It hangs in great blobs of color—nature's way of cheering up the landscape just in time for Christmas. When there is snow on the ground, the red against a white background is almost shockingly vivid. And in the winter twilight, you would swear that the fruit is luminous. We never pick it from the tree, preferring to leave it glowing until the rains come in the New Year.

Kir Provençal

Most people are familiar with the classic *vin blanc cassis,* made by pouring a glassful of white wine over a spoonful of *crème de cassis,* or blackcurrant liqueur. The drink is probably better known as a Kir, after Canon Kir, the mayor of Dijon who is credited with inventing it. Very few people, however, have ever heard of *le Kir provençal,* and it was only by accident that I discovered it.

I had lost my way in the wilds north of Mont Ventoux—an area that is sometimes described as being behind God's back—and I'd stopped in a tiny, isolated village to try to get my bearings. It was a bitterly cold winter's day, and by the look of things, the inhabitants had gone into hibernation. Shutters were closed, streets were deserted, and even the local cats had gone into hiding. The only visible flicker of life came from a string of winking colored lights above the door of what turned out to be the village bar.

It was a bar similar to hundreds of others in rural Provence: a TV set bleating in one corner, small tables, hard chairs, various brands of *pastis* taking up most of the shelf space along the back wall, a coffee machine, a peanut dispenser, a plastic dish containing one lonely hard-boiled egg— and mine host, a young man studying the pages of *L'Équipe.* He and I had the place to ourselves.

Propped up next to the hard-boiled egg on the bar was a homemade sign made from stiff cardboard. The illustration showed a bunch of livid berries cascading into a wineglass. The words scrawled below in matching livid ink announced it as *Le Véritable Kir Provençal,* priced at one euro. This was something I'd never come across before, and I asked the young man what the difference was between this and a normal Kir. Perhaps because it was a slow day, he took the time to tell me.

His wife's family had a few acres of vines not far from the village, and his father-in-law was extremely proud of the wine he produced. Alas, he had a palate like a plank, and his pride was quite unjustified. The red was drinkable, but barely. The white was a sour, nasty liquid, more vinegar than wine. Even chilled to the point of freezing, it was enough to pucker a man's teeth; a shudder came with every mouthful. The problem was that the old man insisted on his wines being sold in the bar, and for the sake of domestic harmony, his son-in-law felt himself obliged to take a few cases each month. But therein lay a problem. How could he get rid of this dreadful swill without offending—or, indeed, poisoning—his customers?

It was clear that a fundamental adjustment to the taste was necessary. Or better still, an impenetrable disguise that would conceal the taste entirely. Experiments were carried out on the wine with mint-flavored syrup, with aniseed, mulled with cinnamon, laced with *marc*, each concoction tasting more disagreeable than the last. Finally it was the turn of *crème de cassis*. Little by little, the dose was increased from the conventional spoonful to double, then almost triple the normal amount. And it worked. The final touch was to give the mixture a name that would distinguish it from a plain old Kir.

As luck would have it, *le Kir provençal,* although too sweet for most men, had proved to be quite popular with young girls, old women, and the sprinkling of tourists who strayed into the village. Out of curiosity, I asked the young man to make one for me, and he watched as I took a sip.

It reminded me of Ribena, an English drink that mothers used to administer to their children in the belief that it contained health-giving amounts of vitamin C. Sticky and cloying though it was, I had to admit that I couldn't taste even the faintest hint of wine. I congratulated the young man on his achievement.

"*Voilà,*" he said. "*C'est le marketing.*"

Korthals de Provence

In 1901, Monsieur Charles Prudhommeaux founded a club whose membership was restricted to owners of a particular and very distinctive breed of dog. For the record, we should give the breed its full cumbersome name: *le griffon d'arrêt à poil dur Korthals*. In other words, a rough-haired pointer, originally bred by Monsieur E. K. Korthals. For those who like their dogs bearded, mustached, shaggy, and extremely affectionate when wet, there is no finer breed to have. We have been owners of Korthals for more than twenty-five years, and so we have become accustomed—even addicted—to having them around. To us, living in a house without one of these hairy and amiable creatures would be to live in a house lacking an important piece of furniture.

Korthals like moist conditions. Show them a marsh, a bog, a pond, or, failing those, a filthy ditch bottom, and they are in their element. It is perhaps because of the shortage of these amenities in Provence that we don't see too many of them down here; this despite the fact that they are formidable hunting dogs with a nose like radar for game birds. As for finding a breeder of Korthals, I had always thought one would have to go north, to the damper areas of France.

But once again, Provence surprised me. We had recently lost a Korthals, who had died after being with us for many years. My wife was determined to find a replacement in time for my birthday, and had discovered one in a most unlikely place. There was a fully accredited breeder only an hour's drive away, in Marseille. His bitch had just produced a litter of eleven pups, one of which my wife had chosen during a clandestine visit. And so, the very day the pups were old enough to leave the bosom of their family, we drove down to pick up my birthday present.

I had never been to a dog breeder's premises before, and I was expecting something rural—if not an estate with a few dozen rolling acres, then at least a house with a good-sized garden. But as we did our best to find our way through the tangled outskirts of suburban Marseille, the houses became smaller and the gardens more and more vestigial, barely big enough for a cat, let alone a litter of young dogs. Finally, we arrived. There was no sign of any garden, however tiny. The house was built above a garage, with narrow steps leading up to a shaded terrace, and there they were: a squirm of pups, one mother, and a nervous quail, pacing back and forth behind the bars of a wooden cage.

The breeder, dressed in shorts and a sleeveless undershirt, came out to greet us.

"Here she is," he said, picking up what looked like an oversized hamster. "All the papers are ready, and she's been tattooed. She's called Sony."

A note of explanation is due here for anyone who has not been exposed to the complications of purchasing a pedigreed dog in France. Documents in triplicate giving vital details such as the date of birth and names of parents and breeder are obligatory. Then there is a personal code, normally tattooed on the inside surface of the dog's ear. This code is registered and stored in a central computer, together with the owner's name and address. Finally, there is the name. Each year is allocated a letter of the alphabet, and dogs born during that year should officially have a name beginning with the official letter. Our pup, having been born in the year of the *S*, had been given the name Sony. (Not wanting to have a dog named after a television set, we immediately changed her name to Nelly.)

She was six weeks old and already showing signs of enormous charm. The breeder put her down next to the caged quail. The two of them looked at each other with mild interest as the breeder said, "I like to get them used to the scent of game as early as possible. You're lucky. Your dog has an exceptional nose. No bird will elude her." Nelly yawned, lay down, and went to sleep.

I said how surprised we had been to find a Korthals breeder this far south, and this seemed to remind him of some important information. His dogs, he told us, were not just Korthals, but Provençal Korthals; indeed, *Korthals de Marseille*. He gave us a significant nod, as if we should know exactly what that meant.

"They have *le caractère marseillais*," he said, "*un peu spécial*. Not like the dogs of the north."

After living with Nelly for the past three years, we now know what he was talking about. By some mysterious genetic process, she seems to have acquired many traits of the classic Marseillais personality. She exaggerates: a small thorn in the paw is treated with all the drama of a major amputation; she flings herself at her food as though she had been starved for weeks; and visitors to the house are subjected, by nose, to an embarrassingly thorough body search. She is boisterous, treating other dogs to the canine equivalent of slaps on the back and digs in the ribs. She is extremely vocal, with a range that varies from the normal bark to a selection of extended falsetto squawks when she can't wait a second longer for her morning walk. She is assertive; despite being the youngest of our three dogs, she is the boss. To use a euphemism I have often heard applied to overbearing personalities, she is *dynamique*. And she is, without a doubt, the best birthday present I've ever had.

Lactaires

Autumn, and the forest teems with crouched, questing figures. Bucket, basket, or plastic bag in hand, they root around in the undergrowth, searching for mushrooms. With luck, they might stumble upon a fungus—mainly orange with greenish stains—that is highly regarded by Provençal cooks: the *pinen*, otherwise known as *Lactarius deliciosus, lactaire délicieux* or just plain *lactaire*.

The *lactaire* family is extensive. More than a dozen varieties exist, and most of them are so tough and so bitter that they are inedible. But the *délicieux* lives up to its name, and in the right kitchen it can be excellent. It thrives where pine trees grow, often on sandy soil—conditions that are common in the Luberon. It has a concave cap, anywhere from two to six inches across, and a short stem. When sliced or squeezed, it leaks a kind of milky, orange ooze.

Do not let this deter you. Cut your *lactaires* into thick slices and fry them in a pan with olive oil, garlic, and parsley, and there you have it; as satisfying as eating a good steak. There is, however, a curious side effect that can be alarming unless you know what to expect. A plateful of *lactaires* can make your urine turn red, a phenomenon not usually mentioned in recipe suggestions.

Lauzes

The limestone of the Luberon is occasionally and unfairly called the poor man's marble. It is certainly less expensive than marble, and it is certainly less smooth than marble, having a more porous, slightly abrasive texture. But it has several virtues. It is a warmer, softer stone than marble. It cuts easily. It ages gracefully, darkening over the years from a pale putty color to a weathered gray. And, in the Luberon at least, it has the great advantage of availability. There are literally mountains of it.

It has one other characteristic that has endeared it to generations of builders. It tends to break off from cliffs and hillsides in massive, flat flakes—irregular flagstones, or *lauzes*. You see them used in drystone walls, in *bories*, and laid along the edges of roofs to add extra weight to the tiles so that they're not blown away by the mistral. Very occasionally, you might see an old church with an entire roof of *lauzes*, put up in the days before cut stone and cement took over.

Some of these seasoned old slabs are more genuine than others. What appear to be authentic weather-beaten *lauzes* are sometimes fresh from the quarry, but prematurely aged by judicious applications of soot and diesel fuel. This is known as cosmetic masonry and is popular with those who like a veneer of instant history applied to their houses.

Lavande et Lavandin

Where would the postcard business be without it? Endless rows of it, vast fields of it, with or without a venerable building in the background or a beaming peasant in the foreground—lavender is the Provençal flag. There is a museum dedicated to it (at Coustellet), there are fairs and festivals celebrating it, and there is an Appellation d'Origine Contrôlée to distinguish the best of the crop from less aromatic varieties. It is, without a doubt, one of the most ravishing sights of summer. But there is much more to it than meets the eye. Lavender is useful.

Making what may seem like an improbable transition—from the high country of Provence to your washing machine—the essential oil distilled from lavender is widely used by such giants of hygiene as Procter & Gamble, Henkel, and Colgate for their cleaning products. And ever since the Romans first added it to their bathwater, lavender and its extracts have found their way into soaps and gels and creams, scenting the air and the

skin with their distinctive, clean, astrin-
gent fragrance.

What we think of as
lavender is, more often than
not, *lavandin*. This is a
hybrid (sometimes known as
"bastard lavender"), a cross between *lavande fine,* which grows
at altitudes of two thousand feet
and up, and *lavande aspic,* which
grows below two thousand feet.
According to expert professional noses,
lavandin doesn't have quite as complex and
refined a bouquet as *lavande fine,* al-though it
does produce more oil; and, growing at lower,
less mountainous altitudes, it is easier to cul-
tivate. For those reasons, there is a great deal
more of it. But the aristocrat of the family will always be *lavande fine,* the
super-bleue, the only lavender eligible for the AOC. Not all of it quali-
fies—only the top of the crop, grown at an altitude of 2,600 feet and
above, and production is, by industrial standards, modest. It takes nearly
three hundred pounds of flowers to make a single liter of essential oil, and
the total output of this connoisseur's essence is no more than twenty-five
tons a year. Lavender farmers are seldom rich men.

The eye and the nose are not the only parts of the body to benefit from
a good dose of lavender, and the French, being world-class hypochondri-
acs, were not slow in discovering its medicinal qualities. Some of these, it
has to be said, might not stand up to modern scientific inspection. In *Flora
Laboratory,* a book published in 1722, we find that ten to twelve drops of
oil of lavender, added to a suitable liquor, will do wonders for "hysterical
vapours." Four or five drops, with a spoonful of wine, help to alleviate
migraine and strengthen the stomach. And, "mixed with oil of St. John's

wort, it makes an excellent liniment for rheumatisms, paralysis and convulsions. It kills not only worms, but also vermins and insects." Swellings and contusions, effusions and luxations, nausea, vertigo, flatulence, laryngitis, jaundice, scrofula, influenza, asthma, whooping cough—these and almost anything else that ails you will apparently respond to the lavender treatment applied in one form or another.

Some applications of this miracle cure-all can be swallowed with pleasure. During the flowering season, you can see (and hear) bees making their rounds in the lavender fields, flying in their drowsy, unhurried fashion from one plant to the next. The result is a wonderfully perfumed honey with—needless to say—remarkable tonic properties. I can also recommend lavender-flavored ice cream. There can be no more delicious way of protecting yourself against a sudden attack of hysterical vapours.

Appropriately enough for the postcard plant, Provençal lavender is seen at its best during the main tourist months of July and August. Flowering dates depend on altitude: the lower the field, the earlier it will be in bloom. This means that lavender addicts can start in the foothills of the Luberon at the beginning of July and work their way up to the Plateau de Valensole by mid-August, with magnificent carpets of purple unrolling before them as they go.

Long after the color has faded, lavender retains its scent. Small bunches of it, hung in armoires or left in drawers, will add a subtle and evocative souvenir of blue skies and hot days to your clothes, your sheets, and your towels. An armful of dried lavender tossed onto an open fire will help you forget winter. And so, one way or another, you can make lavender last from the end of one summer to the beginning of the next.

Librairie Le Bleuet

In these competitive times, it is not enough just to write books. The author, if his publisher is feeling optimistic, will be asked to leave his garret and go forth to promote what he has written. Loved by some authors and loathed by others, the book tour is now part of the job, and it's something I have been doing for sixteen years. Totting up my score the other day, I arrived at a total of twenty-six of these tours in eleven different countries, involving visits to at least three hundred bookstores, from Tokyo to Monaco, by way of Martha's Vineyard and Winnetka. I think I can reasonably say that I know a good bookstore when I see one, and the Librairie Le Bleuet, in Banon, is among the best I've seen.

Banon is an unlikely place to find a literary treasure house. A village high on a hill in Haute-Provence, it has fewer than a thousand inhabitants. The bookstore's proprietor, Joël Gattefossé, gave up his first career as a carpenter and cabinetmaker to become a bookseller about fifteen years ago, and your first sight of his store is a reminder of his previous occupation. A stack of wooden books—the height of a small tree, and beautifully carved—stands outside the entrance.

Inside are between fifty and sixty thousand books, arranged on two floors. Every subject you could wish to find is there: philosophy, travel, classic and contemporary fiction and nonfiction, cookery, photography, sailing, *boules*—shelf after fascinating shelf. There are dictionaries and encyclopedias, guidebooks and children's books, self-help books, crime novels, belles lettres, even an English-language section. It's a reader's paradise, light and airy, and a place in which one could happily spend hours. It is known, and deserves to be known, as *une librairie pas comme les autres.*

Banon is perhaps a particularly literate village; even so, it could hardly support a bookstore this large. But it is clear that the French are prepared to travel, just as they do to support a fine chef, in order to satisfy their appetite for books.

There are other, less intellectual, reasons to take a trip to Banon. The drive up from Apt takes you through some spectacular countryside, glorious at any time of the year, but especially on a winter's morning, when the fields are white with rime and the hills seem to be floating on a sea of mist. Then there are the cheeses of Banon—"from contented goats and sheep"—in themselves worth a detour (as noted elsewhere). And then there are the sausages.

No more than a minute's walk from the Librairie Le Bleuet is the *charcuterie* of Maurice Melchio, a most affable man and a creative force among sausage makers. At Monsieur Melchio's shop, you will find a good selection of local cheese, honey, and wine. But where he truly excels is in his anthology of handmade sausages, including one that I've never met anywhere else. This is the *brindille*, or twig, a slender model no thicker than my thumb and almost as long as my arm, some two feet of pure pork. It comes in seven subtly different flavors, from pine nuts to savory, from walnuts to red peppers. It should also come with a warning, because one or two slices are never enough. And if you have sausage connoisseurs among your friends, Monsieur Melchio can help you send his *brindilles* to them by mail. He has a stock of long, skinny tubes, perfect for *saucissons à la poste*.

Marchés

Some years ago it was reported that, for the first time, more than 50 percent of the food bought in France had come from supermarkets. This was seen as a sad day for the French stomach, an irreversible trend and a mortal blow to the old way of shopping. Gloomy predictions abounded. Small *épiceries* would disappear. Butchers and bakers would be threatened. Cheese makers, fishmongers, and growers of everything from asparagus to olives would be obliged to sell their produce to the big chains or go under. And, needless to say, markets would suffer, too. Who would bother to make the effort of lugging a shopping basket from stall to stall when they could glide from shelf to shelf with a trolley? Convenience, so we were told, was the way of the future.

But it takes more than convenience to destroy an institution, and Provençal markets are not only surviving but thriving, as they have done for nearly five hundred years. Apt market was authorized by good King René and has been held on Saturday mornings ever since 1523. Apt was followed by Roussillon in 1567, Gordes in 1774, and countless others since then. Anyone prepared to drive around Provence can find a different market for every day of the week, all through the year.

There are two basic types. The first is the traditional weekly market, a sprawling mobile emporium where, along with your sausage, honey, and country bread, you can buy camouflage trousers, hunting knives, omelette pans, kitchen gadgets, young trees, heavy-duty brassieres, hats (wool or cotton, according to the season), T-shirts, live rabbits, CDs, and ferociously strong cough drops from the Vosges. These and many other treasures are available throughout the year.

The second kind of market is seasonal, usually limited to produce, and relatively new: the *marché paysan,* which started to appear in Provence a few years ago. At first, it was no more than a few peasants getting together in the village parking lot to sell their fruit and vegetables from the back of their vans. Since then, it has flourished and expanded, and it's now a fixture that begins in the spring and runs through until autumn.

Markets appeal to us for many different reasons, some practical, others social or even educational. Unlike supermarket shopping, which is anonymous, market shopping is personal. The sellers are also the suppliers, often the growers. What's more, they are there, personally accountable for their produce. If they were to sell anything in less than excellent condition, they would be denounced—loudly and at length—by that most demanding of customers, the Provençal housewife. She considers tired vegetables, stale cheese, or suspect fish a personal affront, and she is not afraid to share her displeasure with her friends (or indeed with anyone in hearing range). Consequently, regular stallholders are subject, each week, to searching quality control inspections, carried out in public. They fail at their peril.

A more positive side to this is that it will often encourage a relationship to develop between buyer and seller, in response to a deep-seated yearning in the French soul almost as powerful as those other national passions, anarchy and hypochondria. This yearning can be found in all those who consider themselves gourmets; that is, most of the adult population. It is the need to have a gastronomic support squad of *fournisseurs,* specialists who provide, at appropriate times of the year, delicacies that are fresher, bigger, rarer or more succulent than anything from the supermarket shelves. And there they are, these specialists, each week in the market, greeting you by name and, you are convinced, saving their best just for you. It is not long before you begin to think of them as your personal team.

Obviously, they will know more than you about their particular specialties, which is where the educational aspect comes in. In the course of a single morning, if you care to enroll in the market curriculum, you can take in a series of short but informative lectures. Your professors are the stallholders, who will be happy to tell you about the origins and virtues of everything they have sold to you, together with recipes. In this way, I have learned only to buy fish that still have a twinkle in their eye, what should go into the stuffing of *fleurs de courgettes,* how to cook a double-breasted version of *magrets de canard,* the best way to store olive oil, the most efficient method of skinning peppers, the restorative qualities of a small dose of lemonade added to a vase of cut flowers, the health benefits of fresh almonds, and the subtle allure of green *tapenade.* Try getting all that from a supermarket.

But this, while useful and interesting, is only part of what makes market shopping such a pleasant way to spend a morning. There is a special atmosphere to market days—good-humored and gossipy—and it is rare to see a doleful face. It's also rare for anyone to be in a hurry. In fact, I have even witnessed the extraordinary sight of the French forming themselves into an orderly line, content to wait their turn to be served in the manner of that quaint invention, the Anglo-Saxon queue. They take advantage of the wait to bring one another up to date on the latest episode of the saga that is currently entertaining the village (and there is always something), or to pass judgment on the new postman, or merely to exchange words of wisdom about the weather. The subject isn't important. It's the social contact that's important—a bonus that adds another small pleasure to the morning.

Finally, a few specific notes. Here, for enthusiasts, is a day-by-day selection of some (but not all) of the markets that take place each week throughout Provence. They normally start around 8 a.m. and pack up at lunchtime.

Monday

Cavaillon, Cadenet, Fontvielle, Forcalquier, Goult, Lauris, Mazan, Nîmes, Saint-Didier, Saint-Saturnin-les-Avignon, Tulette

Tuesday

Aix, Beaumes-de-Venise, Caderousse, Caromb, Cucuron, Fontaine-de-Vaucluse, Gordes, La Tour d'Aigues, Mondragon, Saint-Saturnin d'Apt, Tarascon, Vaison-la-Romaine

Wednesday

Aigues-Mortes, Bagnols-sur-Cèze, Buis-les-Baronnies, Entraigues, Gargas, Le Thor, Malaucène, Mérindol, Rognes, Roussillon, Saint-Martin-de-Castillon, Saint-Rémy-de-Provence, Salon, Sault, Valréas, Velleron

Thursday

Aix, Ansouis, Aubignan, Les Baux, Beaucaire, Cairanne, Caumont-sur-Durance, Le Pontet, Mallemort-du-Comtat, Maussane-les-Alpilles, Mirabeau, Nyons, Oppède-le-Vieux, Orange, Robion, Villeneuve-les-Avignon

Friday

Bonnieux, Carpentras, Châteauneuf-du-Pape, Courthézon, Eygalières, Fontvielle, Lagnes, Lourmarin, Pertuis, Suze-la-Rousse, Visan

Saturday

Apt, Beaumont, Camaret, Cheval Blanc, Crillon-le-Brave, Mornas, Oppède, Pernes-les-Fontaines, Richerenches, Sainte-Cécile-les-Vignes, Saint-Martin-de-la-Brasque, Sommières

Sunday

Aigues-Mortes, Camaret, Châteaurenard, Jonquières, L'Isle-sur-la-Sorgue, Mormoiron, Sorgues

As if these weren't enough, there are also specialized markets each year devoted to asparagus, flowers, garlic, truffles, and wine. *Courage—et bon appétit.*

Marseillaise, La

Most national anthems, despite—or perhaps because of—their noble intentions, tend to be dirgelike and rather dull. They remind me of bad hymns: leaden lyrics and plodding, forgettable melodies. In dramatic contrast, "La Marseillaise" is altogether more emotive, both in what it says and how it sounds. It is one of the great anthems, even if originally it had nothing to do with Marseille.

The date was April 25, 1792; the place, Strasbourg. France had just declared war on Austria. Baron de Dietrich, the mayor of Strasbourg and a man brimming with patriotism, was entertaining guests in his salon. One of them was Claude-Joseph Rouget de Lisle, a young army officer who happened to be a keen amateur musician. In the course of the evening, the baron turned to him with a musical request: "Monsieur de Lisle," he said, "you who speak the language of the gods, you who play the harp of Orpheus, give us a battle song for all the soldiers who are answering the call of their fatherland in danger."

Overnight, de Lisle obliged. He came up with a composition that he called "Battle song for the Army of the Rhine," and strong, fierce stuff it was: "The day of glory has arrived, the bloodstained standard is raised, listen to the roar of enemy soldiers rampaging into our midst to slaughter sons and wives"—that was just the start, to be followed by a rousing chorus:

> To arms, citizens!
> Form your battalions!
> Let's march! Let's march!
> Let impure blood water our furrows!

The sentiments were appropriate for the times, of course. But what undoubtedly gave the song its immediate popularity was the melody.

From the very first hearing it stayed in your head, stirring, catchy, instantly memorable. Within three months it became a hit, largely thanks to a battalion of volunteers from Marseille, who sang it as they entered Paris in the month of July. Parisians called it "La chanson des Marseillais," or simply "La Marseillaise," and that has been its title ever since.

In 1795, it was decreed that "La Marseillaise" should be the national anthem. Shortly afterward, the man whose patriotism had inspired it, the unfortunate Baron de Dietrich, was sent to the guillotine. As for Rouget de Lisle, he was later commemorated with a statue by Frédéric-Auguste Bartholdi, the sculptor responsible for the Statue of Liberty.

Martigues (être de)

A pretty port between Marseille and the Camargue, Martigues is locally celebrated for two reasons. The first is that each year, in July and August, there is a Sardine Festival, and a fresh Martigues sardine is well worth a detour.

The second claim to fame is the subject of a number of stories, none of them flattering. Here are two examples.

A man from Martigues was seen riding off on his mule with two large sacks of wheat, which he was taking to be ground at the mill. One sack was balanced on his shoulder, the other clutched to his chest. When asked why he was doing this, he replied that he wanted to take the weight off the mule.

An entire group from Martigues made a special journey to Marseille, where, so they had been told, they would see a prodigious great fish with its head in the Vieux Port and its tail in the Château d'If, some miles away.

From these examples, you will have gathered that the good people of Martigues have a certain reputation for being simpleminded. A false and dreadful slander though this is, it seems to have survived for hundreds of years. Today, when you hear someone (usually from Marseille) describing a man as *"il est bien de Martigues,"* it means that he is inclined to believe everything he's told. Conversely, if you wish to emphasize your own worldliness and intelligence, drop this phrase into the conversation: *"je ne suis pas de Martigues, moi."*

Mas

In the architectural pecking order of Provence, the *mas* comes just above the *oustau*, or small farm. The *mas* is—or was originally—a more substantial affair, a collection of agricultural buildings joined together: a low, rectangular farmhouse with stables, a covered sheep pen, barns, storerooms, a dormitory for doves, a cocoonery for silkworms, and a cellar. Normally, the *mas* faced south or was angled toward the east to keep its back to the mistral. There were no windows on the north side, and trees were used for climate control. To the north, closely planted rows of cypresses formed a buffer against the wind; to the south, plane trees provided shade. The interior was stone and tile. In those winters before central heating, it must have been deeply uncomfortable, like living in a massive refrigerator. No wonder the fireplaces were built with sufficient space on either side of the fire for the farmer and his family to sit and defrost themselves.

Uncomfortable or not, the traditional *mas* is a handsome sight, completely at home in its setting. It blends in with the surrounding countryside, almost as though it had grown out of the rocky earth. Like so much else in Provence, it is seductively picturesque. The very name conjures up visions of an idyllic rural life surrounded by the majesty of nature. This is why real estate agents have seized upon it with such barefaced enthusiasm and a cavalier disregard for accuracy. Today, when house hunters hear a building described as a *mas*, all they can be sure of is that it will have a tiled roof, with little or no provision for their sheep, their horses, their doves, or even their silkworms. *Caveat emptor.*

Melons

In 1895, a journalist passing through town endeared himself to generations of local melon growers by reporting that "There is only one melon: the melon of Cavaillon." The compliment stuck, and Cavaillon is one of the handful of towns in France to be renowned for a particular delicacy, like Le Puy and its green lentils or Castelnaudary and its cassoulet.

The distinction has not been achieved overnight. The first melons reached Cavaillon more than five hundred years ago, coming from the papal domain of Cantalupo, in Italy. Cavaillon must have seemed an obvious destination. It was, at the time, another of the pope's possessions, and it enjoyed a climate that might have been made for melons: dry, hot, and sunny. The descendants of those first Cantalupos prospered. Cavaillon had started what would become centuries of melon cultivation.

Today the Cantalupo has long since been replaced by the Charentais,

and the melon elite of Cavaillon has its own organization—the Confrérie des Chevaliers de l'Ordre du Melon. There is also the Syndicat des Maîtres Melonniers de Cavaillon. There is a melon festival in July, when the center of town smells like a giant melon. And, as you would expect, the whole business of choosing and eating melons has been analyzed, discussed, and codified with the attention to detail that the French bring to all things edible.

Melon experts—and they are thick on the ground in Provence—will tell you that the melon has three seasons spread over five months. The first early melons are brought to ripeness around the middle of May in heated greenhouses; during the second season, from mid-May to mid-June, the greenhouses are unheated; while the juiciest and best-tasting melons come during the long third season, when they have been grown *en plein champ*, in the open fields under the sun of high summer.

You choose a melon by inspecting it, holding it, tapping it, and sniffing it. A melon has a nipple at the top and a *pécou*, or tail, at the bottom. This, the *pécou*, should be the same color as the rest of the melon. A small fissure around the *pécou*, tinged with red, is a sure sign of ripeness—the "drop of blood" that has been formed by sugar seeping out of the flesh of the melon and crystallizing.

Now examine the skin. Nature has conveniently divided the Cavaillon melon into segments, marked by blue-green lines. A good melon should have ten of these segments; no more, no less. This is *un melon de dix*. Pick it up. It should feel dense and heavy. Tap it with your fingertips. It should sound hollow. Finally, apply your nose to the *pécou* (never the nipple) and inhale that clean, sweet scent.

Assuming that the melon has passed all these tests, it is now ready to be eaten. Prepare yourself. There are literally dozens of options. A melon can start the meal—with Parma ham, with crab, with lobster; as a salad with avocado or with celery; as a *coulis* with feta cheese; or fried and flavored with *anis*. As a main course, it goes very well with seafood—with red mullet, with langoustines, with prawns. Or with meat—roasted with pork or chicken, dried and thinly sliced into petals to accompany roast beef.

As a dessert, it is sublime with chocolate, with honey, sprinkled with Beaumes-de-Venise, or made into a sweet soup.

Or you can eat it on its own, as I like to do, with just a pinch of pepper.

Mistral

There is Frédéric Mistral, the Provençal poet and Nobel Prize winner. There is the Chilean Gabriela Mistral, by an amazing coincidence also a poet and also a Nobel Prize winner. And there is *le mistral*, a wind and a word associated with Provence almost as often as lavender.

The name comes from the Provençal *maestral*, the *"vent maître"* that makes an ordinary wind seem like nothing more than a sigh. A winter mistral in full blow can often reach 115 miles per hour on land or a Force 8 gale at sea, making Atlantic-sized waves in the normally placid Mediterranean. If it doesn't actually live up to the Provençal fable of blowing the ears off a donkey, it certainly rips tiles from roofs, unsecured shutters from windows, and topsoil from fields (farmers used to call it the *mange fange,* or mud eater). Trees exposed to the mistral in their youth will develop a decided slant, and old ladies, anyone who wears a wig, and small unattached animals do well to stay indoors while it's blowing.

I had been told that its violent and enervating effect was accepted in French courts as an extenuating circumstance in criminal cases, particularly crimes of passion. This struck me as an interesting legal argument, and so I asked three lawyers to give me their opinions. The first looked at me with some suspicion and asked me what I'd done and whom I'd done it to. The second said that the wind defense was unknown in French law. The third said it was a gray area. As is so often the case when consulting lawyers, I was left no wiser.

What makes the mistral so powerful is that on its way down from north to south it comes through the natural wind tunnel of the Rhône valley, gaining force and velocity along the way before it turns east to sweep across Provence. A cold and mischievous wind, it has little to commend it except for one redeeming virtue: it brings with it blue skies, clean air, and diamond-bright light.

In Marseille, a city that is no stranger to exaggeration, they claim that the mistral blows for a hundred days a year. The gusts often come in a pattern of three, six, or nine days at a time, and it is said that you can always spot people who are used to living with the mistral by the way they walk: tilted slightly forward or slightly back—like a drunkard trying to keep his balance—depending on the direction of the wind.

Moi, Je

In Provence, as in the rest of France, these are the two most often used words in the vocabulary. I find it curious that the French, an articulate and self-confident race, should feel the need to reinforce their clear and perfectly understandable *je* with a totally unnecessary *moi.* And yet they do, all the time. Me and I march through everyday speech like Siamese twins.

They have an opinion: *Moi, je pense.* They order in a restaurant or café: *Moi, je prends.* They agree with you: *Moi, je suis d'accord.* They disagree with you: *Moi, je suis contre.* Is it for emphasis? Does it make an opinion sound more weighty, an order more decisive, an agreement more whole-hearted? Or is it simply a matter of ego? *Moi, je ne sais pas.*

Musée de la Légion Étrangère

My introduction to the Foreign Legion was P. C. Wren's novel *Beau Geste,* which I read with guilty pleasure by flashlight under the blankets as a boy at boarding school. It was what could justifiably be called a ripping yarn—gentlemen in disgrace and criminals with hearts of gold finding refuge, comradeship, and glory in the ranks of France's toughest fighting force. I loved it, and the Legion has fascinated me ever since.

Wren's book, and subsequent contributions from Hollywood, did much to add a romantic coating to the grim realities of war and death in the desert. Romance, however, was far from the mind of King Louis Philippe when he ordered the legion to be formed in 1831. These were dangerous times in Europe, which was seething with uprisings and political unrest. Exiles, many of them undesirable, were pouring into France from other European countries, much to Louis Philippe's concern. His response was to export them en masse. The fugitives, revolutionaries, army deserters, and potential troublemakers of all kinds were formed into a legion "composed of foreigners" and sent off to fight France's various wars in Africa (which would also allow the regular French army to come home and protect the king's interests). As an inducement to join up, volunteers were promised French citizenship at the end of their term of service. What started, in those early days, as an unpromising collection of criminals and misfits has since become one of the best-known and most highly respected and decorated corps of soldiers in the world.

After nearly 120 years in the barracks they had built at Sidi Bel Abbès, the men of the Legion left North Africa in 1962. They took with them their history: the battle flags and banners; the decorations and souvenirs of past colonels; the wooden hand of the hero of the battle of Camerone, Captain Danjou; the coffins containing the remains of the unknown legionnaire and of General Rollet, "the father of the Legion" (to the right)—these were flown back to a new base in Aubagne, a few miles east of Marseille.

The greater part of the Legion's Provençal home is a broad, immaculately kept barracks square and parade ground. Behind this is the museum, a low, white block that you might mistake for a small office building if it weren't for the barbed wire draped along the walls and the artillery and tanks parked in the garden. Everything here is just so, a testament to the military passion for neatness and order. The stone borders are whitewashed, the flagstones swept clean, the grass clipped to within an inch of its life. I couldn't imagine that even a fallen leaf would be tolerated in such disciplined surroundings.

Once inside the museum, it's hard to know where to begin. So many mementos have been accumulated during 175 years of fighting in so many places. The Crimea, Mexico, Tonkin, Formosa, the Sahara, Dahomey, Madagascar, Morocco, Syria, Chad, two world wars, Algeria—the list is long; the list of those who died, much longer. They are commemorated, campaign by campaign, on plaques set into the wall.

Among the displays of medals, bayonets, epaulettes, and pistols, are large glass cases containing life-size figures of Legionnaires through the ages, in the uniforms of the time. How some of the early recruits ever functioned in what they had to wear and carry defies belief. Each man, in full uniform, including thick woollen greatcoat, had to carry an enormous knapsack, his rifle and bayonet, three hundred rounds of ammunition, a pick or shovel, and wood for his fire. He was expected to march with this burden, in the desert heat of North Africa, as much as thirty miles a day. And then fight.

After war, remembrance. At the heart of the museum is the crypt, a simple, dimly lit anteroom that is the setting for some of the Legion's most solemn memories: the first flag, the hand of Captain Danjou, the names of all the officers fallen in battle. In the background, you hear the faint cadence of Legionnaires singing a marching song, low and measured. The sense of history is overwhelming. It is impossible not to be moved.

Musée du Tire-Bouchon

So far as I know, this is unique: the only museum in the world dedicated exclusively to corkscrews. It is quite possibly unique in another respect, as it has its own permanent *caveau de dégustation*, where visiting *pomelkophiles* (as corkscrew fans are officially known) can taste wines of all three colors.

The Musée du Tire-Bouchon is actually part of Domaine de la Citadelle, a vineyard and *cave* situated just below the hilltop village of Ménerbes. The owner of the domaine, Yves Rousset-Rouard, is also the mayor of the village. He lives in the Citadelle on the crest of the hill, with a comforting view of his vines.

He became a museum proprietor almost by accident. On a visit to the auction rooms of Drouot, in Paris, his eye was caught by a particular lot that was for sale: a small selection of corkscrews from different centuries and countries. He was intrigued by the variety of shapes and mechanisms—some functional, some decorative—and, being a wine man, by their historical ties to the bottle. He bought that first batch of corkscrews and soon became an addictive collector. And then, of course, he had to find somewhere to put them. Where better than next to his wine?

The museum is a large, dim, elegant room that would do credit to Cartier. More than a thousand different corkscrews are displayed, like twisted jewelry, in softly lit recesses and cabinets, each corkscrew identified and dated. Alas for the glory of France, the first corkscrew, a simple T-shaped affair, was invented not in Burgundy or Bordeaux, but in England at the end of the seventeenth century, and not even for wine, but for uncorking bottled beer and cider. However, once wine storage changed from hogsheads and bungs to bottles and corks, the corkscrew was on the way to becoming the universal necessity it is today. (W. C. Fields once complained, during an expedition to some remote spot:

"We lost our corkscrew and were compelled to live on food and water for several days.")

Once the basic engineering problem of making a strong, efficient corkscrew from the three basic parts of handle, shank, and worm had been solved, imagination and decoration took over. The evolution from the "bare bodkin" to the Screwpull is marked by some remarkable flights of fancy: the erotic corkscrew (better seen than described); the lethal corkscrew, attached to a pistol, presumably to help celebrate the successful outcome of a duel; the dog lover's corkscrew, with its dog's head handle; the double-lever de Gaulle corkscrew, with both arms raised; the ancestral corkscrew, complete with the owner's family seal; the defiant corkscrew, featuring Representative Volstead (shown above), the man behind

Prohibition; corkscrews disguised as bunches of grapes and clusters of vines; corkscrews with handles of ivory, bone, and sculpted silver; pocket corkscrews; boudoir corkscrews (for uncorking flasks of perfume)—they are all in the museum, a thousand ingenious ways to open a bottle.

And bottles are just a few steps away, in the *caveau de dégustation*. I have found that an hour or so spent studying corkscrews is thirsty work, and a glass of Monsieur Rousset-Rouard's excellent wine is a fitting end to a fascinating visit.

Noël

Each year, while living in England, I was obliged to endure a three- or four-week period of hysteria, culminating in a bankrupt torpor. This was, and still is, Christmas *à l'anglaise*, which, for reasons of commerce, has been extended far, far beyond its natural span. A good three weeks, from early December until the end of the month or beyond, is dedicated to the pursuit of festive jollity. England is under a nationwide injunction to spend money, to eat too much, to drink too much, and to display goodwill to all men. The strain on the wallet, the liver, and the disposition is brutal.

The brevity of Christmas in Provence—just two days—is, for me, one of its great attractions, but there are others. Notably the food: compared with the mountainous and frequently tasteless Anglo-Saxon turkey, the Provençal *gros souper* of Christmas Eve manages to be reasonably light and, at the same time, interesting. A little soup to start with, followed by a few snails, then some cod with winter vegetables, a salad of curly *frisée* (to remind us of the curls of the Infant Jesus), and a modest selection of cheeses. The meal is then interrupted by a *pause religieuse,* when everyone attends Midnight Mass before coming back to attack the thirteen desserts.

The approach of Christmas is signaled on the day of Sainte-Barbe, December 4—the official date to plant some handfuls of wheat in small pots. Regularly watered, the wheat will have grown sufficiently tall and green in twenty days to decorate the family *crèche.* If you want to add a further Provençal tradition to your Christmas Eve, you will need a large, slow-burning log—the *cacho fio*—to place, with due ceremony, on the hearth. The log is sprinkled with a glassful of wine before being lit, and it should burn until Christmas is over.

You will have noticed that Father Christmas doesn't feature in these simple celebrations, and when I first came to Provence, he was very rarely seen. But in recent years he has been making up for lost time. The village of Lourmarin has actually flown him in by helicopter to land on the football field and astonish the local children. And effigies of him—some as large as life—now make seasonal appearances clinging to the outside of houses and peering into windows, like garishly dressed cat burglars. A most disconcerting sight.

Noms

I have heard it said that France holds the world record as the country with the largest number of family names. According to Monsieur Farigoule (of the Avignon Farigoules), this is yet another example of French historical and cultural *richesse*, especially when compared to England where, so he frequently tells me, half the inhabitants are named *Smeet* (Smith). Be that as it may, the fact is that there are approximately 900,000 family names currently in use throughout France.

These vary from region to region, and although the Martins, with an unbeatable countrywide score of 268,000, are well represented in Provence, they face stiff local competition from the Blancs, the Michels, and the Roux. Further down the list, the names become less common and, it could be said, more Provençal. For example, you won't find too many Pinatels in Paris; they tend to be concentrated in the south.

If one doesn't count derivations borrowed from the saints, the origins of family names fall into three broad categories: geographic, occupational, or physical. The first Camoins lived in a hamlet near Marseille known as Les Camoins. The first Latils were makers or sellers of *l'atil*, or military equipment. It is when we come to the third category—the physical origins—that the names become a little more personal; sometimes flattering, sometimes not.

Roux for a redhead and Brun for a brunette are inoffensive descriptions, bland and straightforward. But how would you like to be known for a lifetime as Bondil (short and fat), Pelloux (hairy), Chabas (bigheaded), Hermitte (solitary), Grosso (corpulent), or Cresp (woolly haired)?

As if family names weren't enough of a burden, some Provençal children are given diminutive labels by their fond parents that can become increasingly inappropriate with age. Could you take a politician or captain of industry seriously if you knew his mother called him Nono (Jean), Dèdou (André), or Sissou (Francis)?

Normalement

Here is a word used very frequently in Provence, although rarely in its literal sense. You and I might think that the dictionary definition says it all: "in a normal manner, or usually." The Provençaux have added their own interpretation to the word, turning it into a reminder that life is an unpredictable business, and a warning that the best-laid plans go oft astray. Its most common use is in the context of time, as in "*Normalement,* I will start the job next Tuesday."

Experience has made me wary of sentences that begin with *normalement*. I have learned that a more accurate translation in this case would be: "In the absence of circumstances that are beyond my control and are therefore no fault of mine, and provided nothing more pressing turns up, I should be able to start the job next Tuesday—or, at the latest, Wednesday."

One hears *normalement* so often in Provence that it could be mistaken for nothing more than a linguistic tic. It isn't; it's the great qualifier and a signal of doubt. If a man should ever tell you that *normalement* his dog doesn't bite strangers, my advice is to stay well away from the beast.

Nostradamus

One of the world's most famous pessimists, Michel de Nostredame was born in Saint-Rémy-de-Provence in 1503. He spent his early professional life as a doctor and had some success finding and developing remedies for the plague. These he kept to himself, refusing to pass them on to other doctors, who eventually retaliated by expelling him from the medical profession. But by then he had decided to make a career change: he set himself up as a prophet.

He bought a house in Salon-de-Provence, married a local woman, and in 1555 published, under the name Nostradamus, the first collection of his *Centuries*. This was a mixture of poetry and prediction—more than nine hundred predictions, in fact, but written in four-line stanzas of such impenetrably enigmatic language that nobody could say for sure exactly what they meant. There was, however, a distinct air of impending catastrophe about his verses. War, famine, plague, conflict, earthquakes, and other calamities were his subjects, and then as now, bad news proved to be good for sales. *Centuries* became a best seller. Nostradamus was visited by royalty, prepared horoscopes for Catherine de Médicis, consulted on occult matters, and achieved wealth and celebrity. A most enduring celebrity it has been, too, with scholars and soothsayers over the centuries analyzing his veiled hints of doom and gloom. Some claim to have found references to the Great Fire of London, the French Revolution, the rise of Napoléon, the coming of Hitler, space travel, and the Gulf War. And, of course, every prophet's favorite warning is featured: the end of the world, which will apparently take place in 3797. It depends which scholar you consult; interpretation is all.

Nostradamus was also the author of *Façon et manière de faire des confitures,* a jam-making manual that is undoubtedly his most cheerful literary effort. He died in 1566, and his body lies in the fourteenth-century church of Saint-Martin, not far from the house in Salon where he lived. The address, predictably, is the Rue Nostradamus.

Notaires

Any village in Provence worth the name will have its *mairie,* its café, and its bakery. Some will have butchers and hairdressers, *épiceries,* and garages. These you would expect. What comes as a surprise to many visitors is to find, even in villages of only a few hundred inhabitants, a fully qualified representative of the legal profession: the *notaire.*

Village *notaires* in Provence date back nearly five hundred years. (The earliest one I have been able to find is Maître Bosse, of Lauris, who set up shop in 1555.) They performed then, as they do today, the invaluable role of legal referee. For the settling of a will, for the buying and selling of property, for clarification of

easements and usufructs, for marriage contracts and for land leases, the *notaire* is the man to see. Others might offer their opinions—indeed, try to stop them—but the *notaire* will give you the law, as it exists, in writing.

In addition to his professional skills, he needs to be a diplomat. He lives where he works. His clients are his neighbors. Villages are not always harmonious, and accusations, disputes, and feuds have been known to muddy the limpid waters of village life. The *notaire,* whether he likes it or not, can often find himself in the middle of anything from a family squabble over an inheritance to a war over water rights. And since the law tends to disappoint the losing side, there's a good chance that the unfortunate *notaire* will be blamed, quite unfairly, for pointing out the facts of the matter.

Sore losers can always seek a more favorable decision by going to another village and consulting another *notaire,* but this seldom leads to anything except a second set of fees. As a legal gentleman of my acquaintance once told me: "The French, even in Provence, have a great respect for paper. It is a foolish man who tries to argue with a document."

Ocre

At some unspecified date long, long ago, the Archangel Gabriel, in a struggle to the death against an unruly battalion of fallen angels, slew them all. Their blood stained the earth red, and ocher was born.

That is legend, and although other accounts may be less violent, they are equally colorful. Ocher was prehistoric makeup. It was used by our distant ancestors to paint their bodies, presumably for those occasions when they wanted to look their best. Experience showed them that it was nontoxic, that it didn't fade, and that it was available in what would be described today as a wide range of tasteful colors; twenty-four in all. Not surprisingly, early interior decorators found ocher inspirational, using it to transform the walls of previously drab caves with wildlife paintings or more avant-garde splashes of gray, green, yellow, and the traditional red. And in the forefront of this burst of color and creativity was Provence, where sandy soil rich in iron oxides provided plenty of ocher for anyone who cared to extract it.

Given the obvious decorative attractions of ocher, it is curious that prehistoric man's experiments weren't picked up immediately and developed by future generations. But there was a lull, a long lull, before ocher made a comeback in Provence. Tens of thousands of years after those first efforts at cave and body painting, a man named Jean Étienne Astier rediscovered the virtues of ocher, saw that it was plentiful and available, and became the first official *ocrier* in France. He lived in the red village of Roussillon, near Apt, and between 1780 and 1785 he started what would turn into a Provençal industry.

Many other villages near Apt—Saint-Pantaléon, Goult, Gargas, and Rustrel among them—were close to ocher deposits. But, Provence being

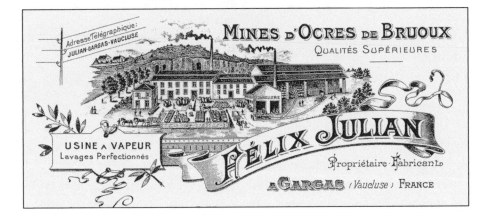

Provence, there was no headlong rush to follow Astier's example, just in case it might turn out to be nothing more than a passing novelty. It wasn't until the end of the nineteenth century that the ocher business exploded.

In 1885, twelve ocher quarries opened in Rustrel and twenty-two in Gargas. By 1890, ocher production in the Vaucluse had reached twenty thousand tons a year, and by 1900, there were fifteen separate enterprises providing ocher for what looked like an ever-increasing demand. Alas, it was not to last. After a final optimistic surge of production—forty thousand tons were made in 1929—it was a steep slide downhill. First the Depression, then the war, then the invention of synthetic coloring agents pretty much killed the industry. Today only about a thousand tons a year are made by the last remaining producer, the Société des Ocres de France, based in Apt. (It is used in paint, pottery, tiles, and cosmetics and to tint the crust of certain cheeses.)

But, in Provence at least, ocher is still very much with us in the form of landscape—an extraordinary jagged landscape, dominated by cliffs and twisted spires of rusty red. Relief from the bare rock is provided by pine trees, clumps of heather and bracken, cistus and broom. The overall effect, seen against the deep blue background of the sky, is like a surrealist painting, hard-edged and vivid.

Roussillon and the *"petit Colorado"* of Rustrel are probably the best-known and most visited sites, although there are others, less dramatic, at Gargas, Villars, and Gignac. I've noticed that you can always tell when a family has been on an ocher expedition: the adults have red feet, and the children have red bottoms from sliding down the rocks—bottoms that stay red for some time despite frequent washing. Ocher dust, as our prehistoric ancestors discovered, lingers on the skin.

Oliviers

Is this the oldest tree on earth? Fossilized leaves found in the Aegean were claimed to date from 37,000 B.C. You may find this hard to believe—how can the experts go back that far with any accuracy? But we know for certain that olive trees were certainly cultivated before 3000 B.C. And the olive, as Lawrence Durrell memorably wrote, has a taste "older than meat, older than wine . . . a taste as old as cold water."

With reasonable care, an olive tree will live and give fruit for five hundred years or more. An old saying has it that "A hundred-year-old olive tree is still a child." It transplants well, which makes it much loved by those *pépiniéristes* who specialize in instant gardens. They are delighted to be able to sell you, at vertiginous prices, childlike hundred-year-old trees that they have uprooted and shipped in from some secret valley. The olive will thrive in its new home; they guarantee it, which is not always the case with living things, especially those that are bundled around the country-side in trucks as unceremoniously as sacks of cement.

The olive's adaptability is only one of its heroic qualities. It is a remarkably tough and forgiving tree, capable of surviving decades of neglect, attempts at strangulation by brambles, and suffocation by weeds. To restore an overgrown olive tree to perfect health, it is enough simply to clean around the base of the trunk, rip out the brambles, and prune severely. (The central branches should be cut away so that the traditional dove, always recruited for this purpose, can fly through the tree without stubbing its wings.) Add a little fertilizer, and the following season, the tree will fruit.

The olive has one mortal enemy: the *grand gel*—extreme and prolonged cold—and olive growers still shiver at the mention of 1956, the most gloomy milestone in recent olive history. That year, the month of January had been unusually mild, and the trees sensed an early spring. Sap began to rise, buds were on the way. And then, overnight, the temperature dropped to below 20 degrees Fahrenheit and stayed there. Disaster. Trunks split, roots froze, a million trees died in Provence, and it was touch and go for millions more. For the half-dead trees, the treatment was extreme. The trunks were sawn off just above ground level in the hope that the roots had survived and would throw out new shoots. Amazingly, many of them did, and fifty years later you can see, all over Provence, trees that have grown up next to the massive amputated stumps of their ancestors.

Even these stumps are impressive, more like sculptured plinths than casualties of the cold, and it is easy to see why artists have found the tree such a fascinating—if frustrating—subject. Van Gogh is said to have painted nineteen pictures of olive trees but complained about the difficulty of doing justice to the subtle, changing colors of the leaves. Bonnard's answer to the problem was to paint them gray. Renoir went even further, painting his trees in gold or pink. But no picture can ever come close to reality—the glorious sight of an olive grove on a fine day, with a breeze through the leaves making ripples of silver and green.

When eventually an olive tree dies, it leaves a wonderful legacy: the wood, dense and smooth and honey-colored, marked by the centuries with a grain of black and dark brown. The Romans had a law forbidding its use for domestic fires; it was to be burned only on the altars of the gods. Today, unless the wood is lucky enough to fall into the hands of a craftsman, much of it will end up in souvenir shops, reincarnated as corkscrew handles. A rather undignified end to a long, useful, and beautiful life.

O.M.

Some people are under the mistaken impression that the O.M.—Olympique de Marseille—is nothing more than a soccer team. It is, of course, a minor but thriving religion.

Its temple is the Vélodrome, where forty thousand worshippers congregate during the season to watch O.M.'s high priest (the current captain) lead his acolytes out to fight the good fight against the forces of evil (the opposing side). The ninety-minute service is accompanied by mystical chants, and ritual imprecations are hurled at the visiting team (especially Paris Saint-Germain). When the proceedings are over, supplicants make their way to designated areas (the bars of Marseille), where they give thanks or beat their breasts in mourning according to the result.

Heretics need to tread very carefully if they should find themselves among O.M. supporters. There is a story—probably apocryphal, but one never knows—of a man who quite innocently mentioned the European Cup match of 1996/97 in which Lyon defeated O.M. 8–0. He was never seen again.

Orage d'Août

It is yet another example of the unfairness of life that one of the most violent storms of the Provençal year occurs at the height of the tourist season. Spring and early summer pass in a blaze of sunshine. July is a month of rainless days, with temperatures in the eighties. Then comes August.

As if genetically programmed, several million French men, women, children, aunts, uncles, grandparents, and dogs squeeze themselves into cars, trains, and planes and submit to the purgatory of the journey down to the south. The *autoroute du soleil,* on that first weekend of August, is a clogged and sweaty nightmare, often with twenty-five-mile-long traffic jams. The trains are stuffed with passengers, each with seventeen pieces of luggage. And at the airports, the baggage handlers have celebrated the beginning of August in their traditional fashion by going on strike. But eventually, exhausted and ill-tempered, the holidaymakers arrive at their destinations and prepare themselves for the *douceur de la vie en Provence.*

It is hot. In fact, it is unbearably hot. The absence of rain and weeks of blistering temperatures have turned Provence into a giant radiator. The sun has soaked into the hills and villages, cooked the grass brown, melted tarmac, carved great fissures in the earth, and fried pale northern skin to a fierce, painful red. Long after sunset, the heat remains. Stone stays warm to the touch, and the night air is thick and close. Life is lived in slow motion; one long, torrid day after another.

Relief, of a sort, usually comes around the middle of August. The air turns heavy, almost suffocating, and a sudden silence descends on the countryside: the *cigales* have stopped their scratchy chirruping as if they've been switched off. This is a signal that the storm will start at any moment, and those of a nervous or prudent disposition go through their houses unplugging computers, phones, fax machines, TV sets, and stereos. Once the storm gets going, it is inevitable that all power will be cut off. But before that happens there will often be one violent electrical spasm—nature's vengeful swipe at high technology—powerful enough to scramble the brains of any sensitive appliance.

Thunder follows, great rolling growls of it, ending with a crack that seems to rupture the air just above your head. Instinctively, you duck. By the time you look up, the next blaze of lightning has started, split seconds of brilliant floodlight picking out the shapes of trees, rocks, and houses against the blackened sky. But still no rain. This won't come until the light show is over.

When the rain does start, it is in the form of fat, gentle drops that cool the air and bring out the blessed smell of wet earth. Within minutes, drops give way to torrents, flattening plants, gouging channels in gravel driveways, bouncing knee-high off flagstones, turning a book left outside into a sodden pulp—two or three months' rain in half an hour. Then it stops, as abruptly as it started, and by the following morning the sky is back to blue.

But inside the house, souvenirs of the deluge linger in the pipes and cisterns and U-shaped crannies of the plumbing system. Subterranean flooding causes curious gurgles as excess water finds its level. Normally mild-mannered faucets have vigorous sneezing attacks, spewing out gouts of muddy water. By some baffling process, items of kitchen waste—odd fragments of lettuce, a sprinkling of tea leaves—take a wrong turn in the pipes and find their way into the toilet bowl, puzzling visitors who are accustomed to uneventful urban plumbing. Well, they say, we never expected *this* in Provence.

Orgues

The organ is the most cumbersome of all instruments, a musical elephant far too big for the average family home, or indeed for the average orchestra. And so the last thing I expected to come across in the Yellow Pages of the Vaucluse telephone directory was a maker of organs. In fact, there are three listed in the current edition, and I now realize I shouldn't have been at all surprised. Provence is organ country, and has been for a long time.

We think of the organ's natural habitat as a church, but for hundreds of years it was viewed with a decidedly unsympathetic eye by religious authorities. During the fourth century, the Council of Arles, in a sanctimonious frenzy, arranged to have organists excommunicated. During the fifth century, Saint Jerome instructed his flock to be "deaf to the sound of musical instruments" (although he gave no useful hints as to how this might be achieved). It wasn't until the ninth century that the organ took its first step toward religious respectability.

A priest, Georges de Venise, was asked by the charmingly named Louis le Débonnaire to make an organ, which he did. He then passed on the secrets of his skill to some of his pupils, who were monks, and over the following years monk-made organs began to appear in chapels and convents. This, naturally, infuriated the spiritual descendants of the excommunication lobby, who wasted no time before starting to foam at the mouth and tell everyone who would listen that the organ was *"la cornemuse du Diable,"* the Devil's bagpipes, a musical prelude to hell and damnation.

Nevertheless, the organ survived. By the fourteenth century it was found in many churches and had come to be accepted as an appropriate instrument for sacred music. Gradually, demand for organs increased beyond the monks' capacity to make them, and a new profession emerged: *facteur d'orgues*—the same job description it has today in the Yellow Pages.

My favorite *facteur d'orgues* is Jean-Esprit Isnard, and the reason I admire him is his total disregard of mundane matters like size and price when in search of perfection. He was brought over from Tarascon in 1772 to build an organ for the magnificent basilica in Saint-Maximin-la-Sainte-Baume. As was the custom with all major works, a *devis* was drawn up that specified the dimensions and other details of the new organ, and Isnard went to work. At some point, looking around him at the vastness of the basilica, he must have decided that the organ that he had agreed to build was altogether too small for its setting. So he enlarged it. And enlarged it. And enlarged it. It took him two years, and by the time he had finished, the organ was twice the size of the one anticipated in the *devis:* eight meters high instead of four meters, with 112 supplementary pipes (some of which weighed three hundred kilos) made from solid pewter. Strangely, there doesn't seem to be any record of the reaction to what must have been a fortissimo increase in the bill.

Isnard's masterpiece, although a giant, is by no means the biggest organ in Provence. In the church of Saint-Vincent at Roquevaire (a town between Aix and Toulon) a modern organ has been installed that is forty-six feet high. There are other heavyweights in the Cathédrale de la Major in Marseille, the churches of Saint-Martin in Saint-Rémy, Saint-Symphorien-les-Carmes in Avignon, Saint-Cézaire in Arles—most Provençal towns of any historical importance have their organs, and there are several organ festivals each year. Those who like to mix culture with nourishment—an admirable French habit—can follow the Route des Orgues from Aubagne to Allauch. In between the guided tours of organ-spotting, there is a break for a *repas gastronomique,* followed by a welcoming drink in Allauch before the evening's recital.

Oustau

Oustau is the Provençal word for the family homestead. It has cozy domestic connotations and is therefore often pressed into service by owners of inns and guest houses who wish to assure clients of a warm and friendly welcome. The undoubted champion of Provençal *oustaus* is the magnificent establishment at Les Baux known as the Oustau de Baumanière. It is not exactly what you would imagine a family home to be—unless you know some indecently rich families—as it has thirteen suites, a Michelin two-star chef, a superb terrace with a view of the Alpilles, and a small army of helpful people to keep you supplied with truffle ravioli and *langoustines.*

Papes d'Avignon

Intrigue, extortion, organized crime—it reads more like something out of *The Godfather* than a religious change of address. The story begins in 1303, a time when Rome was a turbulent and dangerous place. There were riots, there were invasions by foreign armies, there were turf wars between local gangs. Nobody, not even a prince of the church, was entirely safe.

Enter Philip the Fair of France. Using less than respectable tactics, including bribery, he arranged for a Frenchman to be elected pope. Clement V, as he was officially known, was then offered the chance to escape from the perils of Rome to the more tranquil surroundings of Provence, and in 1305 the Avignon Papacy was established. So began a period lasting seventy-three years during which Catholics were encouraged to look to Provence, rather than Rome, for spiritual leadership and guidance. During this time, seven popes came and went: after Clement V came John XXII, Benedict XII, Clement VI, Innocent VI, Urban V, and Gregory XI. There was not a single Italian among them. By a not altogether surprising coincidence, all seven were French.

The papal record during these years was notable—shades of the Mafia—for rampant corruption and a penchant for the construction business. Building a bigger and better palace was the fashion of the times, started by Pope John XXII, who enlarged the existing archbishops' palace to reflect his new eminence. This proved to be too cramped for Pope Benedict XII, who built a new and much larger palace. Not to be outdone, Pope Clement VI built yet another. (Remarkably, he had enough loose change left over in 1348 to buy Avignon outright from the Countess of Provence for eighty thousand florins.)

Meanwhile the town, according to Petrarch, had turned into "the hell of living people, the thoroughfare of vice, the sewers of the earth." This might have been brought on by sour grapes, since Petrarch was Italian and probably thought the papacy had taken a turn for the worse under the French. Nevertheless, it is true that prostitution, violence, debauchery, blackmail, the sale of pardons and indulgences, and every imaginable kind of crime went on under the papal eye, some of it with papal approval. Ironically, much of the crime and overcrowding were caused by the worthy papal policy of tolerance and sanctuary. No doubt it had started with the best intentions, but unfortunately nobody thought it necessary to apply any restrictions. As long as you had money, you were allowed in. Not only could Jews and heretics escape religious persecution, but swindlers, thieves, mountebanks, murderers, and other undesirables on the run could go to Avignon and relax. French justice couldn't touch them. So it was that the town became a haven for refugees of every kind—provided they were able to pay for their safety—which inevitably led to Petrarch's thoroughfare of vice. The pope of the day, of course, was insulated from the nastiness on the streets by the thick walls of his palaces, the old and the new. Both have survived wars and revolutions to create a somewhat gloomy presence in the center of Avignon.

A more refreshing souvenir of those papal times is the village of Châteauneuf-du-Pape, where Pope John XXII built himself a summer residence overlooking the vineyards. Even then, the wine was good; so good, in fact, that Petrarch, unable to resist a final dig, claimed that it was a reason why some members of the papal entourage weren't too keen to return to Rome. Instead, their thoughts turned

> *To happy convents, bosom'd deep in vines,*
> *Where slumber abbots, purple as their wines.*

Appropriately, the name of the poet who wrote those lines was Alexander Pope.

Parfums

It is hardly surprising that the Provence you see receives more attention than the Provence you smell; but there is a rich assortment of treats for the nose, and it would be a shame to neglect them. Here are a few of my favorites.

The café. Slightly less pungent in recent years due to the decline in the smoking of black tobacco, but still distinctive. I particularly like the morning blend: top notes of ferociously strong coffee, with hints of warm milk, buttery croissants, baguettes straight from the *boulangerie* just up the street, and a reassuring whiff of heavy-duty floor cleaner. And the café's copy of *La Provence,* if you get to read it first, has the early morning smell of fresh newsprint.

Lavender. Although delightful in its processed form, in anything from soap to sorbet, the most fragrant lavender comes from the bunch you pick yourself. Rub the flowers between the palms of your hands and inhale. There is nothing like a deep breath of that penetrating, unadulterated essence to make the nostrils tingle and to clear the head.

Garlic. Often overpowering when used, as it often is, with far too heavy a hand, it should be diluted to be appreciated. I think it is at its appetizing best in one of the Marseille restaurants that specialize in *bouillabaisse.* As you walk through the door, there is the faint but unmistakable nip of garlic in the sea air to set up the palate, and you have mentally ordered before you reach the table.

Herbs. Wonderful in the kitchen and even better in the Provençal countryside, where it is possible to go on walks that take you through sage, rosemary, savory, hyssop, and thyme. The difference in scent between fresh herbs and the packets of dried dust found on some supermarket shelves has to be smelled to be believed.

Melons. One of my earliest memories of Provence was driving back to Ménerbes from Cavaillon with a tray of ripe melons. Their scent filled the car, even with the windows open—sweet, heady, and irresistible. The man who wrote that melons "charm the throat and cool the belly" forgot to add that they also seduce the nose.

Truffles. The primeval scent of black truffles may not be to everybody's liking; it's gamy, wild, dense, almost on the turn from ripeness to rot. I am addicted to it, partly because it signals the start of the pleasures of winter: frosty sunrises, long walks in the deserted hills, evenings spent in front of log fires, *daubes* and *cassoulets* and cold-weather wines. And, from time to time, a fat truffle omelette.

Pastis. If there were an olfactory map of Provence, *pastis* would be at its center. The atmosphere of any Provençal bar worth the name is lightly perfumed with that unmistakable tinge of aniseed and licorice, as indeed are many of the customers.

Wet earth. Rain falling on earth that has been baked by week after week of drought brings a blessed drop in temperature and freshens the air with a delicious, cool, life-saving smell. Dying plants revive and the threat of forest fires vanishes. It is a smell that I always welcome, and one that I always associate with a feeling of relief. We can breathe again.

Parisiens

A persecuted minority in Provence, Parisians are the butt of jokes, the source of much amusement, and the subject of many unlikely stories— some of which may actually be true. Here, for instance, is a favorite of mine: A Parisian *en vacances* complains to the local mayor about the insufferable noise made by *cigales* and asks him what can be done about it. It is a tribute to the mayor's sense of humor that he pretends to take the Parisian seriously. The matter will be brought up at the next meeting of the municipal council, says the mayor, and it won't stop there. If necessary, I shall go to the prefect of the Vaucluse with the problem. Come back in the autumn, and I can guarantee that you will see some progress. Of course, by the time the Parisian comes back there isn't a *cigale* to be heard, and he is suitably impressed. How was he to know that with the drop in temperature every *cigale* in Provence was fast asleep, hibernating?

Sitting on the café terrace and trying to spot the Parisian is one of the minor pastimes of summer in the village. It's slightly more difficult than picking out other foreigners because the Parisian speaks a form of French. Even so, he can normally be identified by his appearance. His clothes, although casual, are new—crisp, unwrinkled, unfaded by the sun. One cannot imagine him sweating. His hair has been recently trimmed. His hands show no signs of ever having touched a tractor or a pair of pruning shears. His dog, if he has one, is a model of well-groomed hygiene, an object of fragrant curiosity to the dusty village dogs. His newspaper is *Libération* or *Le Figaro,* rather than the local paper of record, *La Provence.* One way and another, he stands out.

A couple of years ago, I was explaining this to a friend from London when a perfect specimen came to sit at a nearby table: a Parisian from his sleek, well-barbered head to his elegant leather moccasins. He wore a gold watch no thicker than a two-euro coin. He had a copy of *Libération.* He even had a small blond dog with not a hair out of place. He ordered coffee for himself and a bowl of water for his companion before turning to his newspaper.

There you are, I said to my friend, he couldn't be anything but Parisian; probably in advertising, from the look of him. You can always tell. I was about to expand on this when one of the waiters stopped at our table. I asked him to confirm my perceptive anthropological diagnosis, only to be informed that my Parisian advertising man was a computer specialist from Cavaillon. So much for instant deduction.

It has often been said that the highly centralized form of government in France provokes unease and resentment in the provinces, but I think there's more to it than that. I'm sure that the attitudes of Provençaux toward Parisians are similar to the attitudes of country people toward city people throughout the world. The fisherman in Maine regards the New Yorker with some reserve, as does the farmer in Yorkshire when faced with a Londoner. Strangers are suspect. Indeed, we are told that the Parisians themselves are worried in case the extended European community leads to an invasion of Polish plumbers. In fact, I'm sure I saw one of them the other day in the café. You can always tell.

Pastis

A most deceptive drink, *pastis*. With ice cubes, and diluted with the recommended five parts of water until its color changes from gold to an opaque greenish white, it seems light, refreshing, and innocuous. On a hot day, the first one slips down so easily that the empty glass takes you by surprise. You have another. Not until you stand up are you reminded that *pastis*, at 45 percent alcohol, is more powerful than almost any brand of whiskey, vodka, or cognac. How the French manage to drink twenty million glasses of it every day (as they do) and still function is one of life's mysteries.

There are two versions of how *pastis* came into being. The first concerns an unnamed hermit who lived in the Luberon, in a hut festooned with plants and herbs that he had gathered from the hills. Hunters and other passersby would see him from time to time crouched over a cauldron as he simmered his curious concoctions. Many years of simmering passed. And then came the plague.

One of the symptoms in its final stages was a terrible debilitating thirst, which if left unchecked would end in extreme dehydration and death; and one of the villages most severely affected was Cucuron, where 942 inhabitants died. One day, a stranger arrived in the village. The survivors, desperately weakened, were astonished at his appearance. He glowed with health, a rare sight in those sickly times. It was our hermit, who had been protected from the effects of the plague by drinking his herbal potions.

He distributed doses to all the surviving villagers. Miraculously, they were cured, their thirst was quenched, and the hermit, his work there done, moved on to Marseille. He had clearly had enough of the hermit's life, because he opened a bar by the old port. It was called Au Bonhomme Passe-Soif, and the specialty of the house was, of course, the magic drink that banished thirst. In time, the name changed from Passe-Soif to the Latin-inspired Passe-Sitis, and from there to pastis.

The second version of the *pastis* story dates from 1915. Until then, one of the more lethal drinks in France had been *absinthe*, the "green fairy," a distillation of wine, various essences, and the wormwood plant that was addictive and dangerously hallucinogenic. It is said that van Gogh had cut off his ear while under the influence, and that after an *absinthe*-fueled dispute, Verlaine had shot Rimbaud. *Absinthe* addicts could not expect to live long, and the government, alarmed at the premature loss of so many of their beloved taxpayers, banned its manufacture on March 17, 1915.

Not everybody welcomed this public-spirited act—among them Jules Pernod, who had been making *absinthe* at his factory in Montfavet, near Avignon. Fortunately for him, his equipment was ideally suited to the production of another drink, the legally authorized *anis*. It caught on immediately and had the great advantage of not killing those who drank it. But it was not yet known as *pastis*.

This was the inspired idea of Paul Ricard, the son of a Marseille wine merchant. Working for his father, he visited bars and bistros where he saw and tasted dozens of homemade *anise*-based drinks. He recognized the opportunity for a brand. The name he chose to describe it was the

Provençal version of a word that had come across the border from Italy: *pasticcio*, or *pastis*, a word that signified *une situation troublée*, or cloudy— an appropriate name for a liquid that changed color when mixed with water. And so, in 1932, he launched his brainwave as Le Vrai Pastis de Marseille. (In a bar, you will often hear it called *pastaga*, or *un bon jaune*.)

According to Ricard himself, who was not a man overburdened by modesty, it was an instant success. And it has stayed that way, selling millions of bottles a year. Ricard and Pernod joined forces in 1974 and have dominated the market ever since. But that hasn't stopped smaller producers from selling their own blends, which are sometimes called boutique *pastis*. You see them in chic *épiceries*, the labels and bottles carefully designed to look serious and authentic: Henri Bardouin, Lou Garagaï, La Rince, Lousou. There are even a couple of throwbacks to the naughty old days of *absinthe*—or so the makers would have you believe—in the form of the emphatically green Versinthe, and La Muse Verte, which is sold complete with a replica of the old perforated *absinthe* spoon.

All of these, if you happen to like the flavor of *anis*, are delightful, but I have to admit that only in Provence can I drink *pastis* with real enjoyment. Surroundings influence taste, and I am used to sunshine and blue skies with my Ricard. It just isn't the same drink in a London restaurant or a New York bar, possibly because of the dress code. I find that *pastis*, suits, and socks don't mix.

Pétanque

Since prehistoric times, man has amused himself by hurling small spherical objects, or *boules*, at some kind of target. It was a popular pastime with the Egyptians around 3500 B.C. The father of medicine, Hippocrates, used to recommend it as an exercise to develop strength and mobility, and the Greeks enjoyed it so much that they left to posterity a bronze statuette of a player dating from the fifth century B.C. This is interesting for a number of reasons. First, the young gentleman is stark naked, a sight very rarely seen on a modern *boules* court. Second, he is holding his *boule* in his left hand, which is unusual in a world that has always been predominantly right-handed. And third, he is standing in the same way a player would stand today as he enters the throwing circle and prepares to make his throw. His arm is bent, his *boule* is held at waist height, his eye is fixed on the target.

For centuries, *boules* was a game that required players to be reasonably athletic. The court was long, the *boules* were heavy, and players needed to take a run to generate the momentum necessary for a long throw. It wasn't until early in the twentieth century that this changed, and we even have a fairly precise date. It was June 1910, in La Ciotat (incidentally, the birthplace of motion pictures), a town on the coast between Marseille and Toulon. The regular afternoon game of *boules* was in progress, watched by an audience of the local *papys*—wistful old enthusiasts who no longer had the agility or strength to play the long game. None was more wistful

than Jules Lenoir, once nimble, now afflicted with chronic rheumatism, who longed to play again; and it was his great friend, Ernest Pitiot, who found a way for him to do it.

"We will play a shorter game," said Pitiot, "but instead of running to make the throw, we'll play with *les pieds tanqués*, feet together and planted on the ground." And that was the birth of *pétanque*.

The beauty of the game is that it can be played by practically anyone, practically anywhere there is a more-or-less level scrap of land. The preferred surface is hard-packed sandy earth, known in Provence as *clapicette*, smooth enough so that the *boules* can run, uneven enough to cause some interesting deviations from the straight line. Reading a *boules* court is not unlike reading a tricky green on a golf course.

The target is a small wooden ball—variously known as the *but*, the *cochonnet*, the *pitchoune*, the *ministre*, or the *gendarme*—and the winners are those who end up with more *boules* closer to the *but* than the opposition. Each of these scores one point, and the first team to reach thirteen points wins.

This may seem like a straightforward, placid diversion, a gentle to-and-fro devoid of drama. In fact, it's nothing of the kind. It can be every bit as vicious as croquet. An expert, or even a lucky beginner, can scatter an opponent's group of *boules* with a bomb, a direct hit from above, a willful act of savagery that causes outrage and a desire for instant revenge. There is also the delicate and contentious matter of measuring the exact distance between two competing *boules* and the *but* in a closely fought game. Unbiased judgment is available in the form of the *boulomètre à tirette*, a folding measure calibrated in millimeters, which is useful and is sometimes accepted as the final word, but sometimes not.

Usually, the distance in contention is no more than the width of a whisker, and so it is crucial that the measurement be taken correctly. But what is seen as correct by the winner is not always seen the same way by the loser, and it is then that the Provençal fondness for heated debate takes over. Voices are raised, fingers are wagged, accusations of partial blindness fly back and forth, recriminations are exchanged, and the peace of a summer's evening is shattered. To the spectator, it seems that physical violence is imminent. At the very least, it looks unlikely that the two sides of the dispute will ever speak to one another again. And yet, five minutes later, there they are, playing as though nothing had happened.

Pétanque can be enjoyed by two teams of complete novices, and it is one of the very few athletic events that permit players to pause for the occasional restorative glass while playing. This makes it an extremely convivial game, and in Provence it is almost always played under halcyon conditions. The air is warm and still, the *cigales* are in full song, and the other sound effects—the soft thud of a *boule* landing, the clack of one *boule* against another—are pleasantly hypnotic. All is serene. Until the next argument.

Pieds et Paquets

Committed vegetarians and those of a squeamish disposition should probably turn the page now. The dish that appears on menus as *pieds et paquets* is not for anyone who feels faint at the thought of eating the feet and stomach of a ruminant animal; or, as the latter is more widely known, tripe.

This is considered a great delicacy in Provence, especially in Marseille, where it is taken seriously enough to have its own charter—founded by eight restaurants—that guarantees tripe of *"une qualité irréprochable."* Despite the fact that *pieds et paquets* is a stew, which you might think makes it more suitable for winter, it is served in Provence throughout the year, whatever the temperature, a dish for all seasons.

The first of the two main ingredients is tripe, and by the time it leaves the butcher, it is usually stark white, having been "dressed"—soaked in lime, then in brine, then boiled. In Normandy, it is cooked *à la mode de Caen,* with vegetables, spices, cider, and Calvados. This heresy would never be tolerated in Provence, since it lacks the essential *pieds,* the blanched and flambéed sheep's feet. Here, the tripe is cut into small squares and stuffed with salt pork, minced garlic, and parsley. These are the *paquets,* and to them are added tomatoes, onions, carrots, whole cloves of garlic, bacon, pepper, thyme, bay, pimento, cloves, olive oil, and copious amounts of white wine. Everything is then gently simmered for eight hours or so, and served with new potatoes cooked in their skins.

I have always admired the fearless curiosity that led man to try things that were neither obviously edible nor visually appetizing. Snails come to mind, as do sea urchins and the toxic Japanese fugu fish. But there cannot be a more unlikely delicacy than the feet of sheep, and I raise my hat to the gastronomic pioneer—undoubtedly a native of Provence—who first popped them in the pot.

Pierre

Beneath its skin of green, Provence has a heart of limestone. The *tailleurs,* those who turn it into a thousand different forms and functions, say it cuts like a slab of butter. With time and exposure, it ages beautifully, and the raw brightness of freshly cut stone mellows, turning to honey or a pale, weathered gray. Pillars and arches, fountains and statues, flagstones and urns, cherubs and dolphins, the massive blocks of Roman aqueducts, the delicate latticework of an eighteenth-century church—wherever you go in Provence, you will see limestone. And you will rarely be far away from one or another of the quarries that puncture the countryside.

They resemble immense, half-finished amphitheaters, bone white in the sun, the howl of saws and the grind of machinery echoing off the quarry walls. Cut blocks of stone, looking like neatly stacked piles of gigantic sugar lumps, dwarf the figures of the workmen. Everything—man, machine, and the occasional ghostly, long-suffering tree—is blurred by a fine coating of limestone dust, and the unremitting, blinding glare is painful to the eyes. Visiting a quarry is like getting punched in the head. What it must be like to work in one I can't imagine.

Each quarry has its own particular type of limestone: fine or large grained; white, pale blond, straw yellow, or ocher; more or less hard; more or less porous. And there is a curious stoneworkers' vocabulary, dating from premachinery days. A *crocodile* is a saw with fang-shaped teeth, for cutting soft stone. A *crapaud* is a massive dray used for transporting ten-ton blocks of stone. A *gendarme* is a pile of fragments of cut stone. To *battre le beurre* is to make a hole in the stone. A *polka* is a double-edged hammer. A *tête de chat* is a block of stone roughly formed into a sphere. Alas, there don't seem to be any picturesque names for the robotlike equipment one sees in today's quarries.

To see perhaps the world's most frequently photographed—and yet frequently ignored—example of Provençal limestone, you must go to New York and take a careful look at the Statue of Liberty. She is standing on a base made from *pierre de Cassis,* cut from the quarries a few miles east of Marseille.

Pigeonniers

If you could put up with their endless crooning, I suppose that having a bird dormitory fully stocked with pigeons might well be a source of comfort. With a living larder on your doorstep, you are never short of a meal; should hunger strike, you simply have some of the neighbors over for dinner. This convenient access to food explains why you will see, throughout Provence, *pigeonniers* of various shapes and heights, attached to farm buildings or standing slightly apart.

The classic *pigeonnier* is an elegant piece of architecture: tall, slim, and simple, either round or square, with the pigeons' entrance at the top, just under the roof. The more desirable *pigeonniers* have a security system in the form of a wide band of glazed tiles below the entrance. This prevents rats, cats, and other unwelcome visitors from gaining a foothold and climbing in.

Humans are admitted through a door at ground level, and a ladder will take them up through an opening in the first floor to the pigeons' quarters. These are *boulins*, tile or plaster niches that

line the walls, their orderly pattern giving you the impression that you have stepped into an oversize, whitewashed honeycomb. Our *pigeonnier* has about 250 of these niches, which I used to think was quite impressive until I heard about the 700-*boulin* establishment—more like a condominium than a *pigeonnier*—at the Château de Sylvabelle in Revest-des-Brousses.

It is hard to imagine the racket that seven hundred pigeons coming home to roost each night would make, let alone the mountain of droppings they would deposit. I say this with some brief experience of these things. Our local pigeons, despite the spacious accommodation freely available to them in the *pigeonnier,* insist on spending their time on the window sills of our house, with predictable results on the flagstones below. They are unmoved by my bloodthirsty threats. I think they must know that we prefer to eat chicken.

Pistou, Pissaladière, et Pissalat

I once heard a French food snob dismiss Italian cuisine with the damning comment that "after the noodle, there is nothing." Slanderous and inaccurate though that may be, there is a widespread conviction among the French that their national cuisine is more varied and refined than anything one could find east of Menton, where noodle country begins. However, the French are extremely practical where the stomach is concerned, and they know a good thing when they eat it. It is therefore not surprising that some of Italy's gastronomic treasures have found their way onto Provençal menus, suffering only a slight change of name in the process. *Pistou* and *pissaladière* are two popular examples.

. *Pistou* in its original Italian form is *pesto,* a paste made from basil, olive oil, pine nuts, and cheese. Apart from the spelling, the most noticeable difference in the Provençal version is the substitution of garlic for pine nuts when making the paste. This is used to liven up a soup of chopped tomatoes, green and white beans, zucchini, potatoes, leeks, celery leaves, and vermicelli. As you will notice, there is more than a hint of minestrone about the recipe, but here in Provence its Italian origins are ignored, and it is known as *soupe au pistou.* Very good it is too. To make it even more substantial, I always stir in an extra jigger of olive oil.

Pissaladière is essentially pizza without the elastic cheese topping: a bread dough or pastry base, sliced onions, fillets of anchovy, and olive oil. You may sometimes hear it described as *pizza provençal.* What a true pizza connoisseur from Naples would make of that is open to speculation.

Pissalat has its roots, as far as I know, in France, along the Mediterranean coast. It is a purée of tiny young fish, less than an inch long, with brine and olive oil. Nowadays, these fish are mostly anchovies, but a traditional recipe can be found in a book with the memorable title *150 Ways to Prepare Sardines*, published in 1898 by Imprimerie Colbert of Marseille. *Pissalat* is excellent with crudités or spread on thin squares of toast.

Platanes

Forty percent of all the trees in Paris and 60 percent of all the trees in London are plane trees. Yet in spite of the statistics, the plane tree is probably more often associated with Provence than with any city, perhaps for the purely picturesque reason that Provençal plane trees are so much more photogenic than their urban relatives. For a start, they are cleaner: a pale, mottled gray, untinged by traffic fumes. They are planted more dramatically: in pairs guarding the entrance to a village; in lines bordering a straight country road that stretches to the horizon; in elegant alleys that lead to grand old houses; in a courtyard, casting a wonderful dappled shade; and they are pruned in a more imaginative way, according to their function, which might be decorative or practical.

Unlike city trees, they don't have to compete with tall buildings for the camera's attention. The shape of the trunk and the spread of its branches are the dominant elements, and any human beings around or beneath the tree take second place. They may be playing *pétanque,* or sitting at a café table, or kissing on a bench, but they are no more than accessories to the picture. In paintings and photographs and a thousand evocative postcards, the tree is the hero.

It is one of nature's great survivors, apparently able to endure endless abuse. Polluted air, lack of water, savage pruning, and accidental attack by badly aimed cars are normal parts of a plane tree's life. But it doesn't stop there. You will frequently see a variety of unsightly attachments that have been hammered, screwed, or stapled into the trunk. Electric wiring is one of the more popular adornments, snaking up into the branches to be linked to a string of colored lights. Then there is the trunk as communal notice board, with a garnish of flyers alerting us to the arrival next week of an exciting mattress festival, or a circus, or a *vide-grenier* in a neighboring village, or a *soirée musicale,* or an art exhibition, or a lost dog, or even, once in a while, a political election. The final indignity is the metal garbage basket bolted on to the trunk, spilling over with unsavory debris, an affront to the eye as well as the tree.

And yet it carries on, often for centuries. We have a plane tree in front of the house that was planted before the Revolution. This, although huge, is a relative stripling. The Géant de Provence, in Lamanon, is almost 175 feet high. Its trunk has a circumference of nearly thirty feet (seven people, holding hands, can just about encircle it). It is at least three hundred years old, classed as a historic monument, still in the best of health, and looks set for another few centuries.

As if the daily wear and tear suffered by plane trees weren't enough, they also have to submit to the annual coiffure inflicted each autumn by gentlemen with chainsaws. The Provençal *tailleur* prunes with severity and enthusiasm, and to watch him deal with a plane tree is to watch an exercise in disciplined brutality that makes me wince every time I see it. No mercy is shown. Promising shoots are removed, branches as thick as your wrist are lopped off, and by the time the *tailleur* has finished, the tree has the slightly shocked appearance of a man who has just received his first military haircut.

But there is method to this orgy of pruning. If the function of the tree is decorative, it might be pruned *à l'anglaise,* with its branches trained to point up to the sky; or *en gobelet,* with the trunk as a stem supporting branches that echo the shape of a wineglass. When the tree has a practical purpose—as a shield against the sun—it will be pruned *en parapluie,* so that the branches spread out like the spokes of a shady green umbrella.

Since the siesta is such an important part of summer life, you will not be surprised to hear that connoisseurs of shade exist in Provence. They will tell you that the shade under a pine tree is hot, too dry, smells of resin, and is generally disagreeable: *une mauvaise ombre*. Other trees to be avoided are the walnut tree (the shade is too cold), the linden (never take a nap under a linden tree for fear of losing your voice), or the chestnut (bad for the back). The shade of the plane tree, however, is considered to be *une bonne ombre*, clear and cool, with a lovely filtered light.

Finally, a historical note of dubious authenticity: it is said that wood from plane trees was used to construct the Trojan horse.

Pointus de Marseille

You see them being spruced up in the Vieux Port, parked above the waterline on beaches, slipping through currents around the *calanques*, nosing their way back from the Frioul islands, and on countless postcards. They are almost too pictur-esque to be real. Their paintwork is bleached and faded by a thousand days of salt air and sunshine, their shape is thick-waisted and comfortable, and there is a noticeable absence of plastic, chrome, or glass. They are wood from start to finish:

classic, simple, one-man fishing boats, known officially as *barquettes de Marseille*, and colloquially as *pointus*.

The name reflects the design. Instead of the usual fore and aft configu-ration, with a sharp end and a blunt end, the *pointu* is, like Noah's ark, pointed at both ends. A rudder is sometimes slung at one end; if not, steering is done by a pair of oars. Progress through the water is virtually without trace. A *pointu* makes no waves and leaves no wake. It has no keel, and so has no need of ports and moorings; at the end of a day's fishing, you just haul it up onto the beach.

Each *pointu* is unique, made by hand according to the ancient *méthode piffométrique*—that is, the complex system of "guesstimates" developed over the years by highly skilled marine carpenters. The secrets of this system are personal and precious. You pass them on to your son, as the saying goes, but never to your nephews. In fact, there is a rough blueprint for making *pointus*—the *gabarit de Saint Joseph*—but it leaves plenty of room for individual expression.

Nowhere is this more enthusiastically and creatively embraced than with the *capian*, an extension of the stem post at the prow, carefully shaped and painted, that juts toward the sky. To classical scholars, it is a celebration of man's cultivation of the sea and a salute to the sea god Poseidon. To the rest of us (and, I suspect, to most of the boat owners) it's an unmistakable phallic symbol.

In Marseille, *pointu* has a second meaning. Parisians are known as *pointus* because of the clipped accent with which they speak French. This can lead to confusion and a certain amount of low humor, as in: Go down to the port this morning. You might see a *pointu* having his barnacles removed.

Pont d'Avignon

Once upon a time, there was a shepherd boy in the Ardèche named Bénézet, who was instructed by the voice of the Lord to go to Avignon, and there to build a bridge across the Rhône.

Arriving without a penny in his pocket, young Bénézet went to explain his mission to the bishop of Avignon but found precious little in the way of help or Christian charity. The bishop took Bénézet for a crackpot, apparently considered a crime in those days, and sent him off to stand before a judge. After considering Bénézet's story, the judge delivered a masterpiece of judicial logic, which involved a rock of prodigious weight and size. If Bénézet could pick it up and carry it, he was clearly a man capable of building a bridge. And so he proved to be. He picked up the rock, carried it on his shoulder, and tossed it into the Rhône at the point where the future bridge was to be built. From that moment on, fund-raising for the project was assured, and in the fullness of time, Bénézet was rewarded with a sainthood.

Construction took place between 1177 and 1185, and it was the only bridge across the Rhône between Lyon and the Mediterranean. It was not particularly wide; certainly not wide enough for people to dance in a ring, as they do in the song. (Although you do see the occasional group of frisky tourists, carried away by sunshine and pink wine, tripping around in circles and occasionally singing the words: *"Sur le pont d'Avignon, on y danse, on y danse."*) In fact, the dancing took place on the island beneath the arches: *sous le pont,* and not *sur le pont.* Originally, there were twenty-two of these arches, and the bridge was half a mile long, earning Avignon a handsome income in tolls.

Not sufficiently handsome, however, to make up for the high mainte-nance costs. The waters of the Rhône were constantly nibbling away at the stone, and when, in the mid-seventeenth century, the river flooded, the force of the waters broke the bridge. That did it. The people of Avignon, faced with the prospect of enormous repair bills, decided that enough was enough, and left the bridge to take care of itself. One by one, the arches were washed away. Today only four remain.

Printemps

The vivid green blur of young wheat in the fields and young leaves on the vines. A season of firsts. The first butterflies. The first asparagus. The first cuckoo is heard in the forest. The first pair of shorts, revealing bright white knees, is spotted in the village. Sunsets are often no more than pale pink stains in the sky. The smell of a spring night, cool, moist, and fertile. A sudden wind turns the almond blossoms into falling snowflakes. There is the hoarse jabber of frogs as they make their romantic assignations around the edge of the *bassin*. A snakeskin on a rock. The poppy—that glamorous weed—poking its scarlet head above the young wheat.

Provençal

Provençal has been described as the language of the troubadours or, more prosaically, as French laced with garlic. Itself a dialect, it has been divided by scholars into four subdialects. Philologists tell us that it is more like a mixture of Italian and Spanish than French. All in all, it is not a language that a novice can approach with any confidence.

One rarely hears it spoken today, and so I was rather surprised to find, in a local bookstore, a brand-new edition of a fat Provençal-Français dictionary originally compiled by Xavier de Fourvières—priest, philosopher, writer, and ardent defender of the traditional language of the south. The dictionary was entitled *Lou Pichot Trésor*, or little treasure. Here, I was sure, would be the key to some interesting further education.

The dictionary first appeared in *Dou Félibrige an 47*, which, as far as I can make out, was 1901. The new edition sticks closely to the original design, with closely set, turn-of-the-century typography covering more than a thousand pages. Of these pages, 774 are devoted to Provençal words, and a mere 264 to French words, giving the impression that the old vocabulary was considerably richer than its modern counterpart.

The introductory section, however, is in French, under the heading of *Notions Préliminaires*. After some general throat clearing, it plunges straight into the heart of the matter—and what I assume most students wish to learn first—which is how to decline irregular verbs. But I was looking for something a little less technical to ease me into the language, a few words that would be useful if I bumped into a Provençal speaker (that is, a person aged at least seventy-five living in an isolated village in Haute-Provence). Specifically, I was hoping to find the Provençal equivalents of three phrases I remembered with great fondness from an ancient French textbook that I had at school.

They were:

Lo! My postillion has been struck by lightning!

The goat of my uncle's gardener has eaten my hat.

I cannot attend the theatre tonight. I am indisposed. My doctor has prescribed a purge.

I realize that under normal social circumstances there might be little call for these personal revelations, but I thought they would be enough to get the conversational ball rolling. At least they might provoke a reply in Provençal, and that's what I wanted. Reading a dictionary is one thing, but to learn the music of a language one has to listen.

Even so, as I went through the pages, I began to get a sense of what a Provençal conversation might sound like—the *ou*s and *oun*s and *au*s and *olo*s; the long flourish of words like *boumbounejaire* and *estranglouioun*, punctuated by the single-syllable grunts of *té* and *bou, goum* and *ʒou*. No wonder Mistral was inspired by this extraordinary language to heights of epic poetry.

But search as I might, I was unable to put together the necessary elements for my opening sentence, the one that would instantly gain the attention and sympathy of Provençal speakers wherever I might find them. A crucial word—*postillion*—seems to be missing from the Provençal vocabulary. I experimented with possible alternatives: *My hat has been struck by lightning* and even *My doctor has been struck by lightning*, but they are both unsatisfactory. Hats and doctors don't have quite the same dramatic cachet as postillions. I feel sure that Mistral would agree.

Quadrangle d'Or, Le

One of summer's annual miracles, as predictable and regular as the sound of *cigales,* is the rediscovery of the Luberon by the press. Each year we are treated to an update of last year, which in turn was an update of the year before. It's become a tradition, rather like the presummer flood of cellulite articles in women's fashion magazines.

There was a time, not long ago, when the chic part of the Luberon was known as Le Triangle d'Or. This was where those suffering from varying degrees of celebrity—now referred to in French gossip magazines as *les people*—could be seen at play. It was an area defined by the three villages of Gordes, Ménerbes, and Bonnieux. Within this triangle, if you were lucky, you might have caught a glimpse of a cabinet minister negotiating with his *aioli,* an actress shopping for monogrammed linen espadrilles, or a movie star playing *pétanque* with his bodyguard.

Now, so we're told, the triangle has turned into Le Quadrangle d'Or. I'm not sure where the fourth point of the quadrangle is, but that doesn't matter. The important thing is that the chic area has been officially extended—either because of inflation or because of a sudden increase in the number of celebrities. Perhaps we shall one day see it extended still further into Le Pentagone d'Or. Meanwhile, *les people* come, year after year, to relax, let their hair down, and frolic in the sun.

Mercifully, we see few photographs of this actually taking place. The beautiful villages and charming restaurants are shown, but rarely with a famous face in the picture, possibly because many celebrities like their privacy. This inconvenient problem is traditionally solved by the use of a couple of devices dear to the journalistic heart. First, those famous faces are shown not in the Luberon, but in miniature: small mug shots that were probably taken in Paris or Los Angeles. And second, the text is sprinkled with optimistic and largely unconfirmed reports of sightings of *les people*. The cabinet minister—well, we're pretty sure it was him—was once seen at the corner table of a certain restaurant. The actress, anonymous though she hoped to be behind her sunglasses, was almost definitely seen visiting a certain boutique. The movie star, so they say, has a personal *pétanque* trainer. All this is little more than speculation, but who cares? Speculation is a lot more fun than reality.

There is one aspect of *la vie en vacances* that doesn't seem to have reached the Luberon, and one hopes it never will. So far, we have been spared the horrors of paparazzi lurking in the lavender. These gentlemen seem content to hang around Saint-Tropez, in the hope of getting some candid shots of naked celebrity bosoms or buttocks. This, I think, is just as well for the famous names of the Luberon. As anyone who has ever looked through the pages of the paparazzi press can confirm, the unposed, off-duty celebrity often looks disappointing—dowdy and very ordinary; a person, and not one of *les people*.

Quart d'Heure, Un Petit

One of several seemingly precise phrases that decorate Provençal speech and lead the unwary listener into believing that a time or date has been set.

A quarter of an hour, even a small quarter of an hour, is more an expression of general intent than something to set your watch by. It means soon. Or quite soon. Or, at any rate, some time today.

Similarly, *une quinzaine* has a definite air of exactness about it: fifteen days. Should these stretch—as they have a habit of doing—into twenty days or more, it should be seen not merely as an inconvenience, but as an illuminating example of the Provençal attitude to time. This can best be described as philosophical: Time is one of the few things in life that is abundant and freely available to all. If we run out of it today, there is plenty more of it to be had tomorrow. So why panic?

Qu'es Aco?

Literally, this is Provençal shorthand for *Qu'est-ce que c'est que ça?*, but it is also used to express surprise and disapproval, as in: "Some bastard has stolen my *pastis* / broken into my car / run off with my wife. *Qu'es aco?*"

Queue Provençale

Englishmen of my generation were taught as schoolboys to queue. Not just to stand in line, but to do so in what our elders and betters would describe as a civilized manner. That is, no fighting, no elbowing or jostling, and certainly no queue jumping. In life, one must wait one's turn, we were told, and trying to push your way to the front was cheating. Worse, it was un-English.

Lessons learned young tend to stick, and to this day I still find myself waiting my turn—to cash a check, to buy a couple of lamb chops, to go through the formalities at Marignane airport. On these occasions, I am surrounded by Provençaux, which gives me the chance to observe, at close quarters, their response when forced to deal with this irritating Anglo-Saxon habit they dislike so much.

The aim of those who refuse to queue, naturally, is to be served before anyone else, and to hell with who actually got there first. Tactics vary. The most barefaced that I can remember was one employed by a young woman who rushed into the crowded butcher's shop claiming that she was double-parked in the busy street outside. Her ailing grandmother—late for a doctor's appointment, heart fibrillating, nervous about being left alone—was waiting in the car. The story came out in an agitated, life-or-death torrent. What else could a reasonable man do but give up his turn and step aside? Curiously, the young woman seemed to have the time to make a number of purchases, and there was no sign of the car. Perhaps the ailing grandmother had run out of patience and driven off to see the doctor by herself.

The portable phone is an invaluable prop, particularly for the executive who is far too busy to waste precious time waiting to go through passport control. He detaches himself from the crowd, phone stuck to his ear, and drifts away from the back of the long line, apparently absorbed in his conversation. By the time he sidles back into the line, still talking, he has moved to the front and has overtaken fifty or sixty people. But, preoccupied as he is with business matters, he doesn't seem to have noticed.

Going to join an acquaintance at the head of the queue is always useful, even if it turns out to be a case of mistaken identity, and the adroit use of an accessory—a fractious baby or a well-aimed shopping basket—is usually very effective. The fine points of technique don't really matter as long as they work. It's odd, this urge to save a few minutes, since the normally easygoing people of Provence are not noted for hurrying. My theory is that it has something to do with the way in which they drive their cars: a fierce joy in overtaking, whatever the conditions—a competitive instinct that is always there, whether on four wheels or two legs.

Rabasses

In most parts of France, they are called truffles. Gourmets with a weakness for the grandiloquent phrase call them *divins tubercules*. In Provence, they are known as *rabasses*.

The truffle is possibly the most notorious fungus in the world, surrounded by myth and rumor; sought after by pigs, dogs, poachers, and epicures; bought and sold for extravagant sums; revered by chefs; and eaten with a relish approaching addiction. It is more like an obsession than a mushroom, and for unusual reasons.

The first of these is smell. A truffle introduces itself through the nose, with a ripe, gamy, almost rank scent that many (including me) find irresistible. The scent is not only powerful, but contagious and intrusive, able to penetrate almost anything—including the shells of eggs—except sealed containers of glass or tin. Leave a naked truffle in the refrigerator, and within a short time it will have perfumed its neighbors; not only eggs, but bacon, butter, yogurt, cheese, and ice cream will all have a faint but distinct truffly whiff about them.

Scarcity is another part of the mystique. Unlike grapes, corn, or melons, truffles cannot be cultivated; they can only be encouraged, and the results are far from predictable. Years ago the French government, taking a paternal interest in an undoubtedly lucrative if largely undeclared market, attempted to get in on the act by cultivating the official Ministry of Agriculture truffle. After thorough research into the most suitable conditions, fields were planted with carefully selected truffle oaks, and to protect them from poachers and trespassers, sternly worded notices were put up. (Alas for officialdom, these were either ignored or used by hunters for target practice and peppered with buckshot until illegible.) The experiment was not dramatically successful; in fact, the government men seem to have abandoned their truffle initiative altogether. As every Provençal *paysan* could have told them right from the start, truffles grow only where and when they choose to. Nature knows best.

The erratic and unpredictable supply pattern is emphasized each year by market prices. The truffle business is well known for its secrecy, its sometimes suspect sales methods, and its lack of detailed financial records. All we have to go on are the figures declared by reputable dealers, and even these give us only a general indication of whether the truffle season has been bountiful or disappointing. In 2000/2001, the price per kilo was 540 euros; in 2003/2004, it was 720 euros. The average price over the past five years is about 600 euros. This is for unwashed truffles, allowing for between 10 and 15 percent of earth per kilo. And these are wholesale prices, buying direct from the suppliers.

As truffles travel, so they become more valuable, and by the time they reach the public, the prices quoted above will have doubled. Indeed, this can happen before they reach the public. It is a matter of Provençal fact that up to 50 percent of the truffles sold in the Périgord (where truffles are more expensive) have come from the Vaucluse and have been magically transformed en route into Périgord truffles. Like so much else in the truffle world, firm statistical evidence here is nonexistent.

Faced with scarcity and outrageously high prices, what is a truffle addict to do but learn to find his truffles by himself? Here is the traditional way to go about it if you happen to be without a pig or a trained dog.

First, check the calendar (the official season lasts from the first frost to the last, normally from November to March). Then find a group of truffle oaks as far from the public gaze as possible. Inspect the ground around the base of each tree, keeping your eyes open for the "burned patch," a bare, roughly circular area devoid of grass and other vegetation. This is often a sign of truffles beneath the surface (the scientific explanation being that the truffle secretes a form of herbicide, which doubtless adds to the flavor). Having found your burned patch, cut a small branch from the nearest pine tree and trim off the twigs until just a few needles remain at the end of the branch, forming a tiny, primitive brush.

Now, with extreme focus and concentration, go over the burned patch, brushing the surface as you go. You may be lucky enough to disturb *Suilla gigantea,* the tiny fly that lays its eggs in earth where truffles grow. If you see such a fly, keep your eye fixed on the spot from where it took off, and get down on your hands and knees. This is the moment to start excavating.

The equipment required is straightforward: a long screwdriver, wiped clean. Push it carefully into the area of earth recently abandoned by the fly, and sniff the tip of the screwdriver after each probe. The closer you get to the truffle, the more intense the scent will be, even though the truffle itself may be as much as a foot below the surface. Dig carefully, using your hands and sniffing the earth as you dig. When you eventually see the truffle, you will be tempted to seize it with a cry of triumph and pluck it immediately from the ground. Don't; you might damage or break it. Clear the earth around it to make sure that part of it isn't wedged under a stone or a root, lift it out, and let your thoughts turn to how you're going to eat it.

There are entire books devoted to truffle recipes. Many of these are complicated and best left to professional chefs. I much prefer recipes—if you can call them recipes—that I can make myself, and in which the truffle is the hero rather than an expensive addition. Sliced truffles transform scrambled eggs, a runny omelette, or a buttery baked potato into simple masterpieces, but my favorite is the greatest indulgence of all, almost too delicious to be legal.

Take an entire truffle, set it on a slice of foie gras, and wrap it in aluminum foil. Put it in the oven and heat for a few minutes, until the foie gras has melted into the truffle, infusing it with heavenly juices. Remove from the oven, leave it in the opened foil (plates are an unnecessary refinement), and sprinkle it with *fleur de sel de Camargue*. Give thanks and eat.

Raito, Ratatouille, et Rouille

A good sauce reminds us of the principal reason why sauces were invented: to add interest to unassuming foods with little flavor of their own. Thus it is with *raito* and salt cod.

At the heart of a proper *raito* is a generous measure of red wine (about a liter is needed for four people), into which goes a mixture of chopped onion, olive oil, tomato purée, garlic, a little flour, a *bouquet garni*, water, salt and pepper. Let this simmer until it has been reduced by about two-thirds and the consistency has thickened. Add the fillets of fish, some capers and black olives, *et voilà*—cod in triumph. (*Raito* without the cod is also wonderful when scooped onto a fresh baguette to make a spectacularly messy and tasty sandwich.)

Unlike many of the dishes that seem to have been on Provençal menus forever, *ratatouille* is a modern invention. Although the word has existed in Provençal since the eighteenth century, the dish wasn't mentioned in cookbooks until around 1930. One can see why its rise to gastronomic stardom has been relatively quick: it's versatile, easy to make, and can be eaten hot or cold.

Ratatouille is a summer stew of vegetables—tomatoes, eggplant, squash, onions, and sweet peppers, with the obligatory olive oil and garlic—coarsely chopped or sliced, and cooked slowly until the ingredients turn into a fragrant mush. It is especially good with grilled meat. On its own, it makes a tasty filling for a tart. I like it in an omelette, too, or cold, spread on bread like a rough vegetable jam.

Finally, here is a sauce for soup. Rust-colored, thick, humming with garlic, and spiked with chili pepper, *rouille* is the sauce that gives *bouillabaisse* and other fish soups their punch. It also adds to the flavor of subsequent conversations, since, at close quarters, *rouille* makes its presence felt on the breath for some time after eating.

Rideaux de Porte

It was, and still is, one of the dilemmas of summer in Provence. During those long months of heat, should you open your doors to let in the breeze, or shut your doors to keep out the insects? The simple solution,

which has frustrated wasps, bees, and flies for two hundred years or more, was the door-sized, ventilated curtain. This was originally made from short, narrow lengths of wood strung together and hung in closely spaced, vertical strands from a bar attached to the lintel. Air could pass through; flies couldn't. It was easy to install, effective, and attractive. Every village *épicerie* had one.

Times changed, and so did the *rideaux de porte*. Plain wood was replaced by painted bamboo, or colored plastic in tubes or strips. A more recent artistic development has been the use of a particular kind of furry, synthetic fiber, chopped into small, writhing shapes that resemble dead caterpillars. But fortunately, there is still hope for connoisseurs of the traditional *rideaux de porte.*

In Montfavet, just outside Avignon, there is an establishment founded by Émile Reboul after the 1914–18 war. Originally a bootmaker, Monsieur Reboul turned his attention to wood when he returned from military service. He made shoe trees, picture frames, birdcages, bread baskets, brush racks, even lollipop sticks. And, right up until 1970, he made *rideaux de porte.*

He had a granddaughter, Marie-Claude Brochet, who inherited her grandfather's love of wood and who took over the business. Today her wooden curtains are, in my opinion, the most beautiful in Provence.

Each one is made to measure from hundreds of pieces of polished boxwood threaded onto fine wire, usually in a mixture of two classic shapes: the round *perle* or the longer, slimmer *olive.* (There are dozens of more whimsical shapes, from hearts to cones to miniature doughnuts, but traditionalists stick to their pearls and olives.) You might decide to leave it at that—a curtain of unpainted boxwood that will mature over time until it takes on the tint of dark caramel. Or you might ask Madame Brochet if she would make you something a little more colorful.

The existing choice is already large—a menu of designs picked out in green, ocher, dark brown, or black, colors that stand out nicely against the pale, unpainted background. There is the *vague persane,* a wave that starts at the top of the curtain, with wavelets down each side; the *double feston,* a scalloped effect at the top with striped sides; the *serin,* a symmetrical pattern of large vees; the *salernes,* a thick horizontal zigzag; or there are lozenges, cubes and stripes, flames and chevrons, *quinconces* and *quadrillages*—a selection that can make your doors look like a gallery of graphic paintings.

And it needn't stop there. Any clear, uncomplicated design that can be drawn on a piece of paper can be copied: numerals, initials, a simplified version of your family coat of arms, a silhouette of your cat, the shape of a favorite tree, a flag, a flower, the Eiffel Tower, the rising sun, or a short message (Do Not Disturb or Welcome, depending on your disposition).

Once installed, your curtain will keep you informed of the comings and goings in your house. People, dogs, and cats, as they slip through the curtain and pass across the threshold, leave behind them a soft, clicking ripple of sound, wood against wood—another sound of summer, and a most agreeable change from the electronic beeps and squawks that infect modern life.

Ronds-Points

Despite being a nation that prides itself on its logic, France is not without its share of illogical quirks. The popularity of French rap music comes to mind, as does the curious choice of gender for several words in the French vocabulary. *Vagina (vagin)*, for instance, is masculine. And for many dangerous decades, French motorists were subject to a rule of the road that, as far as I can see, had absolutely no basis in any kind of logic: the priority of the right. This allowed drivers joining a road from the right to take precedence over cars already on that road. Obviously, it was a certain recipe for accidents, near misses and stimulating roadside arguments.

Eventually, logic was applied to the roads in the form of the grandly named *carrefour giratoire,* more commonly known as the *rond-point,* or traffic circle. It was an idea whose time had come, and it has been enthusiastically embraced by the authorities. They have been on a *rond-point* spree for years—and still are—adding so many circular detours to the journey between point A and point B that there is a risk of drivers getting dizzy.

You may think of the *rond-point* as nothing more than a practical safety device, but here in Provence it is seen as a chance to add a certain flourish to the landscape. Using the center of the area as a blank canvas, artists, sculptors, gardeners, and stonemasons have shown what can be done to transform an island in the road into an outlet for creative expression. Below the village of Lauris, you will find a perfect example of the *rond-point appellation contrôlée*, planted with neat rows of vines. Outside Apt, there is a large and elaborate affair, more like a park than a *rond-point*, bursting with trees, bushes, and stone walls. In the center of Cavaillon, motorists must drive around a giant star set in beds of flowers, and throughout Provence you will see *ronds-points* decorated with a single olive tree, a cluster of three cypresses, or a miniature panorama of lavender—quite modest, perhaps, but still a pleasant break from tarmac.

The prize for modesty has to go to Cadenet, where one of the road junctions is marked by a raised concrete pimple, so unobtrusive that it's almost invisible, and more often driven over than around. As if to make up for this, the *rond-point* just outside the village is not only much larger but has its own parking area off to one side that has become an unofficial used-car showroom, where hopeful sellers leave their vehicles, marked with price and contact telephone number.

Ronds-points are, yard for yard, some of the most expensive patches of real estate in Provence. Not long ago, the outskirts of Lourmarin were awarded a *rond-point*, and on the official notice authorizing the work was the budget that had been set aside for it: 460,000 euros, considerably more than the price of a good house in the village.

For some reason, despite their cost and their prominent positions, *ronds-points* are usually anonymous. They seem to have escaped the widespread French practice of naming public facilities after illustrious public figures. General Leclerc has his avenues, Gambetta his boulevards, Mirabeau his *cours*, Jaurès his *rues*. The smallest and most insignificant alley will often bear the name of some local dignitary, and I find it odd that *ronds-points* have so far been excluded from this distinction. I can understand that nobody these days wants to name anything after a politician; but why not a poet, an artist, an inventor, a local chef, or even a soccer player?

And let us not forget music. As far as I know, the *rond-point* has never been celebrated in song, unlike the bridge at Avignon or that even more improbable musical subject, the Route Nationale 7. And yet the subject—which is, after all, part of the romance of the road—cries out for a ballad or two. "I've Got Those *Rond-point* Blues," or "Going Round in Circles After You" are a couple of titles I can imagine striking an immediate chord in motorists' hearts.

Rosé

"No sooner made than drunk. No sooner drunk than pissed away." This jewel of scorn was the response of a wine critic—was he sober at the time?—when asked to give his considered opinion of *vin rosé*. It is an outdated and peevish comment, another smudge of tarnish to add to an already much maligned reputation. And yet one can see why pink wines have, until recently, been condemned as being frivolous and inconsequential.

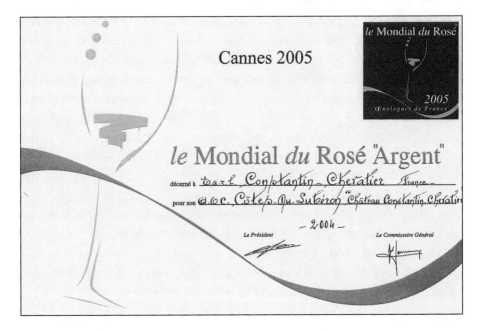

Rosé has always been thought of as a summer wine, more often associated with sunbathing than taste; a wine to drink *en carafe* at a beach restaurant, a wine that is equally happy with a grilled sardine, a barbecued chop, or a *salade niçoise*. It is a simple, obliging wine. Apart from a short period of chilling before serving, it needs no special attention. It doesn't presume to make an appearance on vintage charts. It lacks the complexity and the mystique of good reds and whites. It is neither expensive nor pretentious. Given these homely virtues, it is hardly surprising that it has not been taken seriously by critics.

But things are changing. There are more and more well-made *rosés* to choose from, and they are in a different league from the lurid tipple of the past. While it will take several years for the reputation of *rosé* to catch up with reality, progress is being made, not only in the vineyards but, of all places, in Cannes.

Normally, Cannes is associated with the film festival—starlets losing their clothes on the beach while producers make deals on the Carlton Hotel terrace. For the past two years, however, Cannes has been the setting for Le Mondial du Rosé, an international tasting and assessment of the world's best pink wines. It is a serious affair: 2005 saw fifty professional oenophiles from sixteen different countries, blind tasting 650 wines from wherever good *rosé* is made. In all, twenty-nine countries were represented, from Australia to Uruguay, and the sniffing, sipping, and spitting were spread over three days. There were two pleasing aspects to the proceedings. The first was that the oenophiles, defying well-established Cannes convention, remained fully dressed; the second was that the Provençal *rosés* picked up a hatful of gold and silver medals.

By definition, *rosé* is pink, but not just a single shade of pink. It can be almost as pale as a white wine, with the faintest ruddy tinge. (I hesitate to use the word *blush,* a more elegant and appropriate word, because it reminds me of the bad old days when primitive California *rosés* were called blush and had the sticky taste of boiled sweets.) Or it can be cherry red. Or any rosy tint in between. The color depends on the length of time the skins of the grapes—which are black—are left in the fermenting wine. The currently fashionable extra-pale *rosés* are made from grapes that are barely picked before they are in the *pressoir*. For the darker wines, or *rosés d'une nuit*, the grapes are left overnight or longer.

Rosé has more to recommend it than a pretty complexion. It is a wonderfully versatile wine: light yet satisfying enough to drink on its own, and good with a surprisingly wide range of foods. It goes very well with the *brandades, aiolis*, and grills of Provençal cuisine, as you would expect, and, as I have discovered, with curry and with anything pink, such as prawns, prosciutto, and steak tartare.

But does it keep? I have heard of a venerable *rosé* from the 1985 vintage that was described as still being "vivacious," and of another twenty-year-old that was "remarkably complex" (make of those descriptions what you will), but as a general rule most *rosés* should be drunk within two or three years of being made.

Memories of drinking *rosé* last much longer. On a shady terrace; around a smoky, herb-scented barbecue; outside a café on market day; by the pool before lunch—it is a wine that accompanies some of the most pleasant moments in life. Perhaps that should be marked on every bottle.

Route des Cèdres

Here is the ideal walk for people who don't really like to walk. In other parts of the Luberon, the walker will encounter twisting, overgrown paths; prickly waist-high gorse; and thirty-five-degree climbs under a ferocious sun. The Route des Cèdres, in total contrast, is level, free of clinging undergrowth, and delightfully shady. There are magnificent views. The going is not only flat, but carpet soft. The most pampered and demanding stroller could hardly ask for more.

The route begins just above Bonnieux, and ends at the Gorges du Régalon, a distance of about two and a half miles. Its origins date back to 1861, when cedar seeds gathered in the Atlas Mountains of Algeria were sown along the crest of the Luberon, more than 2,300 feet above sea level. The seeds took, and the trees prospered and reproduced. Cedars being the least flammable of Mediterranean trees, many of them were able to survive the horrendous fires that destroyed thousands of acres in 1952. Today the forest is a true forest, with hundreds of widely spaced trees—tall, dark green, and handsome.

For most of the year, there are more trees than people, and the loudest sounds are the flurries of breeze through the branches. After a day or two of mistral, when the sky has been swept clean and the air is more than usually pellucid, you can see to the south—beyond Aix and the great wedge of Mont Sainte-Victoire—the glint of the Mediterranean. And to the west, the white teeth of the Alpilles.

Under snow, the route is magical. Under the sun, tranquil and cool. At all times, it is a tonic. The poet Karle Wilson Baker put it well: "Today I have grown taller from walking with the trees."

Saint-Germain Sud

This is a description once applied to the area of the north Luberon around Gordes, Bonnieux, and Ménerbes, inspired by the summer population of Left Bank Parisians. This same area is now more likely to be called Le Triangle d'Or, which presumably reflects the rise in property prices. Le Quadrangle d'Or, as noted elsewhere, made its first media appearance in 2005.

The rest of Provence has managed for the most part to escape similar classifications. There was an attempt some years ago to promote the region as "the California of Europe," and Mont Ventoux went through an uncomfortable moment or two as "the Mount Fuji of Provence." Fortunately, common sense prevailed in both cases, and we have heard no more of these fanciful labels.

Saints Patrons

You will be comforted to hear that you have a patron saint, no matter which subsection of society you belong to, which occupation you follow, or even which malady ails you. Businessmen have Saint Expédit watching over them, as he also watches—for some inexplicable reason—over driving students. Gypsies have Saint Sarah. Winemakers have Saint Vincent. Toothache sufferers have Saint Laurent. And on a personal level, I was gratified to discover Saint François de Sales, who is the patron saint not only of writers, but of journalists and deaf mutes. How these three came to be grouped together under the benevolent eye of Saint François is unclear, but it is only one example of some highly unlikely combinations. The flock of Saint Michael the Archangel, for instance, includes bakers, fencers, waffle irons, pastry makers, barrel makers, and parachutists. Try though I might, I cannot see any obvious connection between waffle irons and parachutists, but that is doubtless due to some gaps in my theological education.

Things are simpler in Provence, where patron saints tend to have less diverse responsibilities. Saint Jean has long been one of the most popular saints among the Provençaux because of his links to agriculture. He watches over fruit, vegetables, and the harvest, but leaves the garden to his colleague Saint Roch, the patron saint of gardeners. The winegrowers and barrel makers of the Côtes du Rhône have Saint Vincent, of course, but a number of other patron saints as well, and the church of Roquemaure is dedicated to all of them. (The same church contains the relics of Saint Valentin, the international patron saint in charge of romance.)

Of all the saints, I think my favorite—admittedly for gastronomic rather than spiritual reasons—is the patron saint of truffles. Saint Antoine is officially remembered each January in the church at Richerenches during the Fête de la Truffe, and he is one of the few patron saints to have his own signature tune. A chant dedicated specifically to him is sung as part of the church service, and one short verse will give you the flavor of the proceedings:

> Bon Saint Antoine, donne-nous
> Des truffes en abondance
> Que leur odeur et leur bon goût
> Fassent aimer la Provence

Which, roughly translated, is:

> Good Saint Antoine, give us
> Truffles in abundance
> So that their perfume and good taste
> Make us love Provence

Nobody could argue with sentiments like these, least of all the members of the congregation, whose custom it is to sit down together after church and tuck into a truffle lunch.

A question that puzzles me is how patron saints come to be associated with certain occupations or groups, particularly when these are of fairly recent origin. For instance, who made the decision that parachutists and driving students deserved their own patron saints, and who selected the saints? In search of answers, I consulted Monsieur Farigoule, normally an expert on everything. For once, he was at a loss. *"C'est comme ça"* was all he could manage, and told me to go and ask a theologian.

My research has had mixed results, partly because of the reluctance of ecclesiastical authorities to reveal definitive details of the selection process. I can tell you, however, that the pope has been petitioned to approve the candidacy of Saint Isidore of Seville as patron saint of the Internet. The relevance here is that Saint Isidore, who died in 636, compiled a thirty-volume encyclopedia of all the knowledge that existed in his lifetime, thus establishing the world's first database. So there is a certain logic in this case. Less obvious is the link between Saint Clare of Assisi and her patronage of television, which received papal approval in 1958.

So far as I can tell, this is the way it seems to work: patron saints are chosen by popular demand, which is later authorized by the Catholic church. In Provence, where matters of this sort are never rushed, we are still awaiting the nomination of the patron saint of *joie de vivre.*

Sangliers

We try to lead a quiet life here in the depths of the country, keeping to ourselves and minding our own business. Even so, there are times when we cannot help but become involved in the nocturnal activities of our neighbors. Intrusive, gluttonous, and destructive, they descend on us uninvited each summer, causing sleepless nights and at times arousing murderous instincts. I am not, of course, referring to people in general or even house guests, but to those wild and whiskery ancestors of the domestic pig known as *sangliers*.

Not content with the 165,000 hectares of the Luberon that they have more or less to themselves, the *sangliers* like to drop in, most often at night, for sport and refreshment. During the hot, dry months from June until October, water is scarce in the hills but plentiful in the swimming pool, and this has proved to be a major attraction. So far we have been lucky, and thirsty *sangliers* have confined themselves to drinking from the pool rather than falling into it. (I am told they don't swim.)

From the pool, it is only a short stroll to the patch of grass we water diligently, hoping that one day it will turn into a lawn. This, too, is popular, being moist and nutritious, with worms and other tidbits waiting to be dug up. *Sangliers* excavate with their snouts, which operate like the scoop of an earthmoving machine, leaving deep holes and zigzag patterns of shallow trenches across the grassy surface; a primitive form of abstract art.

For the fruit course, the *sangliers* move over to a nearby field that has been planted with melons, and here they display their connoisseurship. Each morning you can see that a number of melons have been beheaded and eaten; nothing remains but the bottom part of the melon rind, still attached to its stalk. The selection of these melons might appear to be haphazard, but it isn't. Only mature melons, ready for the table, are eaten. The rest are left until they are ripe.

You may wonder how these relatively quiet activities could lead to sleepless nights. After all, the chewing of a melon or the desecration of a lawn can be achieved with very little noise: no more than the occasional hiccup or grunt of satisfaction, which would never disturb us. The problem is with our dogs, who have sharp ears and a profound dislike of trespassers. The merest rustle of a *sanglier* tiptoeing through a flower bed will wake them up. Outraged at the thought of another animal on their territory, they bellow at us until we wake up and let them out. So begins a prolonged and rowdy session of hide-and-seek, with the barking of dogs and the squealing of *sangliers* making any further sleep impossible.

As a rule, the *sanglier* will retreat rather than attack. This is just as well, since he is a formidable creature, far better able to take care of himself than the domestic pig. For a start, there is the armor plating that a mature male *sanglier* develops, a tough subcutaneous sheath, up to two and a half inches thick, that protects his neck and forequarters. Then

there are the two curved tusks that protrude from his lower jaw, and a surprisingly nimble turn of speed when he runs.

A dog wouldn't have a chance against an irate *sanglier,* as I discovered one morning during the hunting season. One of our dogs, Nelly, being young and curious, went to investigate a sound in thick undergrowth. There she found a wounded *sanglier,* shot through the shoulder and unable to run. But he could still use his tusks, and I very nearly had a dead dog to carry home. As it was, she had to have fifteen stitches in her side and was trussed up in bandages for weeks.

But despite the ravages to the garden, the ear-splitting nights, and that one gory encounter, I am happy to have *sangliers* as neighbors. They mean no harm, and they are oddly endearing as they trot across the fields with their tails straight out behind them. And besides, they were here first.

Santons

In northern Europe, as in many other parts of the world, the coming of Christmas is heralded by an onslaught of reindeer, elves, and stout white-bearded gentlemen in red suits, decorated for the occasion with a picturesque dusting of snowflakes. These seasonal invaders, who seem to arrive earlier and earlier each year, have done their work so well that their influence now extends to the Mediterranean, an area not known for either snow or reindeer. But Santa Claus and his crew, successful though they may have been elsewhere, will never entirely replace the quieter, smaller, and more individual characters that gather each year to celebrate the Provençal Christmas.

These are *santons*, handmade or hand-painted clay figurines. They range in height from less than half an inch to sixteen inches, and in subject from the celestial to the commonplace. The Infant Jesus and the village baker, the Virgin Mary and a fish seller, angels and donkeys, the Magi and a Gypsy—they and a host of others are brought out every Christmas to take their places around the family *crèche*.

As Provençal traditions go, *santons* are relatively recent. Until the end of the eighteenth century, there was no need for them. For the traditional

Christmas Midnight Mass, there would be living *crèches* in most of the churches, with a recently born baby from the village standing in for the Infant Jesus, the most placid donkey available brought in from the fields, and various local notables in the roles of wise men and shepherds.

The Revolution put a stop to all that. Religious symbols were banned, churches were disfigured or destroyed, and the Nativity was forced into hiding. But it was still celebrated privately, and each family collected its own group of *santons* as miniature replicas of what could no longer be seen in church.

With time, the antireligious zeal of the revolutionaries dwindled, and the making and collecting of *santons* could come out into the open. In 1803, the entire month of December was devoted to a *foire aux santons* in Marseille, where members of the public could stock up for Christmas without risking official retribution. More than two hundred years later, the Marseille fair still takes place each December, and now there are dozens of others throughout Provence.

One of the reasons for the enduring popularity of *santons* is their variety. You can pick your own team. Apart from the holy family and a handful of principal characters, there is a supporting cast of hundreds, some less obviously festive or religious than others. If, for example, you feel that your Christmas *crèche* would not be complete without the presence of Yves Montand in his role as Papet in *Manon des sources,* you can find him, meticulously dressed in waistcoat, jacket, and hat, with a rifle slung over his shoulder. The arts are represented by Cézanne and van Gogh, Mistral and Daudet. The world of commerce is represented by sellers of cheese, snails, and garlic; knife grinders; chimney sweeps; and basket makers.

You will have noticed that these *santons,* with the exception of Yves Montand, are based on characters from the eighteenth and nineteenth centuries. While I have a great respect for tradition, I hope it won't be long before we see a few figures around the *crèche* that reflect the more contemporary side of Provence. The plumber, the postman, the electrician, the man who installs satellite TV dishes, the driver of the UPS van, the local garage mechanic, perhaps even the occasional tourist—surely they deserve to be involved during what is, after all, the season of goodwill to all men. They certainly have more relevance to Provençal life than reindeer.

Sardines, Les Cinq

The people of Marseille have a fondness for fish and a gift for the colorful phrase, and here the two are combined. In this case, a sardine is equivalent to a finger, and five sardines make a hand. When you hear a Marseillais say he met a friend so briefly they only had time to *toucher les cinq sardines,* he is not, as you might think, referring to some occult fisherman's ritual. He is merely saying that he and his friend shook hands.

Saucisson d'Arles

The sausage is taken extremely seriously in Provence. I can still remember the involuntary expression of distaste on the face of a Provençal friend as he had his first mouthful of a classic English breakfast sausage (brought over from Harrods, I might add, as a special treat). When I asked him what was wrong, he poked at the sausage with his fork and thought for a moment, clearly not wanting to be impolite. "Well," he said at last, "this is a very unusual way of eating bread."

I'm afraid he had a point. English sausages, although they have many admirers, normally contain one-third of their weight in cereals. This gives them a measure of stodginess much prized by the English sausage fraternity, which holds the view that a sausage isn't a sausage unless it sticks to your ribs. In France, where every self-respecting sausage is 100 percent meat, the bread is taken separately or not at all, according to taste.

The sausage capital of Provence is Arles, and one could say it has been since July 6, 1655. On that day the *charcutier* Godard established a recipe that has inspired the master sausage makers of Arles, generation after generation, ever since—a mixture of pork and beef, flavored with pinches of pepper, cloves, nutmeg, ginger, and good red wine. The resulting mas-

terpieces are then dried for several weeks before being hung, like rows of edible stalactites, on an overhead rail in the butcher's shop.

And there we could leave the *saucisson d'Arles* were it not for the ticklish question of another, more controversial ingredient. The addition of donkey meat to the recipe—hotly opposed by some, hotly supported by others—is said to impart a touch of *je ne sais quoi* to the taste. (I have never found it to be that distinctive, but my palate probably needs further education.) I suspect that the controversy arises not over the flavor of donkey, but the very idea of using donkey in the first place. We are accustomed to eating pigs and cows without a qualm, but donkeys, with their soulful eyes and expressive ears, are characters—far too charming to turn into sausage meat. For many people, it would be like eating a domestic pet.

We find an early example of the elevated status of the donkey in Provençal society as long ago as the fifteenth century. In 1480, the farmers of Sisteron and the farmers of Peyruis were at furious odds over the grazing rights for their herds of pigs. Harsh words and worse were exchanged, and in a particularly violent episode, a man and a donkey were killed. Their assassin was brought to justice and duly condemned, but not for killing the man. His crime was that he had murdered the donkey.

Saussoun

Most of us in recent years have been exposed to the experimental cuisine that is so fashionable among chefs seeking to make a reputation for culinary daring. Here is where you will find the most bizarre combinations of ingredients—caviar and white chocolate, fish mousse with bananas, egg-and-bacon ice cream—which are usually presented and described to you with the whispered reverence normally reserved for religious occasions.

The mere thought of these weird inventions makes me shudder, and I have come to terms with the fact that I must have timid taste buds. I can't even work up much enthusiasm for cherries dipped in pig fat or sardine-on-toast sorbet, preferring to see something more familiar and conservative on my plate. This is why I have made the mistake of resisting *saussoun* for so long; the mixture of almonds and anchovies sounded awkward and not at all appetizing. But I should have known better, because this has been a standby in Provençal kitchens for hundreds of years.

The traditional recipe takes peeled almonds, unsalted anchovies, a touch of fennel, and a few mint leaves crushed together in a mortar, then mixed with water and olive oil to form a savory paste. Spread on bread, it was often given to grape pickers during the *vendanges* to keep their strength up between meals. Appropriately, it encourages a healthy thirst. For those of you who have become jaded with the complicated offerings of "molecular gastronomy," *saussoun* on a slab of toasted bread will bring your palate down to earth in the most tasty and satisfying way.

Savon de Marseille, Le Vrai

The personal hygiene program of the ancient Gaulois was a sketchy affair, consisting of little more than a brisk scrub with a primitive pomade of wood ash and goat suet—a kind of rustic, no-frills soap—which they used to wash their clothes and tint their hair. But great moments in soap history were to come, and one of the most important took place in Provence. Quantum leaps were achieved in both hygiene and soap, and much of the credit for that must go to Marseille.

The city's first *savonnier* of record was Crescas Davin, who introduced soap making to Marseille between 1371 and 1401. Then as now, nothing happens fast in Provence, and it took several generations of city elders to realize that soap might have a future. But by 1688 they had established rules and regulations governing manufacture and labeling, and Savon de Marseille was officially on the map. In 1760, Marseille had twenty-eight soap factories; in 1820, eighty-eight factories; and by 1906, the city was riding on the crest of a lather boom, with 140,000 tons of soap being turned out every year.

What made it popular then is what makes it popular among soap connoisseurs today: it is com-

pletely natural and remarkably pure. By law, it must contain 72 percent oil (olive, copra, or palm), with no artificial additives. In its traditional form—that is, without any added scent or coloring—it is so mild as to be hypoallergenic. Babies and others with sensitive skin thrive on it; so do sensitive clothes. Silk, lace, fine wool, gossamer underwear, and lawn handkerchiefs of an almost transparent delicacy all emerge from the wash clean and unscathed. And, since it is totally biodegradable, Savon de Marseille is equally kind to the environment.

It has been called the queen of soaps, and it is not so much made as cooked, in enormous cauldrons that hold twenty tons of basic ingredients. These are simmered for ten days at a temperature of 250 degrees Fahrenheit until they form a liquid paste. The paste is washed, left for two days, and washed again. (The second washing allows the soap to be officially designated as Extra Pur.) Then the paste, still liquid, is decanted into rectangular containers and left to dry before being cut into *pains,* weighing just under 80 pounds, *barres* of 5.5 pounds, and *cubes* of 200, 400, 500, or 600 grams. These are stamped with the soap's pedigree and sent on their way. The process, from cauldron to point of sale, takes about a month.

There are lesser soaps that hope to be mistaken for *l'authentique* Savon de Marseille by copying the distinctive shape, but these counterfeit *cubes* can easily be avoided by reading your soap before you buy it. Nothing is genuine without the guarantee that has been stamped into the *cube.* One side should always be marked *Extra Pur 72% d'Huile.* A second side will state the *cube*'s net weight in grams. Other sides will carry the maker's name and, of course, the description that this is indeed Savon de Marseille.

The colors vary according to the oil that has been used: dark cream for copra and palm oil, pale green for olive oil. Each is as good for the skin as the other. Used as a shampoo, this is one soap that will leave the hair with a healthy gloss. And it would never surprise me to hear that some extreme enthusiasts use it instead of toothpaste.

Scorpions

One of those words—*snakes* is another—that send a shudder down many a spine. And it is true that Provence is home to a great many scorpions, who settle under stones or in the crevices of old stone walls and floors, waiting for insects to devour or, so it is widely believed, for human toes to sting.

In fact, I have never met anyone who has been attacked by a scorpion. It is a nocturnal creature with better things to do than scuttle after your bare feet, and given the choice, it will avoid human company. However, the chances are high that anyone spending time here will come across a scorpion or two, and it is as well to know how to tell the difference between the innocuous and the potentially painful.

Nature has made this easy for you by color coding the two common types of scorpion found in Provence. The first is *Euscorpius flavicaudis,* deep brown in color and harmless to man; the second is *Buthus occitanus,* which is a distinctive yellowy orange. This is the one that should make you tread carefully. The sting in its tail is poisonous and can cause a burning sensation on the skin, muscular cramps, and a general feeling of weakness for up to twenty-four hours; not life-threatening, but unpleasant.

To keep scorpions of both colors at bay, at least in the house, swab down the floors with a mixture of water and lavender essence. I have been told that the astringency of the lavender makes a scorpion's eyes water. This has yet to be confirmed by scientific observation.

Sel de Camargue

Salt. In most parts of the world it is no more than a commodity; necessary, of course, but without any inherent interest. In France it is a delicacy, elevated to a place of honor on the table, with its connoisseurs, its varieties, and its specialist uses and recipes. As any Frenchman will be happy to tell you, French salt is a superior kind of salt (notably *sel de Guérande* and *sel de Noirmoutier*). But as any Provençal will tell you, the most superior kind—the very aristocracy of salt—comes from the flat, marshy areas of the Rhône delta, the *salins* of the Camargue, sometimes called the salt cellar of France.

In the course of a normal year, the Camargue produces about 400,000 tons of salt. During harvest time at Aigues-Mortes, the salt mound becomes a landmark, a miniature alp that can measure 230 feet wide, 75 feet high, and 2,500 feet long. Predictably, this pile of salt is called the "white gold" of the sea, and it has been extracted the old-fashioned way, using a process that has changed very little in more than a thousand years. This is basically a system of controlled evaporation, a natural conveyor belt with sea water at one end and salt crystals at the other. During the hot months of summer, sea water is let into a network of shallow pans, where the drying effects of sun and wind cause the water to evaporate. As it evaporates, so the salt content increases. The water is moved by gravity through a sequence of pans, becoming more and more salty until it reaches the final pan, where the salt becomes crystallized.

And that, you might think, would be the end of it. After all, no matter how good it is, salt is salt. In the Camargue, however, there is a hierarchy, based on grain size and flavor. Starting at the bottom, we have *sel fin*, a fine-grained salt that you would use for everyday cooking. *Sel gros*, coarser and crunchier, is ideal for any recipes that call for a salt crust. And finally, the jewel of the salt pans and the finest salt of all, there is *fleur de sel*.

This is the name given to the tiny, irregular flakes that come up to float on the water's surface; brilliant white, as white as a coating of frost. The flakes are gathered manually, in the traditional way, by a *saunier* using a wooden shovel, the *las*. He works barefoot, to avoid damaging the marshy bottom of the pans, and after a day of working in conditions of intense heat and glare, he will be lucky to collect more than a hundred pounds of salt.

A good *saunier* signs his work. So you will find, on each small, cork-topped pot of *fleur de sel de Camargue*, the name of the man who gathered that particular batch of salt. Naturally, that little pot will cost more than a packet of anonymous, industrially produced salt, but then *fleur de sel* is a great deal more enjoyable to eat. It's at its best, I think, with raw vegetables, which set off the taste and texture of the salt perfectly. Take a fresh radish, slit the top, insert a sliver of white butter, and crown with a sprinkling of *fleur de sel*. Never has a radish been so tempting, so crunchy, or so tasty—a radish resplendent. And it's the salt that makes the difference. *Bravo le saunier.*

Serge de Nîmes

In the days before it became an international uniform, denim was thought of as a purely American institution. Prospectors wore it during the California gold rush. Cowboys wore it at home on the range. Movie stars wore it when they were impersonating cowboys, and large tattooed gentlemen wore it when riding their Harley-Davidsons. If asked who had invented it, nine people out of ten would say Levi Strauss (who, incidentally, was German). Such is the power of American popular mythology.

The truth has several versions, but the most appealing and plausible of these—to me, at least—tells us that denim originated in Provence, long before the birth of America. Since the Middle Ages, the town of Nîmes was one of the more important centers of textile production in Europe. The town's specialty was *serge de Nîmes*, a coarse, sturdy fabric used for sails and protective tarpaulins. When Levi Strauss got hold of some out in California, he had thought to use it to make tents for the gold prospectors. But then—inspired, perhaps, by the sight of a prospector with seriously tattered pants—he had a better idea: work trousers or, as they were originally called, waist overalls. At some point, *serge de Nîmes* was abbreviated to denim, and in time the trousers became known as Levi's.

Records are not too precise about exactly when "jeans" came to take over as the generic description for denim trousers, but there is no doubt about the origin of the word. It dates from the sixteenth century, when England began importing "Genoa cloth" from Italy, a blend of cotton, linen, and wool. The English, with their gift for suspect pronunciation, called it jean cloth, and started manufacturing it in the mills of Lancashire. By the eighteenth century, the original blend had been changed to all cotton, woven from one white thread and one colored thread, a technique that was adopted by textile mills on the other side of the Atlantic. The rest is American history.

Sieste, La

Busy though the Romans were putting down the barbarian hordes and putting up triumphal arches, it seems that they still found time for one of life's small luxuries. *Sexta*—the sixth hour of the day, or noon—was the Roman moment to slip out of the body armor, escape from the heat, and take a nap. Ever since then, the siesta has been part of daily life in those Latin countries blessed by a long, hot summer.

But not, alas, for the Anglo-Saxons, regardless of the weather. Their attitude to the siesta over the centuries has been one of disapproval, probably dating from the time when the British first colonized the tropics, bringing their habits with them. Ignoring the local climate, they dressed for a brisk winter's day on the moors, in layers of thick broadcloth, heavy close-fitting hats, and stout frost-proof boots. They disdained the effete practice of taking a snooze in the shade, preferring instead to go out in the midday sun and do something energetic. Many years ago, Noël Coward observed that "Englishmen detest a siesta," and there is still some truth in this today. It is well known that the Englishman *en vacances*, determined not to waste a second of sunshine, is liable—unless restrained—to spring up from the lunch table and bound onto the tennis court, risking indigestion, dehydration, cramps, and heatstroke in 85-degree temperatures.

Like many customs that have endured in hot climates through the ages,

the siesta makes sense, as we can see from the way in which the traditional Provençal working day was organized. It began at dawn, when the fields were fresh and cool. The day's main meal would be taken at around eleven o'clock, followed by a few hours spent well away from the sun. Work in the fields resumed in the evening, and continued until nightfall. It was a practical, healthy way of dealing with conditions that could fry a man's brains. Now, of course, machinery has largely replaced manual labor in the fields, and the siesta is no longer regarded as a physical necessity; indeed, some consider it a decadent indulgence. This should not be allowed to inspire guilt. Instead, it should only add to the pleasure of a well-spent hour or two after lunch.

I have consulted several authorities—men who have made an art out of indolence—on the finer points of the siesta. Their views and advice, developed from years of horizontal experience, represent a useful guide for beginners. Englishmen please note.

- Although winter siestas have their own cozy charm, the ideal siesta takes place in the summer, out of doors, where breeze and shade combine in a most soothing way to cool the brow and induce a feeling of languorous well-being.
- The principal item of equipment must be full-length. A doze in a chair is only half a siesta. The legs must be given room to stretch out, and they should be more-or-less level with the head, allowing the blood to circulate evenly throughout the body. I am assured that this is very good for the digestion.
- While there are some admirers of the fixed and rigid *chaise longue*, the true expert prefers a hammock slung between two trees, for a number of reasons. A hammock conforms instantly to the contours of the body, and at the same time provides a high degree of lateral security. As any sailor will tell you, it is virtually unknown for even the most restless sleeper to fall out. Another advantage is the gentle side-to-side motion that can be set off by a slight

movement of the hips, giving the hammock's occupant the sensation of floating on currents of air. Add to this the hypnotic effect of watching the scenery overhead as patches of sky and the branches and leaves of the trees sway slowly back and forth, and you have the perfect natural soporific.

- There is a range of optional extras, from books and lavender-scented pillows to cigars and straw hats. Music from an iPod is a more recent refinement, although I prefer the sound effects provided by nature. The scratchy chorus of *cigales,* the rustle of a lizard in the grass, the plop of a frog jumping into a nearby pond, the occasional soft surge of air through the leaves—this is enough of a lullaby for me; at least, while I'm still awake to enjoy it.

Sisteron, Agneau de

For once, here is an example of a food additive that has nothing to do with colorants, preservatives, or those mysterious chemical cocktails conceived in laboratories which are passed off as "flavor enhancers." With Sisteron lamb, the flavor-enhancing process is self-administered, and it takes place in totally natural circumstances.

The countryside around Sisteron, set deep in Les Alpes de Haute-Provence, is mountainous, beautiful, and unpolluted. And best of all, from a hungry lamb's point of view, the grazing is unusually delicious because of the wild herbs that grow on the hills in such profusion. It is well known that you are what you eat, and a daily diet that includes thyme, rosemary, and savory is one reason why the lamb of Sisteron is considered by many to be the finest in France. It has been slowly, thoroughly, and naturally pre-seasoned.

Each July there is a Fête de l'Agneau in Sisteron. The Parc Massot-Devèze is turned into a public picnic area, fragrant with the scent of lamb grilling on barbecues. Take your appetite and follow your nose.

Smollett, Tobias

A fine example of a particular breed of English traveler—critical, superior, and deeply suspicious of foreign food and foreign ways—the sickly Smollett left England in 1763 in search of a healthier climate. He came

south to the Mediterranean, and found so much to offend him that he wrote a wonderfully pithy and cantankerous book, *Travels Through France and Italy*, which was published in 1766.

Here is Smollett on the local population: "The peasants on the South of France are poorly clad, and look as if they were half starved, diminutive, swarthy and meager."

On the local seasoning: "I was almost poisoned with garlic, which they mix in their ragouts, and all their sauces; nay, the smell of it perfumes the very chambers, as well as every person you approach."

On the local toilet facilities: "This is a degree of beastliness, which would appear detestable even in the capital of North-Britain" (a reference to the privies of Edinburgh).

On local food: "I was not disposed to eat stinking fish, with ragouts of eggs and onions. I insisted upon a leg of mutton."

On local wine: "Strong and harsh, and never drank, but when mixed with water."

On local doctors: "A pack of assassins."

The spiritual descendants of Smollett are with us still. You can see them—and, alas, hear them—every summer in the hotels and restaurants of Provence, complaining about the price of orange juice, the odd taste of the milk, the use of garlic, the unbearable heat, and on and on. I'm amazed they keep coming back for more.

Tambour d'Arcole

In the main *place* of Cadenet, a village at the foot of the southern slopes of the Luberon, is a statue of a boy on the run, carrying a drum. This is young André Estienne, born in Cadenet in 1777 and a hero before he was twenty.

He volunteered for the Régiment du Luberon when he was fourteen, serving as a drummer boy. Five years later he was still drumming, this time in the army that Napoléon  had raised to fight in northern Italy. It was a campaign that started well, with victory following victory, until Napoléon came up against a detachment of Austrians defending the bridge at Arcole.

They refused to budge. The French army was blocked. Napoléon, impatient to get at his enemy, had come to grief and had fallen into the river. Prospects for another quick victory seemed remote.

It was then that the young Provençal drummer boy became Napoléon's secret weapon. With his drum on his head and a small group of soldiers at his side, he swam across the river. Once on dry land, he began to beat a series of furious fusillades that the Austrians mistook for gunfire. Assuming that this was the start of a massive attack, they retreated. The French captured the bridge and won the battle. The drum had proved mightier than the gun.

Several souvenirs remain of André Estienne's heroism. Napoléon presented him with two silver drumsticks, which are today on display in the national museum of the Légion d'Honneur. He also has a place on the Arc de Triomphe in Paris, where one of the bas-relief panels commemorates the crossing of the bridge at Arcole. (History has been slightly adjusted, presumably for artistic reasons, and Estienne is shown at Napoléon's side.) And then there is the statue in Cadenet.

Even this has had its wartime adventures. During World War II, the villagers of Cadenet feared that the statue would be taken from them and melted down for German munitions. So they removed it themselves, buried it, and didn't bring it out again until the war was over.

Tapenade

It has been called the black butter of Provence (although it may frequently be green), and it is one of those happy gastronomic inventions that sharpen both appetite and thirst. Normally, therefore, you will find it served with your *apéritif* before you get down to the serious business of making your way through the menu.

The name comes from the Provençal word *tapeno,* or caper, and capers are an essential part of every *tapenade* recipe. Other ingredients can vary slightly according to taste, but I recommend following the instructions of Monsieur Meynier, the Marseille chef who invented *tapenade* more than a century ago. Here's his original recipe:

- Take 200 grams of black olives, with their pits removed. Crush the olives, using mortar and pestle, together with 200 grams of

capers, 100 grams of unsalted anchovy fillets, 100 grams of tuna in oil, a large spoonful of strong mustard, *"pas mal de poivre,"* and a pinch of *fines herbes.*
- As you crush, add, little by little, 200 milliliters of olive oil.
- The final touch: mix in a glass of Cognac.

The resulting thick and wonderfully pungent black paste, gleaming with oil, is traditionally spread on small pieces of toast. But it would be a shame to restrict *tapenade* to toast. Try it with hard-boiled quail's eggs, with tomatoes, with fresh goat cheese, with plain grilled fish, or a cold vegetable omelette. I have also seen it used as a dip for potato chips and eaten, on its own, by the spoonful. It is that good.

I'm told that some people have an aversion to eating anything black, possibly as a result of being exposed to an overswarthy cuttlefish risotto when young and impressionable. For them, substitute green olives for black in the recipe, and the color will change accordingly.

Tarasque, La

Provence has long been a fertile breeding ground for monsters and curiosities—dragons, unicorns, giant sardines, prodigious great snakes— but there is nothing in its bizarre history quite as hideous as the Tarasque of Tarascon.

Picture yourself during the Tarasque's reign of terror, some time around the ninth century, taking a stroll along the banks of the Rhône. The air is balmy, the river flows serenely by, you are at peace with the world. And then all at once, without any warning, this ghastly apparition erupts from the water, looking for lunch. An anonymous eyewitness has described it as "taller than a cow, longer than a horse, the face and head of a lion, teeth like rapiers, a body covered in sharp and spiky scales, six paws with long claws, and a serpent's tail." Add to that a fondness for human flesh, a malevolent disposition, and appalling halitosis, and there you have the Tarasque.

Not surprisingly, the inhabitants of Tarascon lived in dread of this horrible creature, and a variety of methods of extermination were tried. They all failed. A dozen men once set out to trap it, and only six returned; the rest had been eaten. Nothing short of a miracle was needed. And, as in all the best monster stories, a miracle came to pass.

It arrived in the form of Saint Martha, whose mission it was to preach Christianity to the pagans of Tarascon. She too needed a miracle if

she were to convince them of the power of her faith, and she saw her chance with the Tarasque. She sought it out and found it eating someone. Undaunted, Saint Martha sprinkled it with holy water, held up a wooden cross, and, mirabile dictu, the Tarasque immediately became as docile as a lamb.

There are two versions of what happened next. Either the Tarasque was led into town and slaughtered, or it was sent to the bottom of the Rhône and told by Saint Martha to stay there. In any event, it never again troubled the people of Tarascon, although it lives on, once a year, during the Fêtes de la Tarasque. These are held toward the end of June—on Saint Martha's day.

Taureau de Camargue

Grass is scarce in Provence, and so are cows. But for lovers of beef, all is not lost. There is consolation to be found in the black bulls of the Camargue, who provide the only meat in France that has been awarded the distinction of an Appellation Contrôlée.

A POINT

As bulls go, the Camargue bull is small. Males stand no higher than four and a half feet, and weigh between 650 and 1,000 pounds. Females are shorter and lighter. Their lives are spent at liberty in the marshy countryside of the Rhône delta, with flamingos and horses for neighbors, and with Camargue cowboys, or *gardians,* to keep an eye on them.

For years, they have been bred not only for the table, but for a bloodless version of the bullfight, the *course à la cocarde,* a test of speed and courage not recommended for the slow or the fainthearted. A small scrap of red cloth, the *cocarde,* is attached to the bull's head. The human competitors, the *raseteurs,* try to get close enough to snatch the cloth from the bull's head. It seems simple enough, except for two problems: the horns, which are long and extremely sharp. As you can imagine, it pays to be nimble. The winner receives the applause of the crowd and a cash prize. The bull is taken back to his pasture, perhaps slightly confused and irritated, but otherwise unharmed.

Not all Camargue bulls have the aggressive disposition necessary for a career in the ring; it is these, the more docile specimens, that end up as stew. And what a stew it is. *Gardianne de taureau* is one of the classic recipes of Provence—a rich, dark, and wonderfully tasty mixture of chunks of beef, bacon, onions, garlic, herbs, pinches of salt, pepper and flour, a glass of Armagnac, and a bottle (or more) of red Côtes du Rhône. Leave it all to soak for twenty-four hours, then simmer it for at least three hours before serving with Camargue rice or potatoes.

For the full taurine culinary experience, you might like to start the meal with *bouillon pour machos*, or bull's testicle soup. But, like the *course à la cocarde*, it is not for the fainthearted.

Tomates

There is a charming, if slightly untrustworthy, story that provides the first historical link between the Revolution and the stomach, a pivotal moment of *liberté*, *égalité*, and *gastronomie*. The story also gives us some idea of the date the tomato began its popular career in France—a career inspired, so I like to think, by a stroke of Provençal publicity.

In 1792, a battalion of men from Marseille arrived in Paris to join the army defending their country against the Austrians. As everyone knows, they brought their battle song with them in the form of "La Marseillaise." And according to the story, they also brought with them a local delicacy, the tomato, which was then virtually unknown to Parisians. There were tomatoes in every Marseille knapsack, and branches heavy with red tomatoes tied to the end of every Marseille musket. How these had managed to maintain their color and survive the long march up from the south is one of those minor details best left unquestioned, but one thing is certain: by the end of the eighteenth century, tomatoes were well established in Provence.

What had taken them so long? Tomatoes had been brought back to Europe from South America by the Spanish conquistadors in the sixteenth century. But for many years, they were thought to be either aphrodisiac (which probably explains why, in Provence, they are still called *pommes d'amour*), medicine, or ornament. The seventeenth-century master gardener Olivier de Serres cultivated them as decorative climbing plants because, so he said, "they are not good to eat."

Tastes changed, or perhaps the flavor of tomatoes improved, and they gradually found their way onto tables all around the world. Their greatest triumph—and some might say their ultimate destiny—came in the 1830s, with the invention of ketchup. Since then, the tomato has never looked back.

I happen to prefer my tomatoes fresh or cooked, rather than out of a bottle, and one day I came across some of the best I have ever eaten. They were served in a restaurant overlooking the Vieux Port in Marseille, and printed at the bottom of the menu was something I had never seen before. It was a tip of the chef's *toque* to his supplier, a credit that read "Vegetables by Bruno Adonis." Intrigued, I asked for more details, and was told that Monsieur Adonis was remarkable not only for the quality of his produce, but for the restrictions he imposed on his clientele. Vegetables by Adonis were not available to the public, nor to wholesalers; only to chefs. And among chefs, he was celebrated for his superlative tomatoes. Clearly, he was a man of distinction in the vegetable world; I felt I had to go and meet him.

His tomato empire is in the green and undulating countryside above Lioux, a few miles northwest of Apt. He is young, and passionate about his tomatoes, which became apparent as we stood looking at the long, widely spaced rows of tomatoes—actually, more like boulevards—that stretched away until they blended into the hills. With a proprietary flourish, he pointed out the different colors ripening under the evening sun: red, of course, but also pink, green, orange, yellow, black, white, and striped. He rattled off a few names, equally colorful: breast of Venus, green Zebra, black Russian, white Queen, heart of velvet—more than twenty varieties, some barely larger than a plump cherry, others the size of a small melon.

To Bruno's clients, the chefs (including Alain Ducasse, the only chef in the world with three three-star restaurants), this enormous choice is almost as important as flavor. A good chef knows that we start to eat with our eyes, and he will use his ingredients in much the same way that an artist uses his paints, to create a composition of shapes and colors that is visually delicious. And here, he has a spectrum of tomatoes to choose from.

BRUNO ADONIS
HAMEAU LE PARROTIER · 84220 LIOUX

TÉL. 04 90 05 76 46
MOB. 06 84 24 85 44
brunoadonis@free.fr
www.bruno-adonis.com

We walked down the rows, pausing from time to time to squeeze one tomato or sniff another, and Bruno told me that he also takes orders for bespoke vegetables, custom grown for clients with special requirements. Most often, these are miniatures such as tiny eggplants, no bigger than your little finger, bred for taste as well as size. But perhaps there will be a call for striped beetroot, or purple basil, both Adonis specialties. Watching him ride away on his motorbike down one of his tomato boulevards, I wondered what he would come up with next. Caviar-sized peas? Rose-sized cabbages? Green tomato ketchup? I made a mental note to come back in the spring and find out.

Touristes

Seldom can an innocent group of people arouse so much scorn and snobbery as tourists. None of us wants to be mistaken for one. Diligent travel writers, scouring the world in their search for the unspoiled paradise, endure discomfort, inedible food, bedbugs, and surly natives as they look for somewhere the tourist has never set his plebeian foot. (Probably for very good reason.) Towns, regions, sometimes entire islands are dismissed from the sophisticated traveler's plans because they are known to harbor tourists. It is as though they bring with them some terrible affliction. And yet, although we may not care to admit it, we are tourists, all of us.

Tourists have been coming to Provence for two thousand years. If we use the prevailing statistical measure—that vaguely naughty term "tourist nights"—we find that the overall total in the Alpes-de-Haute-Provence, Bouches-du-Rhône, and the Vaucluse is now between 70 and 80 million nights a year. The vast majority of the visitors are amiable and considerate, wanting only to enjoy the sun and the scenery, the food and the wine. But very often, they are treated by their critics as an annual curse, accused of everything from monopolizing restaurants and debasing the local culture to terrifying old ladies and eating ice cream in church. What I find interesting is that these criticisms do not come from those with every right to criticize—the Provençaux inhabitants—but from other tourists.

Of course, they would never call themselves tourists. They have been coming to Provence for several years; they may even have second homes in Provence. And they do not want to share Provence with other foreigners, apart from a few carefully chosen friends. They would like to see Provence frozen in time, just as it was when they first discovered it. They point with horror at the souvenir shop that has replaced the butcher's, the crowds during July and August, the rising property prices, the elusive plumber who is too busy to come and see them, the shortage of water, the strangers who have taken over their favorite café table, the increase in traffic. Their gardener has deserted them to work for a company that installs swimming pools, and their *femme de ménage* has left to run a boutique. In short, my dear, it is the collapse of civilization as we know it. And it is all the fault of those terrible tourists.

There are, to be sure, some parts of the world that have been so over-exploited that they are intolerable, but Provence is not one of them, and it absorbs its tourists very well. The postcard villages *do* have souvenir shops, and in season the streets and markets *are* crowded. But a ten-minute drive from any of these celebrated villages will take you into empty countryside that has been untouched by golf courses, condominiums, spa complexes, or three-hundred-room hotels. If one of the aims of your vacation is to enjoy peace, beauty, and solitude, they are here in abundance.

You might even find yourself grateful for some of the effects of tourism. If it weren't for tourist money, many a church and château would have closed for lack of funds, many a monument would have crumbled, many a public garden would have become neglected and overgrown. Most of those charming country restaurants that everyone loves couldn't exist on local customers alone. The stallholders of small village markets would have to move to the nearest town. It wouldn't be worth putting on concerts. Rural life generally would be the poorer.

Whenever I am cornered by the critics, I try to put it to them that the tourist is not always the monster they claim him to be. That he may, in fact, be helping to make the Provence of today a more lively, stimulating, and enjoyable place than the Provence of yesterday. It never works. You can't beat nostalgia. And so, as a last resort, I suggest to them a guaranteed remedy for all their tourist complaints: we could all spend our vacations in the comfort and privacy of our own homes, and to hell with traveling.

The reaction is always the same. What a ridiculous, unrealistic idea. In any case, they say, it's not people like *us*.

Tremblements de Terre

Anyone with an eye for architecture will notice that certain buildings in Provence have suffered more than others from the ravages of time. There are kinks in the roofline, sagging lintels, wrinkled door frames, windows out of kilter—and, indoors and out, cracks. These are most noticeable on the complexion of a house, its façade, which will often be fissured and pockmarked, seemingly only saved from collapse by the S-shaped iron braces that run from one side of the house to the other. Sloppy building methods are to blame, you might think, or neglect. Or just centuries of wear and tear. In fact, the cause may well have been an especially violent twitch in the climate: the Provençal earthquake.

It is a sufficiently rare and dramatic event to be recorded with some accuracy when it happens. And so we know that the Vaucluse experienced a widespread shock on January 25, 1348; it was the turn of Pertuis on April 14, 1535; 1708 and 1731 were other earthquake years. But the worst was the quake of June 11, 1909, which hit the area around Lambesc. Several people were killed, and there was considerable damage.

Obviously, nobody could see these as anything but disasters. But there are earthquakes and earthquakes, and in their mildest form—little more than a subterranean flutter—they can sometimes come to the rescue of inventive gentlemen in the construction business, as I have discovered. Some years ago, during a moment of domestic masochism, we invited some workmen into the house to replace a large conventional window with plate glass; thick, bulletproof plate glass, of the kind that nervous dictators have fitted in their limousines; solid enough, so we were told, to resist the efforts of burglars armed with sledgehammers. Why, one would need a battering ram to make the slightest mark. The glass was duly installed and admired. The workmen left.

You can imagine our chagrin when, less than three weeks later, we found a diagonal crack that ran from top to bottom of our new, indestructible window. Assuming that there had been some problem during the installation of the glass, we asked the workmen back to take a look.

"What bad luck," said the *patron,* after a disappointingly brief inspection of the damage. "Evidently, the crack has been made by a *tremblement de terre.* There can be no doubt about it."

How could that be? For weeks, the weather had been calm and fine: no storms, no wind, not the faintest suggestion of seismic rumbling. But the *patron* was adamant. Apparently, a minor earthquake had taken place while we weren't looking.

Sometime later, we began to realize that these remarkably discreet earthquakes occurred quite often, and always in the wake of construction work. Some friends discovered cracks in their new swimming pool; others found them in floors and ceilings. In every case, natural causes were blamed. So much for the gentle Mediterranean climate.

Trou Provençal

Here is something that the ancient Roman, for all his civilized ways, failed to do as gracefully as the Provençal peasant.

Roman feasts were lengthy affairs, course after course of lampreys' roe, larks' tongues, milk-fed snails, wild boar stuffed with live thrushes, and a dozen other rich and filling dishes. Inevitably, during the course of the feast, there came a time—perhaps after an injudicious second helping of peacock brains—when a man's toga became uncomfortably tight and his appetite began to falter. But good manners decreed that he must eat on, and on and on, until the last honey-dipped dormouse had been polished off. What was the well-brought-up guest to do?

He would repair to the *vomitorium*, where a slave practiced in such matters would help him throw up what he had just eaten to make way for what he was about to eat. Thus purged, our man would return to the feast with a spring in his step, ready to start again.

A similar result can be achieved in a far less unsavory fashion with the *trou provençal*, which has long been a feature of the more elaborate Provençal lunch or dinner. To make your *trou*, you will need a small glass

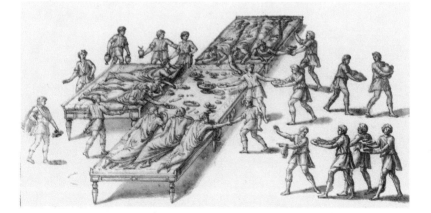

of *marc de Provence,* which, as has been noted elsewhere, is a ferociously powerful member of the brandy family. Taken in the middle of the meal, it is capable of cutting through the heaviest food to provide a measure of relief for the overtaxed digestive system. Its effect is instant: the palate shudders, then recovers, allowing you to look a second helping of *daube* or a selection of cheeses in the eye with renewed enthusiasm.

Those who prefer their *trou* without alcohol should consider another Provençal specialty, the rosemary sorbet: chilled, tangy, and wonderfully refreshing, there is nothing like it for cleansing and reviving the taste buds.

Ucha

This is one of the more explosive and descriptive words in the Provençal vocabulary. If you should suffer from an *ucha,* have someone pat you on the back and give you a glass of water. You've just had a coughing fit.

Unité d'Habitation

Hard though it is to imagine now, there was a time not too long ago when the high-rise apartment building was a rarity in France, and unknown in Provence. Buildings were low and usually made from local stone. Reinforced concrete was something of a novelty until one architect in particular, Le Corbusier, gave it his blessing and made it famous. He deserves much of the credit—or the blame—for inspiring the slabs that have sprouted up across urban landscapes over the past fifty years like monstrous gray teeth.

Le Corbusier's most celebrated contribution to the changing face of Provençal architecture was the Unité d'Habitation, on the Boulevard Michelet in the eighth *arrondissement* of Marseille. His theory was to concentrate living accommodations in what he called a "vertical village," leaving a surrounding area of open parkland for the inhabitants to enjoy. And so, between 1947 and 1952, his twelve-story creation was constructed on a base of giant concrete columns: 337 apartments of varying sizes (each with natural light), a level reserved for shops, and a roof garden. The result was sufficiently ahead of its time to be regarded with some reservation by the locals, who called it *"la maison du fada,"* or the madman's house. But it was, and still is, an ingenious solution to the problem of giv-

ing city dwellers a breath of fresh air and a view of trees and grass.

Le Corbusier's idea has since been copied by lesser architects and greedier developers, with one unfortunate difference. They have embraced the idea of tall buildings of raw concrete—but without the softening contrast of green surroundings. After all, why waste valuable construction land on something as unprofitable as trees?

Urgent

Not part of everyday speech in Provence, *urgent* is a word regarded with a mixture of mild curiosity and amusement. Curiosity, because it signifies the need to hurry, an entirely foreign habit. And amusement at the antics performed by disciples of urgency in their quest for speed and punctuality: the constant checking of watches, the frantic telephone calls, the brutally brief lunches, the explosions of frustration in slow-moving traffic.

I once had a theory that the slower pace of life in Provence could be simply explained by the landscape and the climate, both of which encourage leisurely appreciation. But I think it goes deeper than that. For many generations, the principal occupation of Provençaux was tied to the land and the rhythm of the seasons—the raising of sheep and goats, the cultivation of vines and olives—and impatience was pointless. Nature, not man, dictated the timetable. Over the centuries, I'm sure that this must have had an effect on the Provençal character. "Slowly does it" was the motto, and it became embedded in the genes.

Perhaps this will change. But not soon, I hope, and not quickly.

Usseglio, Raymond

He is proprietor of one of the smallest vineyards in Châteauneuf-du-Pape. Domaine Usseglio extends to just one hectare, with a correspondingly small production, and therefore is unlikely to appear on many wine lists. But if you should see a bottle, seize it. The wine is aged in hogsheads for more than a year before being bottled, and has the warmth and strength of flavor characteristic of the best Châteauneuf reds. Excellent with game.

Valse Provençale, La

One could hardly call it an illness. It is more of a passing inconvenience, an indication that the body is adjusting to changed circumstances. Curiously, it never seems to affect the French; perhaps they are immune from birth. But for many Anglo-Saxons, it is as much a part of the Provençal vacation as the sound of *cigales* or the scent of lavender.

For the first day or two, all goes well for the visitors. There is swimming and sunbathing, long meals taken out of doors, a general air of well-being. "This is the life," they say. "Never felt better." But then there are signs that, while the rest of the body is enjoying Provence, the stomach is not. Preliminary symptoms are a reluctance to take extended trips in the car and an anxious preoccupation with the whereabouts of the nearest bathroom. As the condition develops, the bathroom assumes an increasing importance. Visits become more frequent, and it is at this stage that *la valse provençale* can be seen. A concerned observer will recognize the sudden, hasty scuttle, the body slightly bent, the facial expression fixed and apprehensive. The remedy is extreme, but effective: bed rest and a diet of bottled water while the digestion returns to its former state of health.

Postrecovery, many explanations are put forward to account for the indisposition. Too much sun is often blamed, or too much garlic, or unusually strong olive oil, or the local butter, or a dubious *sauçisson*, or—my favorite—the tap water used for the ice cubes in the Scotch. Oddly enough, the fact that the invalid has been drinking enormous and unaccustomed amounts of pink wine with an alcoholic content of 13 percent is never, ever mentioned.

Veillées

During the cold, slow months of January and February, with darkness falling early, it was once the custom in Provence to invite the neighbors over after supper for a *veillée*. The men would play cards and compare hunting exploits. The women would sew (and probably compare husbands). Children would be allowed to stay up and play in front of the fire, or sit and listen to stories. Biscuits and *beignets* would be served with a glass or two of wine, and the evening would end with an invitation to another *veillée*, perhaps the following week, at another neighbor's house. It was a form of social glue that gave the inhabitants of small rural communities the chance to keep in touch without the formality and expense of dinner parties. A charming habit that, alas, has now been replaced by television.

Vents

Much dramatized by poets and writers, and the subject of a hundred fables, the mistral is the most famous wind in Provence. Indeed, many visitors think it is the only wind in Provence. "Is this the mistral?" they ask, as a passing breeze ruffles the surface of their *pastis,* and seem disappointed to be told that it isn't. They soon find out that when the mistral blows there's no mistaking it. And, should they stay long enough, they will eventually meet the entire family of Provençal winds. Naturally, each of them has its own name.

There is *Le Trémountano,* which comes down from the north with a snap, bringing cold weather. From the south, there is *La Marinière,* which blows up from the deserts of Africa, coating everything in its path with a grimy residue of sand. From the east, there is *Le Levant,* which brings rain. And from the west, there is *Le Traverso.* But it doesn't stop there. Ask any well-informed Marseillais (as if you could find any who aren't), and he will tell you that there are more than thirty different winds. *Le Montagnero* blows from the north-northeast, *La Biso* from the north-northwest, *Le Grégau* from the east-northeast, and so on. Nor should we

forget *Le Mange Fange, Le Vent di Damo,* or *La Cisampo,* each coming from its own particular point of the compass.

Lesser gusts of air, too modest to be given official titles or compass bearings, are conveniently linked to natural episodes that are otherwise inexplicable. I remember the summer evening we were invaded, for no apparent reason, by clouds of tiny black flies. A local expert who happened to be passing told us that this was undoubtedly caused by one of these *petits vents.* I pointed out that it was a perfectly still night with no wind, *petit* or otherwise, but he insisted. There was an undercurrent of turbulence, he said, completely undetectable by humans but quite enough to blow millions of tiny black flies onto our dinner table. I didn't bother to ask him how he knew. There is no point in arguing with a Provençal possessed of supernatural gifts.

Villages Perchés

At the same time the early inhabitants of Provence were practicing the arts of intervillage warfare, they were also discovering the benefits of a particular kind of town planning. Elevated real estate, in the form of the *village perché,* became extremely desirable, for a number of reasons.

First, it enabled you to see your enemies coming from far away. This gave you plenty of time to prepare the oil which, freshly boiled, would later be tipped down onto their heads.

Second, it provided a solution to the problem of municipal sanitation. All kinds of debris, from lamb bones to the local tax inspector, could be tossed away over the ramparts instead of being left to clutter up the streets.

Third, it offered the chance of relief from the solitary nature of country life, with nothing for company but the goat, the ass, and the chicken.

And fourth, it satisfied the primitive urge—still to be found in places as far apart as New York and Shanghai—to live at an altitude that allowed you to feel superior to your less exalted neighbors below.

So it was no wonder that most of the promising hills in Provence were snapped up eight hundred or nine hundred years ago by the forerunners of modern property developers. The *villages perchés* that they built offered security, convenience, companionship, and a certain status, not unlike today's gated communities in Florida or southern Spain (although without the golf courses). Fortunately for us, those early developers, architects, and builders had an innate good taste that is now conspicuously absent. This might explain why the villages they built remain, even after all these years, so attractive.

To start with, there is the view *of* the village, the postcard special: pale limestone walls, a tumble of tiled roofs, the bell tower of a church silhouetted against a sky of the thickest blue. All much as it has been for

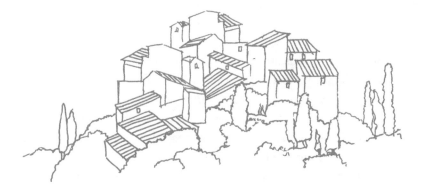

hundreds of years, except for the satellite dishes. Then there is the view *from* the village: mile after mile of countryside, often with a carpet of vineyards stretching toward another village, hazy in the distance—a view that even a scattering of new salmon-pink villas can't spoil.

The most picturesque, and thus most frequently photographed, *villages perchés* are probably the famous Luberon trio of Gordes, Ménerbes, and Bonnieux. But there are plenty of others. Lacoste, Saignon, Murs, Simiane-la-Rotonde, Banon, Les Baux, and dozens more, each of them a handsome reminder of those bygone days before concrete.

Vin

Elizabeth David, who was among the best and most influential food writers ever to come out of a kitchen, once spent a particularly bleak winter in Provence. Day after day, the mistral blew until, as she put it, "we all seemed to come perilously close to losing our reason, although it is, of course, only fair to say that the truly awful wine of that particular region no doubt also contributed its share. It was the kind of wine which it was wisest to drink out of a tumbler so that there was room for a large proportion of water."

More than forty-five years have passed since that was written, and the wines of Provence have changed and improved so much that I doubt Madame David would recognize them. Today they regularly win medals at the annual wine contests at Mâcon. They are respectfully treated in the annual *Guide Hachette des vins* (thirty-three thousand wines blind tasted, of which only ten thousand make it into the guide). They appear on the wine lists of some Parisian restaurants. What can have happened to the "truly awful wine" of the bad old days?

As a general answer, I think it's fair to say that the grape is taken more seriously in Provence than it used to be, possibly in response to the annual influx of thirsty tourists. Even in the cooperatives, where *vin de table* comes in a box as well as in a bottle, standards are much higher than they used to be. Ancient equipment has been replaced, more care is taken with vinification, the choice is wider, the wines more reliable. No longer do you risk a splitting headache every time you buy an inexpensive bottle. But it is the growth of independent, privately owned vineyards that is transforming both the taste and the reputation of Provençal wines.

(Before going any further, I should make it clear what I mean by Provençal wines, because, in true French fashion, the official definition is not at all straightforward. For me, wines coming from the *départements* of the Vaucluse, the Bouches-du-Rhône, and the Alpes-de-Haute-Provence are true Provençal wines. However, due to some byzantine bureaucratic contortions, they are not allowed to give themselves the *appellation* of Côtes de Provence. Côtes du Luberon, Côteaux d'Aix-en-Provence, Côtes du Ventoux—all these and several others are permitted; Côtes de Provence is not. This distinction is reserved for wines grown in the Var and parts of the Alpes-Maritimes. These two *départements,* delightful though they may be, do not, strictly speaking, fall within the boundaries of Provence. I imagine that if you could ever find the appropriate bureaucrat, he would have a logical explanation for this anomaly, but it seems cockeyed to me, and it is a source of great irritation to some of my winegrowing neighbors.)

Since the days when Châteauneuf belonged to the pope, it has always been possible, if difficult, to find decent wine in Provence. In recent years it has become much easier. Old, neglected properties have been bought, restored, replanted, and equipped with stainless steel *cuves* and barrels of the best French oak. Traveling *oenologues,* wine consultants who never used to show their faces in Provence, are now regular visitors to most of these properties. At every step of the winemaking process, the attention to detail and level of investment is remarkable. It's even more impressive when one takes into account the overall state of the wine business: the wine lakes of mythical proportions, the increased competition from the New World, the potential entry of the Chinese (I already have a bottle of Great Wall *rosé*). Where do they come from, these brave souls—the new

LIVRE DE CAVE

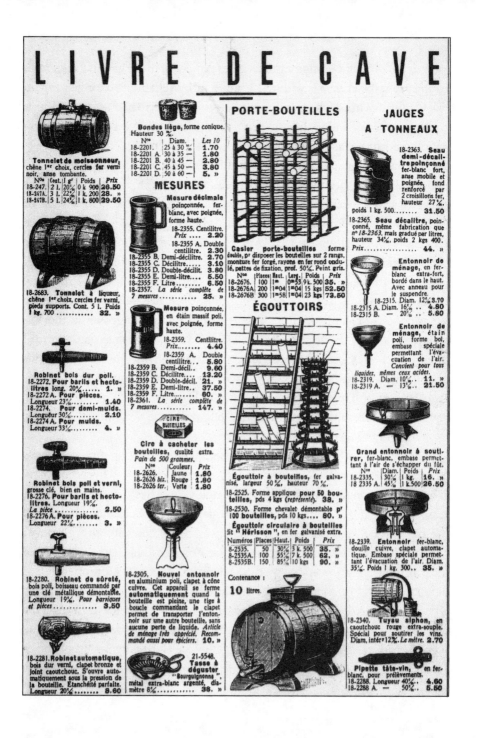

Tonnelet de moissonneur, chêne 1er choix, cercles fer verni noir, anse tombante.

Nos	Cont.	J gr	Poids	Prix
18-247.	2 l.	20‰	0 k 900	**26.50**
18-247A.	3 l.	22‰	1 k. 200	**28. »**
18-247B.	5 l.	24‰	1 k. 800	**29.50**

18-2683. **Tonnelet à liqueur,** chêne 1er choix, cercles fer verni, pieds supports. Cont. 5 l. Poids 1 kg. 700 .... **32. »**

Robinet bois dur poli.
18-2272. **Pour barils et hectolitres** long. 20‰...... **1. »**
18-2272 A. **Pour pièces.** Longueur 23‰........ **1.40**
18-2274. **Pour demi-muids.** Longueur 30‰........ **2.10**
18-2274 A. **Pour muids.** Longueur 33‰........ **4. »**

Robinet bois poli et verni, grosse clé, bien en mains.
18-2276. **Pour barils et hectolitres.** Longueur 19‰. *La pièce* **2.50**
18-2276 A. **Pour pièces.** Longueur 22‰....... **3. »**

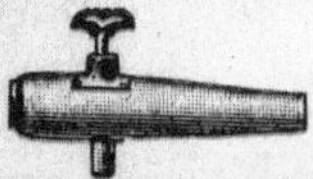

18-2280. **Robinet de sûreté,** bois poli, boisseau commandé par une clé métallique démontable. Longueur 19‰. *Pour barriques et pièces* **3.50**

18-2281. **Robinet automatique,** bois dur verni, clapet bronze et joint caoutchouc. S'ouvre automatiquement sous la pression de la bouteille. Etanchéité parfaite. Longueur 20‰........ **8.60**

Bondes liège, forme conique. Hauteur 30 ‰.

Nos	Diam.	Les 10
18-2201.	25 à 30 m/m	**1.70**
18-2201 A.	30 à 35 —	**1.80**
18-2201 B.	40 à 45 —	**2.80**
18-2201 C.	45 à 50 —	**3.80**
18-2201 D.	50 à 60 —	**5. »**

MESURES

Mesure décimale poinçonnée, fer-blanc, avec poignée, forme haute.
18-2355. Centilitre. *Prix* **2.20**
18-2355 A. Double centilitre. **2.30**
18-2355 B. Demi-décilitre. **2.70**
18-2355 C. Décilitre..... **3.10**
18-2355 D. Double-décilit. **3.80**
18-2355 E. Demi-litre.... **5.50**
18-2355 F. Litre........ **6.50**
18-2357. *La série complète de 7 mesures* .... **25. »**

Mesure poinçonnée, en étain massif poli, avec poignée, forme haute.
18-2359. Centilitre. *Prix*....... **4.40**
18-2359 A. Double centilitre... **5.80**
18-2359 B. Demi-décil.. **9.60**
18-2359 C. Décilitre.... **13.20**
18-2359 D. Double-décil. **21. »**
18-2359 E. Demi-litre.. **37.50**
18-2359 F. Litre..... **60. »**
18-2361. *La série complète de 7 mesures*.......... **147. »**

Cire à cacheter les bouteilles, qualité extra. *Pain de 500 grammes.*

Nos	Couleur	Prix
18-2626.	Jaune	**1.80**
18-2626 *bis.*	Rouge	**1.80**
18-2626 *ter.*	Verte	**1.80**

18-2305. **Nouvel entonnoir** en aluminium poli, clapet à cône cuivre. Cet appareil se ferme **automatiquement** quand la bouteille est pleine, une tige à boucle commandant le clapet permet de transporter l'entonnoir sur une autre bouteille, sans aucune perte de liquide. *Article de ménage très apprécié. Recommandé aussi pour épiciers.* **10. »**

21-5548. **Tasse à déguster** " **Bourguignonne** ", métal extra-blanc argenté, diamètre 8‰............ **38. »**

PORTE-BOUTEILLES

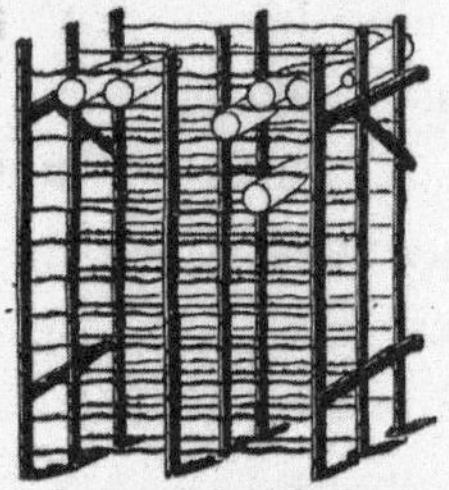

Casier porte-bouteilles forme double, pr disposer les bouteilles sur 2 rangs, monture fer forgé, rayons en fer rond ondulé, pattes de fixation, prof. 50‰. Peint gris.

Nos	Places	Haut.	Larg.	Poids	Prix
18-2676.	100	1m	0m53	9 k. 500	**35. »**
18-2676A	200	1m04	1m04	15 kgs	**52.50**
18-2676B	300	1m58	1m04	23 kgs	**73.50**

ÉGOUTTOIRS

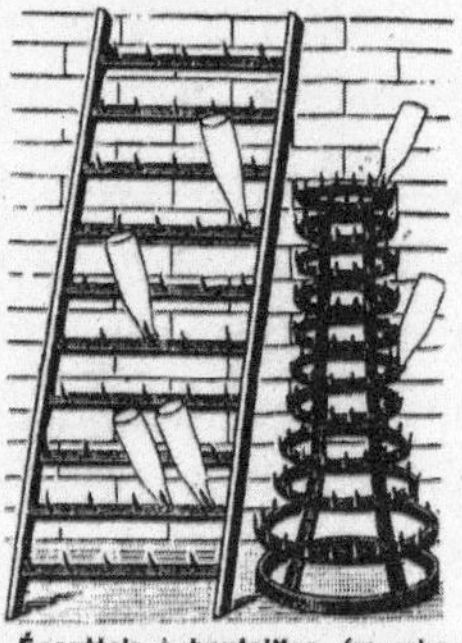

Égouttoir à bouteilles, fer galvanisé, largeur 50‰, hauteur 70‰.
18-2525. Forme applique **pour 50 bouteilles,** pds 4 kgs (*représenté*). **38. »**
18-2530. Forme chevalet démontable pr **100 bouteilles,** pds 10 kgs.... **80. »**

Égouttoir circulaire à bouteilles dit " **Hérisson** ", en fer galvanisé extra.

Numéros	Places	Haut.	Poids	Prix
8-2535.	50	30‰	3 k. 500	**35. »**
8-2535A.	100	55‰	7 k. 500	**62. »**
8-2535B.	150	85‰	10 kgs	**90. »**

Contenance : 10 litres.

JAUGES A TONNEAUX

18-2363. **Seau demi-décalitre poinçonné** fer-blanc fort, anse mobile et poignée, fond renforcé par 2 croisillons fer, hauteur 27‰, poids 1 kg. 500........ **31.50**

18-2365. **Seau décalitre,** poinçonné, même fabrication que nº *18-2363*, mais gradué par litres, hauteur 34‰, poids 2 kgs 400. *Prix*................ **44. »**

Entonnoir de ménage, en fer-blanc extra-fort, bordé dans le haut. Avec anneau pour le suspendre.
18-2315. Diam. 12‰ **3.70**
18-2315 A. Diam. 16‰ .. **4.80**
18-2315 B. — 20‰ .. **5.80**

Entonnoir de ménage, étain poli, forme bol, embase spéciale permettant l'évacuation de l'air. *Convient pour tous liquides, mêmes ceux acides.*
18-2319. Diam. 10‰.. **11. »**
18-2319 A. — 13‰.. **21.50**

Grand entonnoir à soutirer, fer-blanc, embase permettant à l'air de s'échapper du fût.

Nos	Diam.	Poids	Prix
18-2335.	30‰	1 kg.	**16. »**
18 2335 A.	45‰	1 k. 500	**26.50**

18-2339. **Entonnoir** fer-blanc, douille cuivre, clapet automatique. Embase spéciale permettant l'évacuation de l'air. Diam. 35‰. Poids 1 kg. 300.. **35. »**

18-2340. **Tuyau siphon,** en caoutchouc rouge extra-souple. Spécial pour soutirer les vins. Diam. intér. 12‰. *Le mètre.* **2.70**

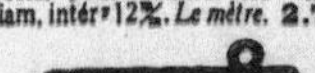

Pipette tâte-vin, en fer-blanc, pour prélèvements.
18-2288. Longueur 40‰.. **4.60**
18-2288 A. — 50‰.. **5.50**

vignerons who are prepared to put their money into a complex and unpredictable venture like a vineyard?

A few of them are young, ambitious, and lucky enough to have inherited the business. They are in the minority. Many more, not quite so young, have taken up wine as a second career. They've done their time in the salt mines—banking and politics, advertising and retailing, medicine and microchips—and they have made enough money to retire and count the butterflies in their gardens. But they're not ready for retirement. They want a project, a challenge, a reason to get up in the morning. A vineyard provides all of these and more: with a bit of luck, there is a handsome old house to live in, there are congenial colleagues to work with (wine people, as a rule, are pleasant and civilized), and there is the enormous satisfaction of producing a respectable wine.

I know several of these new *vignerons* who have given up the city in exchange for the vineyard. All of them feel that their working days have taken a turn for the better. There are no more office politics, no more interminable meetings, no more pig-headed committees, no critical and demanding shareholders. It's true that they have a capricious working partner in nature, which can cause frayed nerves and sleepless nights, but on the whole they enjoy healthier, more relaxed, and more fulfilling lives.

It's also true that they are unlikely to make a fortune in their second careers. There is, so we are continually told, a world wine surplus, and the chances of one small vineyard making a killing are remote, at least for a generation or two. The best financial result that one can reasonably expect is a modest profit over the years, with the bonus of a better life instead of stock options.

Are the wines made by these ex-captains of industry worth the time and effort and investment that have been spent on them? I would say most definitely yes. Elizabeth David would be pleasantly surprised. For the most part, they are not wines to put down for the pleasure of your children, but best drunk young. They are well balanced and fruity and have been described as "very approachable" (which I assume means easy to drink). Or, to steal an extraordinary phrase that has come straight from California's Napa Valley, they offer "accelerated gratification." Quick, pass the bottle.

Vipères

Though you could hardly call Provence an infested region, marked on ancient maps by that infinitely discouraging phrase "here be serpents," anyone who takes regular country walks will see (or sometimes hear) a snake or two. Each spring the snake population emerges from hibernation, coming out to take the air and loll on sun-warmed rocks. There are two principal species, and it is useful to know which is which, as a mistake could prove painful.

The first is the *couleuvre vipérine,* a long, elegantly patterned creature, very partial to frogs, toads, and small fish, and completely harmless to humans. When disturbed, it will slither off into the bushes, making a dry, rustling sound, occasionally leaving behind fragments of discarded winter skin that look for all the world like cracked enamel.

The second species is the one to avoid. This is the *vipère aspic;* smaller, slimmer, and more or less poisonous, depending on your gender. As the old Provençal saying has it: "When a viper bites a man, the man dies. When a viper bites a woman, the viper dies." I have yet to meet a woman who has caused the death of a viper, but Monsieur Farigoule tells me it is a scientific fact, and that a man should never risk a country walk in springtime without a female companion. He also told me that there is no more effective deterrent to burglars and trespassers than a few strategically placed notices around your property carrying this brief warning: *Attention! Vipères!*

Voisins

Life in the city is a life surrounded by *voisins*—neighbors to either side of you, often above you and below you as well. And yet, if you wish, your contact with families who live no more than the thickness of a wall away can be limited to the odd chance meeting on the stairs or in the elevator. Their lives will hardly ever impinge on yours. You can be anonymous.

In the country, anonymity is impossible. Your closest neighbors may be separated from you by the equivalent of two or three city blocks of wheat fields, rows of vines, clumps of trees, hedges, and ditches. Almost too far away to be called neighbors, they are figures seen in the distance or nodded to in the village, vaguely familiar but remote, even disinterested. Or so you think. Unknown to you, the rural telegraph has been at work since your arrival. Your neighbors will very quickly have learned who you are, where you came from, and whether or not you are likely to be an asset or a liability to the little patch of Provence that you share with them.

How should new arrivals behave? Two pieces of advice, given to me many years ago, are worth passing on. First, mind your own business. Second, from the seventeenth-century poet George Herbert, "Love your neighbor, yet pull not down your hedge."

Wood, Matthew

Perhaps because of his unsuitable birthplace (he was English), there is no statue of Matthew Wood anywhere in Provence. Nor is his name commemorated on any street or public building or even a *rond-point*. This seems unfair, as Mr. Wood once rendered a considerable service to the town of Apt and the crystallized fruit industry that is based there.

The *fruits confits* of Apt were well known in Provence as long ago as 1348, when Pope Clement VI appointed Auzias Maseta, a native of Apt, as his personal confectioner. But England's sweet tooth took longer to develop, and it wasn't until the second half of the nineteenth century that English travelers to southern France discovered the sticky joys of sugar-drenched apricots, plums, and figs. Among these travelers was Matthew Wood, a man with a keen eye for commerce, and he started to import crystallized fruits; not only the larger specimens that were eaten at the end of the meal, but also the smaller, pale-fleshed, succulent Napoléon, a veritable emperor among cherries.

History is vague about whether it was Matthew Wood or an inspired colleague who found the perfect home for the cherries that made their way from Apt to England. What is certain is that they quickly became a staple ingredient of the classic English fruitcake, a dense, heavy creation laced with brandy and topped with marzipan that was, and still is, eaten by the ton on the other side of the Channel. Mr. Wood had, in a magnificent single-handed effort, greatly increased the Apt export business. I think they might at least have named a cherry after him.

X

X marks my favorite spot, and I go there with the dogs at least once a week throughout the year, rain or shine.

It's a narrow, overgrown path that cuts diagonally across the south face of a high hill. I imagine it's an old hunter's track, although I've never seen a hunter there. In fact, I've never seen another human being there. Rabbits, hares, and pheasants, but never people.

What you see from the path is a constantly changing picture. Looking to the east, there are ranges of hills, dark green in the foreground, fading to blue in the distance. To the south, there is a silvery grove of olives and a long, flat field, yellow with wheat in the summer, white with frost in the winter, framed by a thick border of trees. To the west, there are the perfectly straight lines of a vineyard, the haphazard roofline of the village in the valley, the tower of a fifteenth-century château. The whole panorama is painted with light and shadow, and as the light varies—with the weather, with the time of day, with the seasons—so does the view.

It is always beautiful and never quite the same. Each time I'm there on the hill, it reminds me of why I came to live in Provence. And, looking ahead, it would be a marvelous place to be buried. (In which case, *X* would mark the plot.)

Xylophone de Vigneron

There comes a moment in the *vigneron*'s year when all he can do is wait. The grapes have been gathered and pressed, the wine is resting, the vines have been pruned, and there are a few weeks when a man can leave the vineyard to look after itself.

It was during one of these quiet periods, so I'm told, that this ingenious homemade xylophone was invented. The inventor was a *vigneron* from the region around Mont Ventoux, noted for his fat, powerful red wine and his hobby, which was playing—not very well, unfortunately—the violin. His musical tastes ran to Saint-Saëns and Mahler, and he greatly admired the way in which the two composers made use of the xylophone, notably in the *Danse Macabre* and Mahler's Symphony no. 6.

One day when he had nothing else to do, he was tidying up a dusty corner of his *cave* when he came across some bottles left over from tastings of the previous year's vintage. Some bottles contained nothing but dregs; others still had a glass or two in them; one was half full. Looking at them, the germ of a musical idea came to him, inspired perhaps by the spirit of Saint-Saëns. Taking the old screwdriver he always kept in his pocket for running repairs to his tractor, he gently tapped the bottles, one by one, and found that the sounds varied according to the amount of wine left in each bottle. Eureka!

From there, it was merely a matter of refining his technique, using a teaspoon instead of a screwdriver, and experimenting with the number of bottles and different levels of wine. (The more wine, the shorter and sharper the note produced by the vibrations of the column of air left in the bottle.)

Eventually, he settled on a grouping of seven magnums—for a richer, fuller note—and concentrated on building up his repertoire. He is still some way from the *Danse Macabre*, but he can perform a brisk but very passable version of "La Marseillaise." Musical *dégustations* are planned.

Yeuse et Yucca

Helping to keep Provence green all through the winter, the *yeuse* is a tree with a number of aliases: *chêne vert*, *Quercus ilex*, holm oak, and holly oak. Whatever you call it, during those months of the year when other trees are leafless and much of the vegetation is drab or dormant, the *yeuse* is a welcome relief from bare crags and brown fields. Its leaves are shiny green on top, gray-white below, resistant to drought, frost, the mistral and any other hardships the Provençal climate can inflict on growing things. Surprisingly, it is seldom used by landscape gardeners.

The yucca, on the other hand, is sometimes to be found making a spiky statement in carefully planned gardens. Also known as the Spanish bayonet or Adam's needle, it is a deeply inhospitable plant, a menace to careless children and curious dogs, and best seen, if at all, at a distance.

Ziem, Félix

A contemporary of van Gogh—who thought him "worthy"—Ziem was a painter of landscapes. He loved Venice and went there every year, but his studio was not far from Marseille, in Martigues, with its Venetian mixture of water and boat-lined canals. You can see some of his paintings in the Musée Ziem, as well as the work of other artists who spent time in Provence. And, should you go to Martigues during the second half of July, you will undoubtedly meet some of the finest sardines in France.

Zingue-Zingue-Zoun

A Provençal word, supposed to be onomatopoeic, that was used to describe the sound of the violin. This would undoubtedly have amused the great Isaac Stern (who often referred to himself as a "fiddler"), but I wonder what Stradivari would have made of it.

Zola, François

An engineer who lived in Aix, and who built the world's first vaulted dam nearby at Le Tholonet. Rather overshadowed by his son, Émile, who turned his back on the pleasures of engineering and took up writing instead.

Peter Mayle is the author of *A Year in Provence, French Lessons: Adventures with Knife, Fork, and Corkscrew,* and eight other books set in Provence, where he lives. A film based on his most recent novel, *A Good Year,* is due to appear shortly.

A NOTE ON THE TYPE

Pierre Simon Fournier *le jeune,* who designed the type used in this book, was both an originator and a collector of types. His services to the art of printing were his design of letters, his creation of ornaments and initials, and his standardization of type sizes. His types are old style in character and sharply cut. In 1764 and 1766 he published his *Manuel typographique,* a treatise on the history of French types and printing, on typefounding in all its details, and on what many consider his most important contribution to typography—the measurement of type by the point system.

Composed by North Market Street Graphics,
Lancaster, Pennsylvania
Printed and bound by R. R. Donnelley & Sons,
Harrisonburg, Virginia

Designed by Virginia Tan